Color and Money

Color and Money

*How Rich White Kids Are Winning
the War over College Affirmative Action*

Peter Schmidt

First published in 2007 by
PALGRAVE MACMILLAN™
175 Fifth Avenue, New York, N.Y. 10010 and
Houndmills, Basingstoke, Hampshire, England RG21 6XS.
Companies and representatives throughout the world.

PALGRAVE MACMILLAN is the global academic imprint of the Palgrave Macmillan division of St. Martin's Press, LLC and of Palgrave Macmillan Ltd. Macmillan® is a registered trademark in the United States, United Kingdom and other countries. Palgrave is a registered trademark in the European Union and other countries.

ISBN–13: 978-1-4039-7601-7
ISBN–10: 1-4039-7601-5

Library of Congress Cataloging-in-Publication Data

Schmidt, Peter, 1964 Jan. 20–
    Color and money : how rich white kids are winning the war over college affirmative action / Peter Schmidt.
        p.   cm.
    Includes bibliographical references and index.
    ISBN 1-4039-7601-5
    1. Affirmative action programs in education—United States.   2. Discrimination in higher education—United States.   3. Universities and colleges—Admission.   I. Title.
LC213.52.S35   2007
379.2'6—dc22

                                                                    2007007039

A catalogue record of the book is available from the British Library.

Design by Letra Libre, Inc.

10   9   8   7   6   5   4   3   2

Printed in the United States of America.

Contents

Dedication

Back in 1971, my father, Jim Schmidt, lost his fledgling political career to our nation's long struggle with racism. I have only vague memories of that time, having been just seven. I recall my father had been a city commissioner in my hometown of Birmingham, Michigan, where he and my uncle owned an appliance store. I can still see myself scrawling "Vote for Schmidt" on a poster board to try to help his reelection campaign. I remember my parents taking late-night phone calls and looking rattled afterward. My father lost the election badly, quit politics, and never discussed what had transpired.

In June 2004 my father died after years of being pulled away by Alzheimer's disease. As I researched his obituary, I finally learned how he had come to be rejected by so much of the community he loved. His downfall had been supporting a proposal by a nonprofit group, A Better Chance, to let a few bright black kids from nearby Detroit live in a group house in our community and attend well-regarded Birmingham public schools. Those calls to our home had been from people voicing hatred, fear, and rage.

My father certainly had his flaws. But, at one key juncture, he stood up for something he believed in, knowing full well it would turn people against him. I'll always regret not knowing that about him while he was around.

Dad, if you are out there, this book is for you. Help me do the right thing.

Acknowledgments

I am deeply indebted to several people whose generosity made this book possible.

My agent, Sara Crowe, had faith in this book at times when I had lost it and never hesitated to stand by me and my work. She was a joy to work with, and I can't thank her or her literary agency, Harvey Klinger Inc., enough.

This book had an editor who actually gave it a careful editing—a rarity in the publishing world these days. Amanda Johnson Moon at Palgrave Macmillan took a dense, overgrown manuscript and gently but resolutely instructed me where to prune with shears and where to swing an ax. I cursed her at times but now realize I am in her debt—as, my reader, are you. Also deserving my appreciation are her assistants, Emily Leithauser and Aashti Bhartia, as well as Palgrave Macmillan and St. Martin's Press, Palgrave Macmillan production manager Donna Cherry, and attorney Peter Karanjia of Davis Wright Tremaine.

I had the luxury of being able to take a sabbatical to write *Color and Money* because *The Chronicle of Higher Education* is a humane workplace, and I was able to acquire the background necessary for this book because *The Chronicle* stands out in its commitment to authoritative, in-depth reporting. Its chairman, Corbin Gwaltney, deserves credit for caring deeply about his employees and championing journalism's highest professional and ethical standards. Among others there, Jeffrey Selingo, Phil Semas, and Bill Horne gave me support from above. Sara Hebel, Karin Fischer, and Stephen Burd shared their journalistic insights and helped pick up the slack while I was away. Sarah Hardesty Bray offered me invaluable guidance on authorship. Joan Waynick and Dana Sobyra assisted my research. Bob McGrath kept snapping my book-jacket photo until I looked presentable. Robert Boggs, Daphne Sterling, Faye Phillips, Becky Pendergast, Gene Stamper, Marissa Lopez-Rivera, Jeff Young, and David Glenn helped in various ways, but it's their encouragement and friendship I valued most.

Speaking of friends, I could not have made my trek through the dark woods of authorship without Bruce Kluger, Danny Postel, Jim McNeill, and Welch Suggs, who helped guide me as a fellow writer. Volunteering as careful readers were Patrick Filbin, Mary Weiss, Christen Stumbo Leonard, Michael Hartman, and Alene Hokenstad and her father, Terry. This book also has made me even more thankful than I was before for Ray Yau and Anne McGuire, Peter Mosley, Michelle Carroll, Gayle Filbin, Hugo Flores, John Finnigan, Michelle Leonard, Erik and Pam Wertz, Lauren Brown, Timothy Mayer, Tom Sullivan, Marc Damman, Michael and Beth Fitzsimmons, Jennifer Yachnin, and Mai Nguyen.

Much research points to the importance of mentors for young people, and I have been greatly helped by several: Ben Guerrini at Holy Name, Marcel Gagnon at Brother Rice, Donald Flesche at Kalamazoo College, Theodor Veiter at the Association for the Study of the World Refugee Problem, Mike Wagner at the *Detroit Free Press,* and Gary Hoffman at *Detroit Monthly.* Among other editors who were valuable influences were Owen Eshenroder at the *Ann Arbor News,* Joe Strohmeyer and John Horan at the *Northern Virginia Daily,* and Greg Chronister and Martha Matzke at *Education Week.* I am eternally indebted to all.

Finally, I might never have been in the position to write this book without parents who were willing to help put me through college. Thanks, Mom.

A Celebration of the Few

Who should run our society?

Who should we trust to make our laws or preside over our courts? Who should we be counting on to come up with tomorrow's scientific break-throughs or to steer the large corporations that drive our economy? Who should decide when to send our nation's sons and daughters off to war?

In modern American society, many of us assume—or, at least, desperately hope—that the people in leading positions in government, business, and the professions are our best and brightest. We acknowledge that there are exceptions, that luck and personal connections sometimes play a key role in determining who rises. But, perhaps more than at any point in American history, we believe we live in a meritocracy that elevates those who are smart and work hard—that the people at the top, for the most part, are our top people.

How do we decide who deserves such status? Generally, we rely on academic credentials. We entrust the task of identifying and training our best and brightest to our elite higher education institutions—to the venerable members of the Ivy League, to top research universities such as Stanford, to "public ivies" like the University of Virginia, and to the scores of small-but-solid liberal arts colleges that serve as feeders for our most prestigious medical, law, and business schools. Our higher education system functions as a great sorting machine, with prestigious colleges determining much of the membership of our nation's elite by sifting through huge stacks of applications from teenagers barely old enough to drive.

This book inspects the sorting machine, asking two central questions:
Who should get into our selective higher institutions?
Who actually does?

The question of who *should* get into such institutions is a value judgment at the heart of the long-running war over college affirmative action that continues to be fought out in courtrooms, at the ballot box, on campuses, and over dinner tables. It's an important enough question that the U.S. Supreme Court has weighed in on it several times.

Writing for the majority in the Supreme Court's 2003 decision upholding the consideration of applicants' race by the University of Michigan law school, Justice Sandra Day O'Connor made it clear that she believed the case at hand dealt with much more than a rejected white applicant's complaint of discrimination. Noting that such law schools produce many of the nation's leaders, Justice O'Connor suggested that the very fate of the republic rests on the freedom of elite higher education institutions to assemble racially diverse classes rather than to simply admit only those applicants with the best academic profiles and highest standardized test scores. She wrote, "In order to cultivate a set of leaders with legitimacy in the eyes of the citizenry, it is necessary that the path to leadership be visibly open to talented and qualified individuals of every race and ethnicity. All members of our heterogeneous society must have confidence in the openness and integrity of the educational institutions that provide this training."[1]

An impressive array of the nation's leaders had joined colleges, higher education associations, and civil rights groups in submitting briefs to the Supreme Court supporting the university's policies. When the court decided to basically maintain the status quo in college admissions, cheers arose from the halls of Congress, the headquarters of large corporations, the ivory towers of academe, and the humble storefront offices of community organizations dedicated to helping minority kids overcome discrimination and poverty. Stepping onto a balcony of the Washington, D.C., office of *The Chronicle of Higher Education*—for which I had been covering affirmative action for several years—I half expected to hear popping champagne corks and a marching band triumphantly playing "The Battle Hymn of the Republic" on its way to the Lincoln Memorial. My eyes might not "have seen the glory of the coming of the Lord" but they had read the opinion of Sandra Day O'Connor, and in the view of many who call the shots in this town that was close enough.

Justice O'Connor's talk of "the path to leadership" being "visibly open to talented and qualified individuals" conveyed a deep understanding of the belief system that helps keep the United States largely free of social disturbances, class warfare, or other serious challenges to its established order. Political scientists and sociologists often assert, based on polling data, that as long as people believe in the existence of equal opportunity, they are willing to put up with severe inequities in the distribution of wealth and power. Social unrest is rare among those with faith in the American dream.

Colleges were specifically motivated by a desire to keep the peace when, in the mid- to late-1960s, they first adopted various affirmative action practices ranging from aggressive efforts to recruit black students to the use of quotas and race-based double standards in admissions. As the nation watched smoke rise over Detroit, Newark, and other riot-torn cities, the presidents of our top higher education institutions reckoned that African Americans would be much less likely to take part in violent uprisings if they felt adequately represented in the establishment. There was no more efficient way of absorbing some African Americans into the elite—while, equally as important, offering the rest potent symbols of hope—than to ensure the presence of plenty of black faces in photos of Ivy League graduation ceremonies.[2]

The Supreme Court's 2003 ruling in the Michigan law school case showed that a majority of the justices believed it remained symbolically important to have racial diversity at selective colleges, to convey the impression that any teenager who is smart enough and works hard enough can end up strolling the verdant lawns of Princeton, Oberlin, or their home state's flagship university.

The problem for those who are truly concerned with promoting equal opportunity—and not just promoting acceptance of the status quo—is that such an image has very little to do with the reality of selective higher education.

Setting aside the subjective question of who *should* get into such institutions and turning to the question of who actually *does*, it is hard to escape the conclusion that Justice O'Connor's words ring hollow. Rather than being "visibly open to talented and qualified individuals of every race and ethnicity," selective colleges can much more accurately be described as bastions of privilege, with no more than a tenth of their enrollments coming from the less fortunate half of American society.

Despite Justice O'Connor's assertion that all members of our society "must have confidence in the openness and integrity" of our elite colleges and professional schools, these institutions routinely cloak their admissions practices in secrecy, and they annually turn away tens of thousands of excellent applicants in favor of individuals whose chief qualification is a connection to a generous donor, a powerful politician, or to a member of the alumni, faculty, or administration.

Most applicants who resort to pulling strings do so because they have failed to make a decent showing in a game systematically rigged in their favor. Much in our society serves to elevate the children of the wealthy and well educated while keeping down the less fortunate. Our public elementary and secondary schools are vastly unequal and generally cannot compare to prestigious private schools. Our selective colleges rely heavily on admissions criteria—such as SAT scores and high school reputation—that sort applicants by race and class every bit as reliably as they predict collegiate academic performance. Take into account the effects of regressive trends in the financing of higher education—such as a long-term decline in the share of financial aid dollars going to the truly needy—and it is easy to see why a rich child has about 25 times as much chance as a poor one of someday enrolling in a college rated as highly selective or better.[3]

Four of the five justices who signed on to the majority opinion in the Michigan law school case had followed a parent's footsteps into one of the nation's most prestigious higher education institutions, or had enrolled their own child in their alma mater, or both. Surely they must have known the score.[4]

Of course, the Supreme Court had not been asked to give its opinion of the various ways that colleges favor the wealthy and well connected. Such admissions policies may offend our sense of fairness, but they don't obviously amount to acts of racial or ethnic discrimination that bump up against the Fourteenth Amendment or federal civil rights laws.

Nevertheless, considering that most nonacademic admissions preferences disproportionately benefit white applicants, it seems curious that colleges and higher education associations insisted to the court that the only effective way of ensuring diversity on campuses is by giving minority applicants an edge, that any other approach would erode admissions standards and academic quality. Did they fear that turning down the underachieving children of donors and professors to make room for overachievers from housing projects and trailer parks would somehow cause colleges' *U.S. News & World Report* rankings to plunge?

The situation was different for colleges where race-conscious admissions policies had already been banned through state ballot initiatives, court decisions, or, in the case of Florida, through the actions of state officials. Scrambling to find ways to prop up minority enrollments in the absence of minority preferences, such institutions had rethought their admissions practices. They generally stopped accepting applicants based on who the students know rather than what they know. They experimented with new admissions standards that considered whether an applicant comes from an impoverished background or has overcome some other obstacle, such as being raised in a home where no one spoke English. They began accepting students through "percent plans" that offered automatic admission to applicants who had made the most of the opportunities offered them and were at the top of their high school class—even if the high school stood in an urban war zone or somewhere out past the cornfields. Colleges of education were deployed to help improve the quality of elementary and secondary schools in poor communities, to help ensure that more low-income minority students would gain the academic preparation they needed for college. Financial aid offices devoted a growing share of their resources to covering the tuition costs of truly needy students, rather than spending the money on "tuition discounts" to woo applicants deemed desirable precisely because their families have enough money to pay their way and to donate generously down the road. One key reason many other colleges rallied behind the University of Michigan in its Supreme Court battle is that they did not want to adopt such policies, which they denounced as ineffective and regarded as threats to their bottom lines.

Significantly, most of the leading advocacy groups waging war against affirmative-action preferences, such as the Center for Equal Opportunity, the Center for Individual Rights, and the Heritage Foundation, also were not eager to see colleges making many such changes. They looked with suspicion on any policy—such as class-based affirmative action—that seemed to be a backdoor mechanism for colleges to continue accepting some minority students over whites with better grades and standardized test scores. Being fiscally as well as socially conservative, they had little enthusiasm for the idea of pumping tax dollars into social programs and public schools for the sake of leveling the playing field.

In upholding race-conscious admissions policies, the Supreme Court concluded that colleges should have the final say over whether any alternative to affirmative action would work for them and should feel free to reject any policy they view as not meeting their needs. The court's ruling ensured that, for the foreseeable future, legal battles over affirmative action in admissions would be focused on the narrow question of whether any given college had taken its consideration of race too far—by, for example, failing to look at applicants as individuals. With the Supreme Court having just tackled the bigger legal questions raised by higher education's affirmative action debate, the lower federal courts were unlikely to do anything to seriously shake up the field of college admissions any time soon.

As things now stand, if anyone is winning the war over college affirmative action, it's wealthy white kids. Those from families making well over $90,000 annually are the population most overrepresented on campuses, especially among those who could not have gotten in without the bar being lowered. They account for the largest share of overall enrollment and the vast majority of white students.

Working-class whites, by contrast, quietly exist as one of selective colleges' most underrepresented groups. They generally lack connections that might shield them from competition, and those who overcome their circumstances and become solid contenders for admission are vulnerable to being bumped in the name of diversity. Not only do wealthy white kids dominate such colleges, but race-conscious admissions policies exist primarily for their benefit—at least, that is, according to every major Supreme Court ruling on such policies so far. Higher education leaders have strenuously argued, and the court has accepted, that colleges and professional schools need such policies to make sure their students are able to deal with people from other racial and ethnic backgrounds. Most minority students arrive on campus already having received plenty of exposure to members of other races and ethnicities, according to student surveys and analyses of college admissions data. The students usually lacking such experiences are the white ones, many of whom have been meticulously sheltered from contact with the nonwhite and nonwealthy throughout their childhood and adolescence—often because their parents knew that many selective colleges would be favorably impressed by a transcript from an expensive private school or a public school in a ritzy suburb.

Asian Americans, too, are overrepresented at selective colleges, with their share of the enrollment often being two to four times their share of the overall population. But their prevalence on campus is largely a result of the high achievement levels of many Asian ethnic groups. Most colleges' race-conscious admissions policies work to their detriment by either treating them like white students or holding them to the highest standards of all. Supporters and foes of affirmative action debate whether it or simple discrimination is to blame when Asian Americans have less chance of gaining admission than equally qualified whites. Still, at most colleges that have been prohibited from giving any consideration to race, Asian American enrollments have gone up sharply.[5]

Many people assume that blacks, Hispanics, and Native Americans were the big winners in the Supreme Court's Michigan rulings, especially considering that the gist of the court's decision was to uphold the freedom of colleges to grant them preference. The truth, however, is that race-conscious admissions policies have been a decidedly mixed blessing for the minority groups they seek to help.

Yes, such policies inflate the numbers of minorities on selective college campuses and offer many the opportunity to earn degrees from prestigious institutions that otherwise would have been beyond their reach. Most leaders of black, Hispanic, and Native American advocacy groups will tell you that they would much rather live in a world where their children could enter selective colleges in large numbers without the help of affirmative action, but until such a world exists, it is better to gain admission through race-conscious policies than not to gain admission at all. But several educational researchers who have looked at such policies pragmatically say they have clear drawbacks for the students they are intended to benefit, and many such students find themselves on campuses where they feel overwhelmed, actually hurting their chances of earning advanced degrees or going far in their fields. Although these findings have been disputed, there is little debate over research showing that students from the favored minority groups end up stereotyped as beneficiaries of admissions' double standards and are exposed to resentment and doubts about their capabilities, often eroding their confidence so badly that their academic performance is hindered.

Considering that many of the black and Hispanic students who gain admission to college through affirmative action are the children of either well-to-do professionals or well-educated recent immigrants, it is also becoming harder to see such policies as tools for promoting social justice and uplifting the residents of our nation's ghettos and barrios.[6]

Meanwhile, this nation is full of bright, talented white and Asian American kids who are working diligently and doing everything right—taking challenging classes, earning great grades and SAT scores, winning academic competitions, playing leadership roles at their schools—only to receive thin rejection letters from the colleges of their dreams. Many are blaming affirmative action for their rejections even though, statistically speaking, they are much more likely to have lost their seat to an unqualified white applicant than to a beneficiary of racial preferences.

While this book focuses on admissions to the elite institutions that serve roughly 15 percent of four-year college students, the inequities described here shape the entering classes of every higher education institution, and the preferences discussed here come into play at nearly every four-year college with admissions standards beyond the simple requirement that applicants have a high school diploma.

Some moderate-to-liberal thinkers say one of the chief flaws of affirmative action is that it creates only the illusion of social mobility and equal opportunity and pits those beneath society's upper echelons against each other. Lani Guinier, a Harvard University law professor who has written extensively on class and race, alleges that selective colleges use racial and ethnic diversity as "a fig leaf to camouflage privilege," and she expresses frustration that the affirmative action debate fails to take into account "how the conventional 'merit-based' criteria that we assume to be fair systematically exclude poor and working-class people of every racial group, including whites."[7] Others have suggested that highly selective colleges embraced affirmative action precisely because it has enabled them to stave off a broader attack on their admissions policies.[8]

At least a few scholars concerned with issues of class, such as Michael Lind, a senior fellow at the New America Foundation, see affirmative action in an even more devious light. They believe that it has been used by those in power to co-opt the best black and Hispanic minds—thereby leaving those two minority groups without strong leaders willing to challenge the establishment—and to politically pit members of the working class against each other, clearing the way for the government to adopt policies that clearly favor the haves over the have-nots.[9]

Cornel West has argued that racial conflict over issues such as affirmative action has been a key force holding white America together and preventing popular uprisings among the white poor. He asserts that "without the presence of black people in America, European-Americans would not be 'white'—they would be only Irish, Italians, Poles, Welsh, and others engaged in class, ethnic, and gender struggles over resources and identity."[10]

Many of the changes in federal and state higher education policy made over the past three decades have had the effect of making it harder for those beneath the top rungs of the economic ladder to gain access to selective institutions. Fewer than one out of eight young people from the poorest fourth of society enroll at *any* four-year college within two years of graduating from high school; among those in the top fourth, the share promptly moving on to a four-year college is about two out of three.[11] On the campuses of selective colleges, the children of the middle class are becoming harder and harder to find. Midlevel managers, shopkeepers, and schoolteachers have much less chance of watching their kids go off to a selective college than they did 40 years ago.[12]

It may be no coincidence, given such trends, that the United States has less intergenerational social mobility than nearly every other wealthy industrialized nation, with the class-bound United Kingdom among the few exceptions.[13]

If one subscribes to the belief that the United States is a plutocracy, an argument can be made that ensuring the children of the rich get into our best colleges actually is in society's best interest. After all, if the wealthy are going to run the country no matter what, it makes sense to give them the best education possible, so they won't be as inclined to make decisions that screw up life for the rest of us. Records from Harvard and other elite colleges show that their officials actually have at times worried that raising their admissions standards too high would put them at risk of losing their status as training grounds for society's leaders.[14]

Some critics of the current admissions regime argue, however, that the ascension of children of privilege to high-status positions is no longer automatic—they need academic credentials if they are to be elevated above everyone else—and thus selective colleges that favor the wealthy play an active role in helping rich families maintain their standing from one generation to the next, thereby thwarting social mobility. Plato wrote that it is possible for golden parents to have silver sons, and silver parents to have golden sons, but today's golden parents know enough to slip a few coins to the appraisers.

Such arguments are based on the assumption that going to a prestigious college actually matters, that getting a degree from an Ivy League college leaves you measurably better off than you would be graduating from a less prestigious institution. A few studies that have tracked college graduates over the long term and measured their success based on financial earnings have concluded that the benefits of attending a selective college have been greatly overstated, that earning a degree from an Ivy League institution doesn't leave people any better off than attending an ordinary four-year state college.[15]

The benefits of an elite-college degree are so heavily debated by sociologists, economists, and education experts that it is worth looking at what is known and what is disputed.

Clearly, students at most elite colleges have advantages over those at schools with lesser reputations. Because elite colleges tend to have large endowments, for example, they can spend more per student and subsidize a larger share of their students' educations. They also tend to have higher graduation rates than less selective institutions, a result likely related to the high qualifications of their applicant pools, the culture of achievement that they foster, and the superior resources they have available to help students who are struggling academically.[16]

Students at highly selective colleges also have an edge when it comes to earning advanced degrees. Nationally, about 21 percent of all four-year college students continue their education at graduate or professional schools, but among those enrolled at one of the roughly 160 institutions ranked by the well-regarded *Barron's Profiles of American Colleges* guide as "highly competitive" or "most competitive," about 35 percent pursue advanced degrees.[17] It is well established that most graduate and professional schools favor the graduates of prestigious undergraduate programs in their recruiting.[18]

The tough part about determining the payoff of an elite-college degree is separating out how much of a graduate's long-term success can be attributed to the college and how much reflects the intellectual or financial assets that the graduate possessed going in. Researchers have found that the more money your parents have, the more money you are likely to earn later in life, even when the financial benefits of inheritance are removed from the equation and you are compared with people who have equally good educations. It clearly pays to have close relationships with wealthy, successful people who can pull you up through the ranks, bankroll your endeavors, or at least demonstrate to you how it is done.[19]

If there is one segment of society that has been shown to derive long-term financial benefits from attending a selective college, it is, ironically, the low-income Americans who are the least represented at such institutions. A study that gathered data on people who entered college as freshmen in 1976 and checked on how they were faring as of 1995 found that those who came from low-income families and entered selective institutions were making substantially more money than the graduates of colleges with less prestige, even when compared with people of similar academic ability from wealthy backgrounds. About the only people faring better financially were people from wealthier backgrounds enrolled at equally prestigious institutions.[20]

A shortcoming of such studies is that they measure success purely in financial terms and fail to account for the less tangible payoffs of an elite education, such as prestige and power. Justice O'Connor noted in her Michigan ruling that a handful of law schools had produced a fourth of all U.S. senators and nearly a third of all judges presiding over federal district courts. Other studies have found that the graduates of elite colleges are disproportionately represented among the lawyers at major firms, the top officers of large companies, and the members of the foreign service.[21] Seven of the 18 U.S. presidents inaugurated since 1900 earned their bachelor's degrees from Harvard, Princeton, or Yale, and all but three attended prestigious colleges or professional schools. George W. Bush may have the most impressive academic pedigree of them all, having completed his early education at the exclusive Phillips Academy (Andover) boarding school before earning his baccalaureate degree from Yale and his MBA from Harvard.

Maybe we miss a bigger point in concerning ourselves with who is admitted to selective colleges and how much they benefit from it. The late Christopher Lasch, a prominent social historian, lamented that both sides of the affirmative action debate are so focused on the question of who gains access to an elite education, they fail to see how much our democracy would benefit if such learning was made available to all.[22]

This book might not democratize access to selective colleges, but it seeks to at least democratize the debate over who should be gaining admission to such institutions. I have written it to help ordinary people see how the opportunities available to America's children—and how our nation's future—are being shaped both by the decisions of an elite and by the choices all of us make in the home, the workplace, and the voting booth. I examine the role played by race and class in determining who gets ahead in America. I explore the history of affirmative action in selective higher education and its impact on college campuses. I chronicle the political and legal struggle over such policies, scrutinizing the motives and methods of all sides. And I look at where the conflict is headed and what choices this nation has yet to make. For those who are interested, I have set up a Web site, colorandmoney.com, with additional readings, news updates, useful links for both researchers and ordinary readers, and suggestions for book discussion groups.

I think a little honest discussion will do us all some good.

Chapter 1

Skimming the Top

How Money Rises Above Merit

"And to the C students I say, You, too, can be President of the United States."

—George W. Bush, Yale University commencement address,
June 2001

Bear with me as I walk you through a thought experiment.

Do you remember the cheap cardboard "X-Ray Glasses," advertised in comic books as giving you the power to see through the skin of everyone around you? Imagine opening a magazine and finding an advertisement that says:

"Smarts" detecting glasses! Be able to see who is elite college material!

And suppose that you order a pair for kicks, only to slide them on and discover that, lo and behold, the darned things *actually work.*

When you put the glasses on, you can easily spot people with the intellectual qualities top colleges say they look for, such as the ability to consistently earn excellent grades and test scores; or brilliance in a certain field, like physics; or the sorts of leadership skills one sees in class presidents; or even artistic gifts such as virtuosity at the violin. Through your lenses, those with such traits have a certain aura or glow to them. You can see it emanating from well-regarded surgeons, leading high-tech researchers, business executives who successfully steer big companies, and lawyers who rise to partner in large firms.

Now imagine that you decide to really put your glasses to work by visiting a prestigious four-year college or university, one selective enough to be consistently ranked by the widely used *Barron's Profiles of American Colleges* in one of its top two tiers. Because there are roughly 160 such colleges around the nation and they vary greatly in their size, program offerings, and student populations, let's try to come up with an imaginary college that represents a composite of nearly all of them, at least in terms of its admissions criteria and its student body. Given its reputation for serving the intellectual elite, let's call it Briterdan U.

At first you keep your glasses tucked in your pocket, just to see how Briterdan's students look without them. You'll notice that Briterdan is much whiter and more Asian than the world just outside its gates. Its enrollment is about 77 percent white, 11 percent Asian American, 6 percent Hispanic, and 6 percent black. It has few, if any, Native American students.[1]

When you put the glasses on, you end up feeling amazed—not at the sight of so many students who shine brightly, but at the sight of so many students with no glow to them at all. As you walk around campus, 15 percent of the undergraduates that you encounter will be white students with no aura. That's more than one out of every seven undergraduates, and nearly one out of every five white ones. If everyone out there were to put on a pair of your glasses, the single largest minority group on campuses would be dim white kids.

That 15 percent estimate is based on the research of Anthony Carnevale, a prominent education researcher and former vice president of the Educational Testing Service, and Stephen Rose, a research economist who also worked there. In the course of a broader study on whether class-based affirmative action might work, they decided to look into how many of the students on selective college campuses actually met the admissions criteria that those institutions claimed to use. They constructed a hypothetical, merit-based admissions process for each of 146 colleges in *Barron's* top two tiers—based entirely on those colleges' advertised academic standards—and then fed the academic profiles of the colleges' students through it.[2] Their academic-merit-based admissions models rejected that white 15 percent just as surely as you or I might spit out bad sushi.

How did that subset of students get in? Carnevale says that colleges did not provide the sort of data that could tell him, so one has to extrapolate the answer from other research and whatever else is known about the college admissions field. He says a sizable share of the 15 percent consists of athletes, but many more gained admission based on some personal connection— either they were related to alumni, or they were the child of some college employee, or strings were pulled on their behalf by a donor, a college official, or a politician.

The number-crunching performed by Carnevale and Rose also produced some bad news regarding minority students. If the selective colleges were to consider only academic qualifications—as measured by grades, test scores, teacher recommendations, and demonstrated leadership ability— their total black enrollments probably would plunge from 6 percent to 1.6 percent, while their Hispanic enrollments would fall from 6 percent to 2.4 percent. Although Asian American students generally don't benefit from affirmative action, their share of the enrollments of such institutions also would drop, from more than 11 percent to about 7 percent. The researchers attributed the anticipated decline in Asian numbers to the willingness of many Asian families to push hard to get their children into the best college available, which results in a number of them occupying college seats passed up by students who were more qualified but less eager.

Wearing your "smarts" detecting glasses thus would offer you an insight into one of the chief ironies of the affirmative action debate. Because blacks and Hispanics are more likely than others to receive admissions preferences, many whites who are rejected by colleges wrongly assume that a less qualified minority applicant took their seat. Because the admissions preferences that whites benefit from are largely hidden and offered only to some, few people ever question whether a given white student on campus is academically underqualified, and you almost never hear a rejected white applicant complain that he or she lost out to a less deserving white student.

The colleges in *Barron's* top two tiers serve about 15 percent of all of the nation's four-year college students. Another 20 percent of students enroll in the next tier down—colleges that generally require applicants to have at least a B-average and solid SAT or ACT scores, and that reject one-fourth to one-half of their applicants. The next tier below that—colleges that require at least a C average and comparable test scores, and that reject less than one-fourth of applicants—register about 40 percent. Although plenty of very bright people find a place at third- or fourth-tier institutions and go on to lead fulfilling lives, it is also the case that many colleges in these tiers lower the bar for some students while turning away others with better qualifications.

Put aside the "smarts" detecting glasses for a moment, and now imagine opening a magazine and seeing an advertisement for yet another strange breakthrough in optometry. This one says:

Privilege detecting glasses! See how advantaged people were as children!

Encouraged by your last experience, you order a pair of these and discover that they too work as advertised. The instructions packaged with them rightly caution, however, that the detection of privilege is a fairly tricky business. The glasses have shortcomings in that they cannot tell you whether someone's parents were loving or abusive, or whether there was someone else in their young life, perhaps an older sibling or grandparent, who offered them support. But the glasses are sophisticated enough that they don't just measure parental income. They also account for parental occupation, and they detect how well educated someone's parents were—a variable found by education researchers to play a bigger role than parental income in determining educational achievement. They'll show the child of rich Harvard MBAs to be better off than the child of middle-class Harvard MBAs, but they won't trick you into seeing the 17-year-old child of two janitors who just won $100,000 in the lottery as better off than the child of two physicians who just went broke as a result of a bad investment.

When you put the glasses on, you can see a blue tint—hinting at blue blood, perhaps—in the skin of people who grew up in the most privileged fourth of society (or what social scientists refer to as "the top socioeconomic quartile"). You see the green of money in the faces of those who grew up in the next quartile down, whose parents generally had at least some college education and live fairly comfortably. People from the third quartile down, coming mainly from working-class families, exhibit a red tint. Those who grew up in the bottom quartile, whose parents were poorly educated and struggle to pay their bills, end up looking yellow.

It occurs to you that by wearing your new glasses around Briterdan U., you might gain some insight into what role selective colleges play in determining where people get in life. You look forward to sighting yellow or red people on Briterdan's campus as evidence that it is helping people rise above their circumstances and fulfill their dreams.

When you get to Briterdan, however, you are hard pressed to find any yellow students. Carnevale and Rose have determined that just 3 percent of the students at colleges in *Barron's* top two tiers come from the bottom socioeconomic quartile, or families that generally earned less than $27,000 in 2006.

You also have trouble finding students who are working-class red, as just 7 percent of Briterdan's students are from that segment of society, characterized by family incomes roughly in the $27,000 to $51,000 range. Even green students, the ones from comfortably middle- to upper-middle-class families, are a lot less prevalent at Briterdan than outside its gates, accounting for just 16 percent of its undergraduates.[3]

No doubt about it, Briterdan is a very blue place. The sons and daughters of the top fourth of society, those typically earning well over $83,000 annually, account for 74 percent of its students. They are more than four times as likely as those from the middle class, more than 10 times as likely as those from the working class, and nearly 25 times as likely as the poor to be enrolled here.

All told, the 146 top-two-tier colleges in the Carnevale and Rose study enrolled 170,000 freshmen. If such institutions were to adopt a policy of having student bodies that reflect society, their first-year enrollments from the less fortunate half would rise from 17,000 to 85,000, and more than 83,000 young people from wealthy families would have to go to college elsewhere.[4]

Other research on college enrollments suggests that the wealthier the background, the greater the overrepresentation. A 2004 survey of freshmen at Northwestern University, for example, found that 20 percent came from families earning more than $250,000 annually.[5] Fewer than 2 percent of the nation's families had incomes that high at the time.

Moreover, the wealthy have tightened their grip on most selective colleges in recent decades. A 1998 study of college freshmen found that of those from families earning more than $200,000 annually, 27.9 percent were enrolled at highly selective four-year colleges, up from 20.5 percent of freshmen from the same economic stratum in 1981. Such institutions continued to serve less than 5 percent of college freshmen from poor or working-class backgrounds.[6] It is not the children of impoverished families whose numbers have shrunk as the ranks of the wealthy have grown. It is the children of the middle class who are being displaced.[7]

Differences in academic preparation that are linked to class and race account for some of the skewing of college enrollments toward the wealthy, but hardly all of it. Even among those high school graduates with exceptionally high SAT scores, those from wealthy families are more than three times as likely to enroll in the most selective colleges as those whose parents are working class or poor.[8]

Moreover, many of the selective colleges with low enrollments of students of modest means are institutions with vast resources to draw on for financial aid. *The Chronicle of Higher Education* looked at colleges that had $500 million or more in their endowments in the 2004–2005 academic year to see what share of their students were receiving federal Pell Grants, typically available to undergraduates from families earning $40,000 or less. Such students accounted for less than 15 percent of the undergraduate enrollment at the University of North Carolina at Chapel Hill, the University of Michigan at Ann Arbor, the University of Wisconsin at Madison, and 42 of the 59 private colleges on the list. Among the colleges where they accounted for less than 10 percent were Notre Dame, Northwestern, the University of Pennsylvania, Harvard, Princeton, the University of Virginia, and Washington University in St. Louis.[9] A separate study of state flagship universities by the Education Trust found that from 1992 to 2003, the share of their enrollments that were on Pell Grants declined from 24 percent to 22 percent, even as the share of all American college students who were grant-eligible increased from 29 to 35 percent. The share of flagship university enrollments that is black, Hispanic, or Native American rose slightly, but not nearly as quickly as the share of the college-age population belonging to one of those minority groups.[10] The overrepresentation of the children of privilege at flagship universities is not just an issue in prosperous states. Richard Bayer, dean of enrollment services at the University of Tennessee at Knoxville, acknowledged at a January 2007 higher-education conference that the average family income of students enrolled at his institution is more than $100,000, even though the average Tennessee family's annual income is just over $40,000.

As much as some conservatives like to accuse them of being leftist indoctrination camps, most selective four-year colleges probably would impress Marx as bastions of the bourgeoisie. Not only are most of their students wealthy, but most of the people setting admissions policies and making admissions decisions are, at the very least, comfortably middle class.

Consider faculty members who frequently sit on admissions commit-tees and, as a result of academe's revered tradition of shared governance, have a great deal of say over colleges' policies. In addition to being mem-bers of the nation's elite in terms of their own education and professional status—they have, after all, earned doctorates and landed much-sought-after jobs in academe—they also tend to have come from well-off and well-educated families. Among the studies documenting privilege among the professoriate is a 2001 survey of faculty members at the University of Illi-nois at Urbana-Champaign. It found that the professors were three times as likely as Illinois residents or the rest of America to have had parents with master's or professional degrees, and were disproportionately likely to be the children of lawyers, civil engineers, and physicians, and people even far-ther up the social totem pole.[11] Professors from humble backgrounds are a distinct minority, and many report feeling out of place.[12]

Although many faculty members could be making more money doing something else, most full-time professors earn enough to wear something nicer than worn tweeds. According to the American Association of Univer-sity Professors, as of the 2005–2006 academic year, the average full profes-sor received an annual salary of $70,333, while those at private, independent, doctorate-granting universities made an average of $131,292.[13] The AAUP survey does not count medical school professors, who are among the highest-paid members of academe, or the income that many faculty members derive from outside sources, such as consulting gigs or profits from the commercialization of their research.

Many college administrators make great money, especially those at the top. During the 2006–2007 academic year, the median income of presidents of public research universities exceeded $370,000. More than 100 public and private colleges paid their chief executives over $500,000.[14]

Of course, being paid well does not preclude one from caring about the less fortunate. Many selective colleges have adopted admissions philosophies that espouse the goals of rewarding the hard working, socially committed, or academically successful, whoever they may be; or seeking out and nurturing talent; or promoting the best interests of society; or even assuming the role of the "great equalizer" by promoting social and economic mobility. But colleges cannot do any of these things if they don't have the money to stay in business and award financial aid. More than half of public college presidents and four-fifths of private college presidents say that their institution, when pulling its freshmen classes together, needs to make sure a large enough share is able to pay full tuition.[15]

Derek Bok, a former president of Harvard, and William Bowen, a former president of Princeton, note in their influential book *The Shape of the River* that the admissions process at selective colleges has four broad aims: to admit an ample number of students who show promise of excelling academically; to assemble a class "with a wide diversity of backgrounds, experiences, and talents"; to attract students who seem especially likely to go on to make contributions to their professions or broader society; and "to respect the importance of longstanding institutional loyalties and traditions."[16]

Jerome Karabel, a professor of sociology at the University of California at Berkeley who has extensively researched colleges, takes a more cynical view, positing what he calls the "Iron Law of Admissions." It holds that a college "will retain a particular admissions policy only so long as it produces outcomes that correspond to perceived institutional interests"—for example, a college that is not enrolling enough students might lower its standards, or one that has exhausted its budget for need-based financial aid might take steps to keep out other applicants from poor families. He describes a college's admissions policies as being the product of a negotiated settlement among the various constituencies that help decide what its interests are, such as, internally, the faculty and athletics department, and, externally, alumni and the administrators of key feeder high schools.[17] Experts on college admissions note that individual applications often are the subject of negotiations as well, especially if the applicant is on the fence in terms of admissibility. Lloyd Thacker, the executive director of the Education Conservancy, a nonprofit organization committed to reforming college admissions, observed in an interview: "The more prestigious the college, the more political the admissions process."

In looking at selective colleges' policies, it is important to keep in mind that such institutions don't fashion their own admissions polices out of whole cloth. Driven by the rival spirits of competitiveness and cooperation, they often guide or copy each other.

Also worth remembering is that their admissions policies did not spring up overnight like mushrooms. They're actually a lot more like old trees, the product of decades of growth and adjustment, shaped by the winds that blew them, the storms they weathered, the constant efforts of colleges to grow toward sustenance.

The Origins of the Sorting Process

Although many of our nation's most selective colleges are among its oldest, none was very academically selective prior to the Civil War. Throughout the 1800s, most private colleges had fewer than 100 students, strong ties to churches and their local communities, and admissions criteria that were so distinct that young people prepared themselves for entry into specific institutions. The entrance examinations that colleges gave the applicants who knocked on their doors gauged knowledge of specific subjects, and bore a much closer resemblance to the placement tests that today's colleges give incoming freshmen than the SAT. Many of the students who performed poorly were admitted on a conditional basis. Neither private colleges (which survived on tuition revenue) nor the public land-grant colleges that arose over the course of the 1800s (mainly to provide training in agriculture and engineering) were in the business of turning people away.[18]

As the twentieth century dawned, Harvard, Princeton, and Yale admitted just about anyone who applied from one of the exclusive boarding schools that were their primary feeders. Once on campus, such students were not pushed to develop their intellects so much as traits like "manliness" and "character," freeing them to focus their energies on extracurricular activities and social organizations. Princeton's president, Francis Landley Patton, famously called his institution "the finest country club in America."[19]

Already, however, the nation was changing in ways that would cause its colleges to grow and be transformed into gateways into the professions. Industrialization gave rise to large national companies and management trends associated with their operation, such as quests to improve efficiency and to make society operate more systematically. Employers were asking applicants to have college credentials showing they were up to the task of overseeing complex organizations. Many colleges were establishing graduate programs to provide specialized training, and institutions geared toward graduate instruction, such as Johns Hopkins University, opened their doors.[20] Colleges began reaching out to the high schools sprouting up around the nation, both to recruit their students and to help them develop college-preparatory curriculum.[21] Immigrants pouring into the United States came to see a college degree as the ticket to the good life.

As elite colleges took stock of the broader societal trends around them, they decided they needed to open their doors to a larger segment of society while improving the quality of the students that they brought in. Accordingly, they raised their overall admissions standards while abandoning requirements that applicants have credits in subjects, such as Latin, offered almost exclusively by elite prep schools.

Then something happened that disturbed much of the Ivy League greatly: Smart Jewish kids from competitive public schools in Boston, Philadelphia, and New York—many of whom came from families that deeply valued education and had left Europe mainly to flee persecution—began showing up at the doors of elite colleges and blowing their admissions tests out of the water. Given the rising tide of anti-Semitism at that time, the Jewish influx did not sit well with the wealthy Protestants—mainly Congregationalists, Episcopalians, and Presbyterians—who had long regarded the Ivy League as their own.[22] The University of Pennsylvania, which took no steps to keep Jews out, and Columbia University, which failed to act quickly, lost much of their upper-crust enrollment and, arguably, a substantial portion of their prestige as their Jewish enrollments surged.[23] Most elite private colleges, which had not even been all that enthusiastic about taking in Catholics, saw putting a lid on Jewish enrollments as a matter of survival. Harvard, Princeton, Yale, and Columbia were among the institutions that adopted quotas limiting how many Jews they would admit.

It is amazing how many common features of today's college admissions processes arose or gained currency for the sake of restricting Jewish enrollments. The idea of using subjective admissions considerations to ensure a diverse student body was a reaction to the realization that objective admissions criteria had opened doors to a Jewish influx. Although selective colleges had long brought in subsequent generations of the same families, they did not feel a need for formal policies giving legacies an edge until those kids began losing their seats to Jews. Colleges started trying to gauge applicants' character through personal interviews and letters of recommendation out of a conviction that good character was something most Jewish applicants lacked. Many Ivy League colleges adopted the goal of having geographic diversity in their student bodies based on the assumption that they could bring in more bright gentiles by casting their nets far away from the large cities of the eastern seaboard.[24]

In *The Chosen*, a history of admissions at Harvard, Princeton, and Yale, Jerome Karabel says the admissions process that arose from that era had as its defining feature "the categorical rejection of the idea that admission should be based on academic criteria alone." Its cornerstones "were discretion and opacity—discretion so that the gatekeepers would be free to do what they wished and opacity so that how they used their discretion would not be subject to public scrutiny."

Another series of developments early in the twentieth century led to the creation of one of the most crucial sorting devices in the college admissions process, the Scholastic Aptitude Test (now officially known simply as the SAT), as well as its offspring, the Law School Admission Test (LSAT), the Medical College Admission Test (MCAT), the Graduate Record Examination (GRE) for graduate schools, and the Graduate Management Admission Test (GMAT) for business schools.

It all began with the French psychologist Alfred Binet's development of the IQ, or "intelligence quotient," test in 1905. When the U.S. Army began using the IQ test on a wide scale to select officers in World War I, it was found to sort people in a way that closely mirrored the social stratification of American society, with the sons of well-established families of Northern European descent outscoring recent Southern European immigrants, who in turn outscored blacks. For just that reason, the test was embraced by members of the then-flourishing eugenics movement, which espoused that intelligence was inherited and the human race could be bettered through selective breeding. Among them was Carl Campbell Brigham, a Princeton University psychology professor who adapted the IQ test into the SAT.

Brigham eventually recanted his eugenicist writings, but his enthusiasm for the SAT remained intact, and he helped persuade the College Entrance Examination Board—an organization established in 1900 to coordinate the activities of the Ivy League and its feeder New England boarding schools—to administer the SAT to about 8,000 high school students in 1926 as an experiment to see how it would predict their college performance.[25] The SAT would in fact prove to be a decent predictor of students' grades as college freshmen, but what really set the stage for its widespread use were two events that would test the entire nation: the Great Depression and World War II.

The Depression not only left colleges desperate for paying students, but shook the nation's faith in its leadership. Among the prominent thinkers who began calling for a reordering of American society was Harvard University's president, James Bryant Conant, whose ideas would transform how elite colleges picked their students.[26]

Conant drew his inspiration from a formerly obscure letter that Thomas Jefferson had written to a fellow retired president, John Adams, on October 28, 1813.[27] In it, Jefferson mused that "there is a natural aristocracy among men" based on "virtue and talents," and this natural aristocracy—not "an artificial aristocracy, founded on wealth and birth"—should be leading and teaching America.[28] In a series of widely read magazine articles seizing upon Jefferson's words, Conant said the nation needed to reject the leadership of its largely hereditary upper class and instead create an elite based on intellectual merit, its members coming from all classes and all regions but sharing a commitment to the common good. In a world that had watched rebellions against the old order give birth to communism and fascism, Conant argued that America could walk a better path by promoting social mobility.

Conant's writings did not transform higher education, or even Harvard, overnight. As of 1940—a time when only half of the nation's young people were earning high school diplomas—Harvard drew 60 percent of its students from the wealthiest 2.7 percent of the population and continued to accept virtually anyone from the elite boarding schools that were its traditional feeders.[29] But Conant established a new scholarship program to pull in bright students from all over the country and persuaded several other Ivy League colleges to join Harvard in administering it. The SAT was the instrument they chose to identify the worthy. When America was drawn into World War II, it seemed impractical for colleges, given the national emergency, to continue to select applicants based on batteries of essay tests administered over several days. The College Board turned to the SAT as a means of assessing students quickly.[30]

By 1947, demand for the SAT was so strong that the College Board could not keep up with it. Working with other higher education groups, it set up a nonprofit organization, the Educational Testing Service, to handle SAT testing. Within a year, ETS was administering the LSAT and MCAT as well. American College Testing, the administrators of the ACT test, set up shop just over a decade later.[31]

The Second World War set in motion other developments that would profoundly change college admissions. The horrors of Nazi concentration camps inspired a backlash against anti-Semitism in America that led colleges to stop discriminating against Jews. As returning black veterans began demanding fair treatment, the civil rights movement stirred. The GI Bill of

Rights, signed into law in 1944, established a federal role in ensuring college access, triggered a massive enrollment boom, and helped convince the nation that higher education should be widely available. The returning GI enrollments, combined with the ensuing baby boom, left state governments scrambling to build new public colleges. Meanwhile, the cold war as well as the U.S.-Soviet space race sent federal spending on academic research skyward and convinced selective colleges that they not only needed to become meritocratic, but also should rethink how they defined merit to make room for students who were not necessarily well-rounded but excelled in certain strategically critical fields such as science, mathematics, and engineering.[32] Simultaneously under pressure to both train brilliant minds and educate the masses, state higher education systems became more stratified, operating everything from flagship research universities with tough admissions requirements to humble four-year commuter colleges and community colleges open to nearly all.

The mid-twentieth-century transformation of American higher education further weakened the hold that the nation's wealthiest families had on its most prestigious colleges and prompted many of them to send their children to colleges that were less selective or farther from home. A 1990 analysis of the backgrounds of families listed in the *Social Register*—which includes fewer than 3 out of every 10,000 Americans and generally excludes anyone who does not come from an old-money background—determined that the number of students from such families graduating from their most prestigious local colleges dropped sharply from the 1930s through the 1960s.[33]

It is important to note that it was not students from poor and working-class families who were the beneficiaries of prestigious colleges' shift toward meritocracy. Their numbers at Ivy League colleges actually declined significantly after World War II. Instead, students from families with financial capital—the children of business executives—were displaced at elite colleges by the those from families with *cultural* capital, so that, by 1976, the children of college professors accounted for 12 percent of Harvard's entering freshmen.[34]

While the children of alumni—commonly known as "legacies"—became somewhat less prevalent on campuses, there was another group of applicants for whom colleges became steadily more willing to lower the bar: athletes. Many top colleges began setting up sophisticated athletic recruiting operations in the late 1950s and, with the growing commercialization of college sports, showed a willingness to forgive academic mediocrity in applicants who could excel on the athletic field.

The affirmative action policies that most selective colleges first adopted in the mid- and late-1960s created new categories of applicants who would be at least partly exempt from the rising academic standards. Colleges would alter their affirmative action efforts over the years—generally expanding them in response to minority student protests or declines in minority enrollment, sometimes curtailing them in the face of real or expected legal challenges—but they would remain focused on trying to strike the right balance between merit and racial and ethnic diversity.

The transformation of many selective colleges from all-male to coed—another key development of the 1960s—greatly increased the size of the applicant pool for these institutions, allowing them to raise their admissions standards for most students even higher but also forcing them to work harder to make sure various preferred categories were not crowded out.

The baby boom eventually gave way to the baby bust, causing a sharp decline in the college-age population in the 1980s. Colleges found themselves frantically competing for dwindling numbers of high school seniors and using mass-marketing techniques to reach as many potential students as possible. Although the number of students graduating from high schools rebounded in the early 1990s, other forces—such as rising operating costs and recession-induced declines in their endowments and their government support—have kept colleges under pressure to try to take in growing numbers of students who can afford tuition.

The *U.S. News & World Report* college rankings that premiered in the 1980s and similar college guides that have since emerged also profoundly influenced colleges' behavior. The *U.S. News* ranking system broke new ground by claiming to be objective and scientific, with scores based on the hard numbers that colleges provided in response to questionnaires. In an attempt to gauge colleges' selectivity, for example, it looked at the SAT scores of their entering students and what share of applicants they turned down. To get a sense of whether a given college was winning the competition for students, the magazine looked at that institution's "yield," or the share of its admitted applicants who actually showed up on campus rather than going elsewhere. Other numbers that the magazine threw into the equation were average faculty salaries, the share of alumni who donated (as a measure of customer satisfaction), and various measures of financial resources.

Of course, colleges cared about all of these things before the *U.S. News* rankings came along. But with the *U.S. News* guide out there, performance data previously kept hidden away in file cabinets now triggered measurable changes in reputation and marketability. Dropping in the *U.S. News* rankings can cost a college dearly. Not only is it likely to experience a significant decline in the number of applications it receives, it may have a harder time recruiting faculty or soliciting outside support. It may even experience a downgrading of its bond rating, forcing it to pay higher interest rates when it borrows money.

Some college administrators worried about such outcomes simply lie to *U.S. News* or withhold information from it. In providing the information used by the magazine to construct a profile of their entering freshman class, they may exclude minority students, legacies, recruited athletes, or students who were admitted from waiting lists or arrived on campus ahead of other freshmen to go through remedial programs.[35]

The more common strategy colleges employ for dealing with scrutiny, however, is simply to adopt policies and priorities that will make their numbers look better. The best way to look more selective, for example, is to get more high school students to apply. Realizing this, colleges have been steadily pumping more money into recruiting; as of the 2003–2004 academic year, more than four out of five colleges were spending at least $1,500 on recruiting for every student that they took in.[36] In the book *Admissions Confidential,* based on her three-year stint as a Duke University admissions officer, Rachel Toor confesses that her job included coaxing applications out of kids that Duke did not really want, just "so that we can deny them and bolster our selectivity rating."[37]

In an attempt to improve their yield rates, some selective colleges may actually be denying admission to many of their most qualified applicants. A 2004 study found, for example, that applicants with an SAT score in the ninety-third percentile had a better chance of gaining admission to Princeton than those with scores in the ninety-fourth through ninety-eighth percentile range, who presumably were weighing offers from other top institutions such as Harvard. (For applicants with SAT scores above the ninety-eighth percentile, the likelihood of gaining admission to Princeton increased, probably because Princeton saw competing for the best-of-the-best as worth the risk of losing some of them.)[38]

The desire to boost yield rates has been one of the key considerations prompting colleges to adopt "early action" or "early decision" plans and to enroll a growing share of their students through them. Under the regular admissions process, high school seniors apply to colleges by midwinter, get a response by early April, and have until May 1 to make their decision. Under early action plans, students generally apply for admission by mid-November and learn whether they have been accepted by mid-December, giving those who have been rejected time to apply to their backup colleges. Early decision plans, which have come to replace early action plans at many selective colleges in the past two decades, operate with roughly the same timetables as early action plans, but students who gain admission through them must agree not to apply anywhere else.

Colleges say allowing students to apply on an "early decision" or "early action" basis helps them identify those with the strongest interests in their institutions. One study of eight selective colleges found that about 96 percent of their students admitted through early decision, and just 31 percent of the regular applicants they admitted, showed up for class in the fall.[39] But both types of plans have come under heavy criticism for offering an edge to wealthy families with the savvy to know about them and for pushing kids to commit to colleges before they may have made a careful, informed decision.[40] Early decision plans have come under the heaviest fire because they require students to commit to a college before they know how much financial aid it will offer and thus give an admissions edge to those who don't need financial assistance.

Admissions Today

After taking a century of dramatic change in higher education into account, what exactly are we left with? Returning to the image of colleges' admissions policies as trees shaped by what they have weathered, we end up with a very twisted, knotted forest.

The nation's oldest, most prestigious colleges have not forgotten their roots and still look kindly on applicants from the venerable Eastern boarding schools that have traditionally sent them students. Students from the ex-

clusive old Eastern prep schools, known as the Select 16, have been found
to have a substantially better chance of getting admitted to Harvard, Princeton, or Yale than students from public schools with much better SAT
scores.[41] In general, it is common for admissions officers at selective colleges
to give extra consideration to students from their chief feeder schools, to try
to maintain good relations with those institutions.

Early action and early decision applicants to selective colleges also generally appear to have a substantial edge over applicants with comparable academic profiles. The authors of *The Early Admissions Game* took admissions
data from 14 selective colleges and found that applicants with SAT scores of
1300 to 1390 on a 1600-point scale increased their chances of being accepted by more than 50 percent when they applied under early action and
by 70 percent when they applied under early decision.[42] In analyzing 1995
data from 19 selective colleges for the book *Equity and Excellence in Higher
Education,* William Bowen and other researchers found that legacies and
early decision applicants generally had about the same edge.[43]

Although legacy preferences have come under criticism over the years,
most colleges appear unlikely to abandon them any time soon. It is easy to
see why. Because legacies have been found to be more likely than other applicants to enroll once accepted, admitting them helps colleges boost their
"yield" rates. Most colleges also assume that a policy of favoring legacies
helps inspire the generosity of alumni and their offspring. When the University of Virginia looked at the results of a major fund-raising campaign
that ended in 2001, it found that 65.4 percent of legacy alumni had donated, giving an average of nearly $34,800 each. By comparison, just 41.1
percent of other alumni contributed, and their donations averaged about
$4,100. Being (by definition) the children of graduates of the colleges to
which they are applying, legacies tend to come from homes that value education and academic achievement.

In rejecting an individual legacy applicant, a college may alienate or embarrass an alumnus, but in broadly curtailing legacy preferences, it runs the
risk of provoking an organized alumni revolt. In the late 1960s and early
1970s, efforts to reduce legacy admissions caused an uproar at Princeton,
where administrators ultimately retained the old legacy policy, and at Yale,
where administrators decided to restore legacies in response to an alumni rebellion led partly by prominent conservative pundit William F. Buckley.[44]
Harvard considered an admissions model based strictly on academic merit

in 1971, but then abandoned it after a test run showed that it would benefit high-scoring kids from the New York, Philadelphia, and Chicago areas at
the expense of legacies, athletes, blacks, and the graduates of private schools
in New England.[45]

As of 2004, Harvard was accepting about 40 percent of legacies applying for undergraduate admission, compared with about 11 percent of its
overall applicant pool. At most Ivy League colleges, about 10 to 15 percent
of undergraduates were the children of alumni. Few institutions showed as
much love for legacies as Notre Dame, where 23 percent of undergraduates
were the children of Fighting Irish. More than three out of five presidents of
public colleges and four out of five presidents of private ones say they believe
that legacy considerations should play a role in admissions.[46]

Many administrators at highly selective colleges note that being a legacy
applicant no longer guarantees admission. In fact, such institutions generally turn well over half of legacy applicants away, although it is probably safe
to assume that many of the rejected are kids with mediocre records who only
bothered applying because they thought being a legacy gave them a shot.
Many colleges assert, and the *Equity and Excellence* research confirmed, that
legacy considerations mainly come into play as colleges choose among applicants with solid SAT and ACT scores.[47] Although the academic performance of legacies in college is slightly worse than predicted based on the
academic credentials on their applications, they nonetheless hold their own
in college, with a median class rank slightly above that of other students.[48]

In comparing an individual student's grades or SAT scores with the average for a college, however, it is important to keep in mind that the average is probably being pulled down by other subsets of students for whom the
bar has been lowered. And because selective-college admissions is a zero-sum
game—given limits on class sizes, every seat taken usually is one less seat
open—any admissions preference given by a college comes at another applicant's expense. Admissions preferences also can have harmful long-term
effects on the students who received them; the more a college lowers the bar
for legacy applicants, one study found, the more likely such students are to
eventually drop out.[49]

While happy to remind alumni of the existence of legacy preferences,
colleges generally hesitate to discuss them with the public at large and tend
to insist that they play only a small role, as something that might "tip the
scale" or break a tie between two equally qualified candidates. Harvard long

used such language to characterize its legacy preferences, but when the federal Education Department's Office for Civil Rights reviewed Harvard's admissions practices in the 1980s, it found that the admitted nonlegacies outscored legacies in every area (except athletics) in which applicants were rated. For the most part, however, it's mainly public colleges that have seen their legacy preferences scrutinized and debated, because of their obligations to taxpayers and the large degree to which their affairs are subject to open-meetings and open-records laws. Some public institutions, such as the University of Virginia and the University of North Carolina at Chapel Hill, offer little extra consideration to in-state legacy applicants out of a belief that doing so would be unfair to state taxpayers, but give legacies a substantial edge in weighing applicants from elsewhere.

Two sociologists at Princeton University, Douglas Massey and Margarita Mooney, analyzed the records of freshmen who enrolled in 28 selective colleges in the fall of 1999 and found that while slightly less than half of legacy students had SAT scores below the institutional average, the advantage conferred on legacy applicants who received extra consideration amounted to about 47 extra points on the SAT (compared to 108-point bumps for underrepresented minorities and athletes).[50] A separate study of three highly selective private research universities found that the boost conferred from legacy status amounted to 160 SAT points.[51] Other research has found that throughout the full range of applicants applying to selective colleges, legacies are substantially more likely to gain admission than other applicants with comparable academic profiles.[52]

Much of the controversy surrounding legacy preferences stems from the advantages that they provide the already advantaged. One study of selective colleges found that their legacy applicants were about a fourth again as likely as other applicants to come from the wealthiest fourth of society, and that blacks, Hispanics, and Native Americans were about half as represented among legacy applicants as they were in the overall applicant pool.[53] The dearth of minority applicants in the legacy pool is especially an issue at colleges that were off-limits to blacks under Jim Crow. Although the University of Virginia has become much more integrated in recent decades, its pool of legacy applicants is not expected to mirror the racial diversity of its student body until 2020.[54] At least one study of selective private universities has found that their minority enrollments would rise, albeit slightly, if they did away with admissions preferences of legacy applicants and athletes.[55]

Considering that one of the chief motives for legacy preferences is a desire to raise money, it's no surprise that colleges also would take the more direct route and simply give a big edge to applicants connected to contributors. Middlebury College's dean of enrollment planning, Mike Schoenfeld, told the *New York Times* in 2003 that he was certain "every admissions office in the country is paying attention to families' ability to make a major donation." The Vermont private college's president, John M. McCardell Jr., estimated that its tuition would rise from $36,000 to nearly $60,000 in the absence of donated funds.[56] Duke University has acknowledged accepting annually 100 to 125 students based on their family wealth or connections, up from 20 a year in the early 1990s. The *Wall Street Journal* has estimated, based on interviews with education consultants, that a donation of as little as $20,000 can help get an applicant into some small liberal arts colleges, while a gift of $250,000 or more will get one of the nation's top ten universities to open the door for someone. It also can help an applicant's chances if the student's parents are employed by, or sit on the board of, a corporation or foundation that the college is hoping to hit up for money.[57] Rachel Toor recalls that, by meeting with development office representatives to hear them lobby on behalf of certain applicants, Duke's admission officers were able to get the scoop on the university's long-term plans. "Here," she says, "we would learn about plans for a new Center for Jewish Life, a Genomics Institute, and an addition to the gym."[58]

Because nearly every college depends on the government for at least some of its support, and public colleges are very much at the mercy of state legislatures, politicians also have pull in the admissions office. Several public college lobbyists, working in both state capitals and with the federal government in and around Washington, D.C., have told me that they spend a significant portion of their time lobbying their own colleges' admissions offices to accept certain applicants at the behest of public officials. Especially when it comes to public colleges, the desire to keep state politicians happy is also one of the driving forces behind admissions policies that give certain applicants an edge based on geography. Legislators from throughout a state can take umbrage if a public college does not seem to be admitting enough in-state students, and legislators from both big cities and the hinterlands sometimes take swipes at a public college's budget if they think that institution is not accepting enough of their constituents' children.

Both private and public colleges argue that promoting geographic diversity in their student body helps them expand educational opportunity and bring together students with different backgrounds to better learn from each other. Critics of the practice wonder if Harvard's students wouldn't learn more from the daughter of a Boston bus driver than the daughter of a Denver doctor. On a more practical level, favoring students from underrepresented areas helps colleges expand their alumni networks and makes it possible for them to boast that they draw students from far and wide.[59]

Selective colleges also like to keep those on their payrolls happy, and most have therefore adopted a little-discussed practice of giving the children of administrators, faculty, and staff extra consideration in admissions, plus free or discounted tuition, to show appreciation and promote employee retention. It's understandable how tuition benefits and admissions preferences go hand in hand. If a college woos a new faculty member with the promise that his or her child won't need to pay tuition there, and then tells that professor after years of service that the child was just not quite smart enough to get in, the result is likely to be a very disgruntled professor. Many colleges decouple their admissions and benefit policies by making their tuition benefit "portable," meaning that it can be applied at several colleges or, in some cases, any accredited higher education institution. But colleges generally don't offer their employees an admissions edge elsewhere, and a 2003 study of the children of faculty members at 25 private selective colleges with fully portable tuition benefits found that 10 percent ended up enrolling where mom or dad worked.[60] In the fall of 2004 I surveyed about 50 selective colleges, both private and public, for *The Chronicle of Higher Education* and found that most gave at least some extra consideration to the children of full-time employees. Colorado College had a standard abbreviation for such applicants, CER, for "college-employee relative," and pulled their applications from the pile for a separate review after two screening rounds. MIT, which put its applicants through five levels of screening, let its admissions dean take one last look at the applications of employees' children who had not survived that process, to see whether there may be any reason to grant them a reprieve. The University of Maryland at College Park specifically asked applicants if they are related to anyone on its payroll and assigned an admissions counselor to shepherd the applications of employees' children through the process, answering the families' questions and letting them know if anything was missing. Cornell University was twice as likely to admit the child of an employee as the average applicant.

Most colleges describe the level of preference given the children of employees as "a tie-breaker," "a tip," or "a thumb on the scale." But the University of Virginia's dean of admissions, John Blackburn, has acknowledged that if faculty or staff children "come close to qualifying under our comprehensive evaluation, we'll try to offer admission." Anthony Carnevale says his research into the admissions practices of selective universities showed him that steep bias in favor of employees' children "was pretty universal," though few institutions had a formal policy explicitly calling for it. Although most colleges extend such preferences to the children of all employees regardless of rank, people like janitors, groundskeepers, and cafeteria workers do not stand much chance of seeing their children rise to the level of being plausible candidates, he notes. The beneficiaries generally are the children of administrators and professors—a population that is already educationally advantaged as well as disproportionately white. Whatever views college administrators and faculty members may have regarding affirmative action, most rest assured that, at least when it comes to getting into the college where they work, their own children stand very little chance of losing out to the less qualified and a good chance of being picked over better applicants.

At most selective colleges, the biggest admissions preferences of all go to recruited athletes, many of whom would stand little chance of admission based solely on their academic credentials.[61] Much of the pressure on admissions offices to lower the bar for such students comes from coaches, but coaches would not be allowed to have such a voice in admissions decisions were it not for the benefits that winning athletics teams provide colleges as a whole. By keeping alumni fired up about their alma mater, winning teams help colleges' fund-raising arms—their development offices and foundations—take in money. Admissions offices point to successful athletic teams and the traditions associated with them—tailgate parties and packed stadiums, to name two—in selling their colleges to prospective students. It is common for colleges to experience a huge surge in applications after one of their teams achieves glory on national television.

A few prominent higher education leaders, including William Bowen, who now serves as the president of the Andrew W. Mellon Foundation, have begun to study how much colleges are willing to lower their academic standards to put together winning teams, and to question whether institutions that do so have their priorities straight. While many of us associate admissions preferences for athletes with high-profile Division I university teams, research has found that athletics programs actually have less impact on the student bodies of big universities than on those of smaller institutions that most Americans have never seen play. Athletes may account for 5 percent of all undergraduates at a Big 10 school such as the University of Michigan, but they easily account for 25 to 40 percent of each entering class at a selective Division III liberal arts college, and 20 to 30 percent of an entering Ivy League class. Although the coaches at smaller institutions appear to have learned not to waste their time trying to recruit athletes who stand no chance whatsoever of being admitted, recruited athletes are nonetheless overrepresented at the bottom and underrepresented at the top of applicant pools.

Admissions officers often argue that athletic accomplishments signal positive traits such as strong discipline, leadership ability, self-motivation, and a belief in teamwork. But Bowen and a fellow researcher found, based on an analysis of data from 33 selective colleges, that recruited athletes perform worse academically than might be expected based on their high school grades and standardized test scores, one likely cause being that coaches prefer to recruit those who are committed to their sport above all else.[62] Other researchers have found that the farther a college lowers the bar for an athlete, the more likely he or she is to drop out.[63] Before establishing the Education Conservancy, Lloyd Thacker worked 17 years as a counselor at Jesuit High School in Portland, Oregon. He told me in an interview that the only students he ever saw the Ivy League accept from his school, which sends nearly all of its graduates to four-year colleges, were recruited athletes, one of whom was such a bad student with such a bad attitude that his acceptance into the Ivy League dismayed people at Jesuit High. "The kids go to these schools and they say to me, 'I did not get an Ivy League education because I had to practice 30 or 40 hours a week,'" he said. Although minority students account for a disproportionate share of the men recruited to play football or basketball at some colleges, on most teams at most institutions the recruited athletes are disproportionately white. They also are less than half as likely as other students at selective colleges to come from the poorest fourth of society, although there is some evidence that they also are underrepresented among the richest students at such institutions.[64] Those who worry that colleges are putting too much emphasis on sports question what good the recruitment of academically mediocre athletes does for society in the long run. It may be much more fun to spend a Saturday afternoon watching a fullback on the field than a brilliant biology student at the microscope, but 30 years out, the biology whiz may be curing diseases while the former fullback's glory days are but a distant memory.

To justify their various admissions preferences that disproportionately benefit the well-off, many colleges say they also give preference to applicants from low-income backgrounds. Under the Michigan undergraduate policy considered by the Supreme Court, for example, applicants were eligible for a 20-point bonus on a 150-point scale if they gave some indication of socioeconomic disadvantage, such as revealing on application essays that their parents worked a low-wage job, or that they were raised by a single parent, or that they worked excessive hours while in high school. But a recent analysis of records from 19 selective colleges found that economically disadvantaged applicants fared no better or worse than others with the same academic credentials in the admissions process.[65] And a separate analysis of 2003 data from 28 selective colleges found that the only low-income students who appeared to receive any extra consideration in admissions were those who had both very poor families—making less than $24,000 annually—and SAT scores well above 1300. Some experts on college admissions use the term "the knighting effect" to refer to the tendency of higher education institutions to smile upon students who have obviously excelled in the face of great challenges. It appears that one has to be an extreme case to benefit from it—in the 28-college study, it played no role at all among students who had SAT scores below 1300 or whose families earned more than $24,000 annually.[66]

Before becoming dean of admissions at Reed College, Paul Marthers worked as an administrator at Bennington, Boston College, Duke, Oberlin, and Vassar. He says that nearly every college where he has worked has some form of "admission by category." They determine what types of applicants they wish to give priority—be they legacies, or athletes, or members of some other favored group—and shield such students from competition with the whole applicant pool by comparing them only against each other. Colleges generally allot enough seats to high-priority categories that, if an applicant falls into one, the competition will be mild. Students who don't fall into one of these categories—or, in the parlance of college admissions officers, don't have a "hook"—end up "in fierce competition for a limited number of spaces, once the institutional priorities are filled."[67]

Harvard annually rejects more than 2,000 valedictorians, and its admissions director, Marlyn McGrath-Lewis, told the *Atlantic Monthly* in 2003 that it rejects more than half of the applicants with perfect SAT scores, which it no longer regards as "that great a distinction."[68] The competition for seats in selective colleges' entering classes has been intensified as a result of more than a decade of growth in the number of students graduating from America's high schools, as well as various innovations, such as the development of online applications and the Common Application form, that have made it easier for students to apply to a long list of institutions to hedge their bets. Yale announced in the spring of 2006 that it had just had the most selective admissions cycle in its history, accepting 8.6 percent of its 21,099 applicants for the following fall. Also reporting record-low acceptance rates were Columbia University, Dartmouth College, Johns Hopkins University, the Massachusetts Institute of Technology, and Stanford University.[69]

Returning to our thought experiments with the "smarts" and "privilege" detecting glasses, it seems that selective college officials have ordered both, and have concluded that they cannot begin to offer admission to everyone who is bright, and that the well-being of their institutions depends on making sure a large share of seats are taken by the privileged. The colleges maintain that they don't admit anyone who seems incapable of doing the work and graduating, but their critics argue that, considering the effects of grade inflation and the availability of student-support services at selective colleges, to say that their students are able to keep their heads above water is not really saying much. Considering how many bright kids colleges are turning away, the test of applicants should not be whether they can simply get by, but whether they represent the best.

Of course, to even be seriously considered by a college, a young person needs to convince the admissions office that he or she can at least get by. The troubling truth is that black, Hispanic, and Native American students, as well as students from working-class and poor families, are substantially underrepresented among those graduating from our high schools with the qualifications necessary to make that case.

Anthony Carnevale says that any honest look at what is keeping poor and minority students out of selective colleges has to acknowledge that outright admissions preferences that benefit the wealthy are just "the tip of a very large iceberg." The effects of race and class on children's academic preparation and general well-being are so huge that, in effect, "the larger mass of students at selective colleges are given preferences long before the admissions officers get into the act."

As the next chapter makes clear, those who are white and wealthy have found a long list of ways to ensure their children get a superior education while limiting how much competition they will face from the less fortunate.

Chapter 2

Crossing Eight Mile

How the Rich Deny Education to the Poor

I had an epiphany while being shown around Hartford, Connecticut, on a tour that started in the dirt parking lot of the city school system's central office, in the shadow of a soup kitchen and a liquor store with bars over its windows.[1]

There are Hartford neighborhoods where you can set out on a ten-block walk and soon wonder if you will live to make it five. Yet this city is home to more than 24,000 schoolchildren. About nine out of ten are African American or Puerto Rican, and the overwhelming majority live below the poverty line. Several Hartford parents have waged a long-running legal battle to force the state to do something about the racial, ethnic, and economic segregation that has rendered the city's schools so inferior to those of its suburbs. I was there covering the lawsuit for *Education Week* in 1992, back in its early stages, and Jeffrey Forman, an assistant to the district's superintendent, had offered to drive me around so I could see the lay of the city.

Forman and I marveled at how the forces of segregation had managed to cause pockets of such intense poverty here in Connecticut, the wealthiest state in the nation in terms of per-capita income, and had left 16 of the state's 166 school districts serving 80 percent of its minority students. The Hartford school system, like many others that have been at the center of de-segregation lawsuits, was actually hoping that the plaintiffs would prevail, so judges could order the kinds of improvements that elected officials had long been unwilling to bring about.

As we headed into the city's downtown with its tall bank and insurance buildings, I asked Forman exactly what he would like to see happen here if the plaintiffs won. Pointing to a nearby corporate tower, he said, "I would like to walk into an office and see a former poor minority kid as the boss, and the kids from the suburbs as data entry workers."

I sat there in stunned silence, wondering if he really knew what he was saying.

We often hear people express hopes that poor and minority children will go far. But never before had I heard an educator express a desire to see the downside of true social mobility, the relegation of many children of wealthy suburbanites to low-paying jobs.

As I contemplated Forman's wish, a lot of the educational controversies I had been covering suddenly made more sense. I understood more clearly how people who professed liberal values could haul their kids out of schools that were becoming more integrated, or oppose efforts to make the financing of public schools more equitable, or put their homes on the market to leave school districts that refused to place their academically mediocre children in "honors" or "gifted" programs to shelter them from contact with poor or working-class kids.

Suddenly I could better put myself inside the heads of community leaders in Hartford's suburbs, who had done everything they could to keep low- or moderate-income housing projects from being built in their neighborhoods, and now, in fighting to preserve the school segregation that their actions helped cause, denounced any suggested remedy as "social engineering" and a threat to local school control.

When Americans talk about discrimination, they often use the word "ceiling," as in references to the "glass ceilings" believed to keep women and minority members from climbing the corporate ladder. Yet it is clear that *floors* really play the key role in determining educational opportunity.

It almost goes without saying that all caring parents, regardless of race or income, want their children to do well in school and life. Those with wealth and a strong educational background just have more resources available to them to nurture and protect kids, to place them in the best schools possible and push them along. If their toddler has developmental problems, they make an appointment with a specialist. If their child falls behind in a class, they hire a tutor. They enlist the help of a psychologist if their teenager exhibits emotional or behavioral problems, and if the kid gets busted spraying graffiti or smoking pot, they hire a good lawyer to make the charges go away. If they believe a school employee has done wrong by their child, they drive straight to the school and raise hell.

Just imagine, for a moment, what would happen to any teacher in an exclusive suburban high school who told the parents of an unmotivated kid with horrible grades, "Hey, somebody out there has to mop this building's floors when they grow up." Teachers consign impoverished kids to dead-end fates all the time, but they know they can't get away with doing that to the children of privilege.

The wealthiest parents generally provide their children so many advantages that it can take sheer determination and a lot of effort—often in the form of years of sustained rebellion—for those kids *not* to end up qualified for admission to a decent four-year college.

Of course, what is a floor to those above it can be a ceiling to those below it. When wealthy and well-educated parents seek to shield their children from contact with the poor, they often are, in effect, imposing a ceiling above the kids being shunned or avoided. Yet few of the people who contribute to the segregation of society through their personal choices and political decisions express outright malice toward minorities or people with less money. Rather than talking about keeping people down, they almost always speak in terms of just wanting the best for their own children. They seem to know, at least intuitively, that true integration of the races and classes would rob their children of an edge in life.

The Swedish economist Gunnar Myrdal chose An American Dilemma as the title of his landmark 1944 study of race relations in the United States because he saw this nation as torn between, on the one hand, its high-minded ideals and, on the other, the interests of groups and individuals with lesser motives such as prejudice, jealousy, and pride.[2] Horace Mann, the renowned nineteenth-century Massachusetts education leader, popularized the American ideal of public schools as the great equalizer, but this collective vision is constantly being undermined by the actions of people who would rather give their own children an advantage than everyone else's a fair chance. Although the nation's poor surely are better off than they would be if there were no public schools at all, much research suggests that our public schools reinforce inequality, because the quality of the education they provide is strongly correlated with the incomes of the families they serve.

Jim Crow has been gone for decades now. The segregation of schools no longer is something the laws require or people claim to support. Although 68 percent of white Americans opposed having black and white children in the same public schools back in 1942, by 1995 their ranks had dwindled to a fringe 5 percent. [3]

As a practical matter, however, our nation's schools remain almost as racially segregated as they were in the mid-1960s, when the real push to integrate them began. Studies have found that white parents consider the racial composition of neighborhood schools in choosing where they live, and when presented with an opportunity to send their children to magnet or charter schools some distance from their homes, they choose schools with low nonwhite enrollments. What is vexing to advocates of integration is that these parents may in fact be making a rational choice by seeking to raise and educate their children in the wealthiest, least-diverse environments possible, and they would sabotage their children's chances of someday getting into a selective college by doing anything else. As a rule of thumb, the whiter and wealthier a school's enrollment, the more likely it is to have well-paid and experienced teachers, a healthy budget, new facilities, small class sizes, few disciplinary problems, a well-stocked library, challenging and advanced instruction, high expectations of students, and parents who are active and influential in its affairs.[4] It may be a mistake to continue laying the blame for racial segregation on the stereotypical rural southern white Bubba in a pickup truck flying the Confederate flag. Today, the chief enemy of racial integration and minority progress may be the well-educated, SUV-driving suburban soccer mom who professes not to have a racist bone in her body and to be motivated only by love for her kids.

When Bill Clinton was elected president in 1992, many public educators were hoping that he and Hillary would make a gesture of support for public education by placing their daughter, Chelsea, in the District of Columbia's public schools. Did they? Hell no. They enrolled her at Sidwell Friends, an elite private school that serves Washington's upper crust, at which about three out of five students are white and annual tuition stood at $24,545 in the 2005–2006 academic year. Except for a few conservative gadflies, no one faulted them for their decision. It seemed to pay off: Chelsea went on to earn a bachelor's degree in history from Stanford University and a master's degree in international relations from Oxford.

Ellen Brantlinger, a professor of curriculum and instruction at Indiana University in Bloomington and author of *Dividing Classes: How the Middle*

Class Rationalizes School Advantage, spent weeks interviewing 20 white, middle-class mothers in an unnamed Midwestern college town. (She says she initially excluded the husbands simply because they showed little interest in participating, but her subsequent research established that it is mainly the mothers in families who make decisions regarding schooling.) Her research subjects included five public school teachers, four college professors, and four administrators at agencies that provided social services. She describes most as being "esteemed as the most intelligent, liberal, well-meaning people in society," yet found that they readily abandoned their liberal ideals when sticking to them meant putting their *own* children in classrooms alongside those from disadvantaged backgrounds. Her subjects held negative views of the poor, blamed poor children's problems on their home environments, and sent their own children to those schools in their district with the smallest low-income enrollments.[5]

In considering the nation's debate over affirmative action at colleges, it's worth exploring the broad societal forces that cause many white students to grow up with little exposure to diversity and leave a disproportionate share of black, Hispanic, and Native American students unable to meet college admissions standards based strictly on common measures of academic merit. The most powerful stratifying force out there may be residential segregation, which determines what kind of neighborhood environments kids grow up in and where most go to school. Parents shield children from contact with other races and classes simply by choosing to live in communities inhabited by their own kind.

In the Detroit metropolitan area where I grew up, Eight Mile Road serves as the symbolic border between black Detroit and the white northern suburbs, a racial iron curtain. Truth be told, even the words Nine Mile, Eleven Mile, Fourteen Mile, and Sixteen Mile have meaning. By knowing which major road people live near, it is possible to venture a good guess whether they are working class, middle class, upper-middle class, or rich, and maybe even whether they are Jewish, Polish, Italian, or Arab. In *The Origins of the Urban Crisis,* his award-winning history of Detroit after World War II, Thomas Sugrue notes that real estate agents and developers in that area "targeted their markets carefully, quickly giving suburbs reputations based on the class and ethnicity of their residents." Simply being regarded as too "swarthy" could get you redlined out of Grosse Pointe.[6]

Stephen Richard Higley, a geographer at Oklahoma State University, extensively studied the housing patterns of the wealthiest one half of one percent of the nation's population, people who reside in posh homes in places like Long Island's Gold Coast, San Francisco's Russian Hill, the North Shore suburbs of Chicago, West Palm Beach, and the towns along suburban Philadelphia's Main Line. He concluded that, although this nation has never had laws cementing the classes in place, its laws governing property and municipal governance have accomplished nearly the same thing, resulting in "a stratified place hierarchy with profound consequences for all society."[7]

As of the early 1900s, it was still common for blacks to live near whites, the wealthy to live near the poor. But several trends already underway at that time would cause society to segregate over the next century. Suburbs began popping up, their development initially driven by wealthy families that wanted to escape the ills of the city and the reach of urban politics and to assert more control over their local public schools and other aspects of their affairs. Comprehensive local zoning ordinances gained widespread use as a mechanism for keeping the less affluent out of certain communities by, for example, prohibiting the construction of multifamily dwellings and requiring houses to sit on lots too large for many to afford. "Restrictive land covenants" became a common way for the sellers of properties to dictate to the buyers how land could be used, and commonly had provisions barring the sale of property to certain races, religions, and ethnic groups. Even after such provisions were declared illegal by the Supreme Court in 1948, people often entered into unwritten "gentlemen's agreements" to the same effect.[8] Various federal policies such as the development of the interstate highway system, the destruction of working-class black neighborhoods in the name of urban renewal, and the construction of enormous public housing complexes for the poor, had the effect of promoting segregation by race and class.[9]

Although social scientists and policymakers have devoted a fair amount of attention to the plight of poor people in the cities, it is important to keep in mind that poverty remains a problem in much of rural America as well. In 11 states, more than half of the students in rural schools are poor enough to be eligible for free or reduced-price school lunches.[10]

The distribution of rich and poor, black and white has changed somewhat in the last 50 years. With the decline of cities in the Rust Belt and the rise of those in the Sun Belt, poverty has become less associated with the South and more a feature of life in the Northeast and Midwest. The share of families living below the federal poverty line declined from 36 percent in 1950 to 23 percent in 1970 and since then has remained at about that level, while the share of families considered affluent has more than quadrupled over the last half century, reaching 23 percent in 2000. As more people have become wealthy they have chosen to live in the same neighborhoods as other people with money, contributing to an increase in class-based residential segregation.[11] Not only has the middle class shrunk, but the supply of middle-income housing in large metropolitan areas has declined markedly as well.[12]

The racial and ethnic segregation of America's neighborhoods and public schools has withstood the growing presence of minority groups in the suburbs. Although the share of the overall suburban population that is minority rose from 18 percent in 1990 to 25 percent in 2000, the Hispanic and Asian American newcomers to the suburbs were not evenly dispersed; as with the new suburbanites before them, they settled in close proximity to other members of their own racial and ethnic groups. African Americans also have consistently moved into suburbs inhabited mainly by other black people.[13] Where they have been faced with a choice between living in well-to-do areas that are predominantly white or low-income neighborhoods that are black, many with good incomes have carved out new upscale black communities, in some cases by moving into low-income black neighborhoods and gentrifying them. Some researchers suspect the presence of large numbers of highly educated blacks in a metropolitan area may contribute to its residential segregation, by enabling those who are doing well financially to cluster in neighborhoods that are neither integrated nor low income.[14]

In the early 1990s, Camille Zubrinsky Charles, a sociologist at the University of Pennsylvania, conducted an experiment to gauge attitudes toward housing integration in metropolitan Detroit, Atlanta, Boston, and Los Angeles. Borrowing the methodology pioneered nearly two decades earlier by the sociologist Reynolds Farley, she showed to black and white people cards that depicted various combinations of houses with black and white residents and asked her subjects which represented neighborhoods they would like to live in. In Boston and Los Angeles, she threw Asians and Hispanics into the mix, both as test subjects and people depicted on the test cards. Charles found that whites, although more tolerant of residential segregation than they had been in Farley's day, still preferred neighborhoods in which they were clearly in the majority, and they showed more tolerance for a substantial Hispanic or Asian presence in their neighborhood than large numbers of blacks. Meanwhile, blacks, Hispanics, and Asians wanted to live in integrated neighborhoods and were comfortable being in the minority. But they wanted a larger minority presence in their neighborhoods than most whites could tolerate, and they saw neighborhoods that were overwhelmingly white, or visibly lacking members of their racial or ethnic group, as hostile and unwelcoming.

In her research in Boston and Los Angeles, Charles found a clear hierarchy in terms of what groups people were willing to live with. More than 95 percent of the Asians surveyed held negative views of Hispanics and blacks and only desired integrated neighborhoods if their neighbors would be white. Hispanics desired integration most with whites and least with blacks; blacks desired it most with whites and least with Asians. All of the groups surveyed associated living near whites with social status and living near blacks and Hispanics with a lack of it. But the chief consideration driving the choices of most was the degree to which they held negative stereotypes of the other group shown to them on the card.[15] In the case of Hispanics, skin color appears to play a role in housing patterns, with those who self-identify as white living near whites and those as black living near blacks. Those who self-identify as Hispanic are most likely to live around other Hispanics.[16]

Much residential segregation may not be by choice, as there is substantial evidence that discriminatory practices remain widespread in the real estate industry. In a 2000 study of 23 metropolitan areas, financed by the U.S. Department of Housing and Urban Development, researchers from the Urban Institute posing as home buyers found that real estate agents were even more likely to steer people toward certain neighborhoods based on race than they had been in a similar 1989 study. Class discrimination factored into the picture—whites were much more likely than blacks to be steered away from communities with high poverty levels. The researchers found that Koreans and Chinese in the Los Angeles metropolitan area and Native Americans in the Phoenix area faced about the same levels of discrimination as Hispanics and blacks, and that Southeast Asians in the Minneapolis area experienced significantly more.[17] The National Fair Housing Alliance has conducted similar paired tests and found that real estate agents used the racial composition of schools as a proxy for the composition of neighborhoods, intentionally steering whites away from the same heavily black or Hispanic school districts that members of those minority groups were steered toward. The agents frequently raised schools as an important consideration when dealing with whites, but rarely mentioned them when dealing with Hispanics and blacks.[18]

Race plays such a pivotal role in housing patterns that it trumps class in determining where Americans live. For example, among people who were earning annual incomes of $60,000 in 2000, the median income in the average white's neighborhood was $60,363, in the average Asian's, $64,129, in the average black's, $44,668, and in the average Hispanic's, $48,819.[19]

There are some communities that stand as notable exceptions to the residential segregation that pervades most of America. Some are older, inner-ring suburbs (such as Shaker Heights outside Cleveland, Oak Park outside Chicago, or Park Hill outside Denver) where well-educated, middle- or upper-middle-class whites have learned to live alongside blacks with similar education levels and incomes. Others are "multiracial islands" (such as Rogers Park in Chicago, Fruitvale in Oakland, and Adams-Morgan in Washington, D.C.) where no racial or ethnic group predominates. Researchers have found, however, that many of the whites in integrated inner-ring suburbs have stayed because they can afford private schools, while many whites in "multiracial islands" are childless.[20] Other studies have found that having children makes whites more predisposed to prefer predominantly white neighborhoods and that America's children are more segregated than its population as a whole.[21]

In Search of the Rare "Common" School

The fates of neighborhoods and the public schools that serve them are closely intertwined, with one key reason being that most such schools draw from well-defined attendance zones. As of 2000, the enrollment of the elementary school attended by the average white child was 78 percent white, 9 percent black, 8 percent Hispanic, 3 percent Asian, and 30 percent poor. The average black or Hispanic child, by contrast, attended an elementary school in which 57 percent of students were members of his own race or ethnicity, and about two-thirds were poor. Asian Americans, who were about 4 percent of the elementary school population, attended schools that on average were 19 percent Asian and 42 percent poor.[22] Such aggregate statistics fail to convey just how little racial diversity exists at many top public high schools in prosperous communities. When *Newsweek* ranks the nation's top 100 public high schools, most on the list have disproportionately small black enrollments, with the few exceptions tending to be selective urban magnet schools that draw talented students from far beyond their neighborhoods.[23]

The United States is unique among advanced nations in its reliance on local property taxes to finance public schools. With more than 40 cents out of every dollar spent on public schools coming from local sources, the wealth of a community generally plays a key role in determining a school's financial support. Partly because wealthy parents tend to be more skilled than poor ones in advocating for schools in their neighborhoods, there often is considerable disparity in school funding even within districts.

The relationship between schools and neighborhoods is reciprocal, with harm and benefit flowing both ways. Research has confirmed what real estate agents have long told young couples: a house is worth more if the schools that serve it are good, with the correlation being strong enough that improvements in a public school's median test scores or on a state "report card" can trigger an increase in home values in the neighborhoods it serves.[24] Given how much the socioeconomic composition of a school's enrollment influences student achievement, it can only help a school's perceived quality if low-income students are priced out of its service area. Conversely, when people are steered away from a neighborhood because of its schools, the result is downward pressures on home values. If the school district is forced to raise the property tax rate to maintain the same level of services, the higher property taxes in that area become yet another reason to steer people away.

There is nothing in the U.S. Constitution that establishes the right to an education or requires states to finance their schools equitably. That, at least, is what the U.S. Supreme Court held in 1973 in *San Antonio Independent School District v. Rodriguez*, involving a lawsuit brought against Texas on behalf of its impoverished schoolchildren. Most state constitutions, however, have clauses specifying that their citizens shall be provided public education and shall be guaranteed equal treatment under the law. Over the past 30 years, advocates for poor children have seized upon such language in suing state governments to compel them to change how they finance public schools.[25] Yet even when states have lost such disputes, lawmakers have been reluctant to overhaul school-finance systems if doing so meant raising taxes.

A 2005 study by the Education Trust found that after decades of school finance litigation, the nation's poorest school districts continued to have about $900 less to spend on each pupil than the wealthiest ones. In some states the gap was much larger; in Illinois and New York, it exceeded $2,000. Predominantly white school districts had about $600 more to spend on each pupil than districts with large minority enrollments.[26] Such gaps are substantially smaller than a few decades ago, but it is important to recognize that many in the education field believe it costs much more to adequately educate children from economically disadvantaged backgrounds than those from privileged backgrounds, given the deficits that poor children bring to school with them.

Social scientists are divided on the question of how much bearing school spending has on student achievement. Some contend that there is no correlation between the two, an argument that first gained currency as a result of a landmark 1966 federal study of thousands of schools, headed up by the late sociologist James S. Coleman. Widely expected to produce recommendations that the federal government pump much more money into schools serving the disadvantaged, the Coleman study instead produced the sensationally counterintuitive finding that school quality has no bearing on student achievement, that students' home environments and peer groups determine how well they learn.[27] Its conclusions have been backed by some researchers and challenged by others. Among the recent research arguing a link between school quality and achievement is a study by Edward B. Reeves, a sociologist at Kentucky's Moorehead State University who analyzed federal data tracking the long-term educational attainment of students who were in eighth grade in 1988. Comparing students with similar family backgrounds, he found that those who attended better high schools were more likely to earn a college degree, and those from affluent families benefited from good high schools and suffered from bad ones most of all.[28] But even those researchers who argue that school quality affects achievement acknowledge that students' homes and communities play a bigger role.[29]

As Coleman's findings suggested, the real payoff from attending a public school in a wealthy community may come from being surrounded by students from privileged backgrounds, who generally show up at the school door with more advantages than deficits, have families that push them to achieve academically, and benefit from teachers' high expectations. Richard Kahlenberg of the Century Foundation has found that low-income children in predominantly middle-class schools perform better academically than middle-class children placed in schools that are overwhelmingly low income.[30] Other studies focusing on students who had similar family backgrounds and academic credentials found that those who attended a high school where the student body was of high social status were more likely to enroll in a selective college.[31]

Partly in response to this research, a growing number of school districts have experimented with class-based integration to ensure that no schools serve a disproportionate share of low-income students. In many cases, these efforts have met resistance from wealthy communities on par with the resistance that white communities mounted against race-based busing in the sixties and seventies. I covered the first experiments with socioeconomic integration in the La Crosse and Wausau, Wisconsin, school districts in the early 1990s, and it was clear back then that such plans would be so controversial that they would be difficult to sustain. When the school systems began busing children away from their neighborhood schools to distribute low-income students more evenly, parents rebelled and mounted efforts to throw their school boards' members out of office. Within about a year, the Wausau district had begun losing students to private schools, the board members behind the policy had been ousted, the superintendent had been forced to resign, and the busing plan had been scrapped. La Crosse voters also tossed out several of their board members, but the district's leaders managed to defuse the opposition and keep much of their plan intact by giving parents a chance to opt out.[32] The Wake County, North Carolina, school district, which includes Raleigh, has likewise had to alter its class-based desegregation efforts in response to a rising tide of opposition from suburban parents.[33]

Within schools, many wealthier parents secure an edge for their children by getting them placed in programs for honors students or for the gifted and talented, or, at the very least, in college-preparatory tracks. The debate over "tracking" or "ability grouping" remains one of the most contentious in education. Civil rights groups often attack such policies as discriminatory because disproportionate numbers of the students in the bottom tracks are minority and low income. Some education researchers argue that low-ability students are immensely harmed by being placed in separate settings, and children of all ability levels can learn well together if the instruction is handled right. On the other side of the issue, advocates for gifted and talented programs persuasively argue that some exceptionally bright children are ill-served in regular classrooms, and many educators see ability-grouping as a sensible means of tailoring instruction to children's needs.

Although racial discrimination in classroom placement decisions is less of a problem than it used to be, educators continue to struggle with how to assess and place immigrant children with limited English proficiency. And class continues to play a key role in ability-grouping decisions—three times as many high-income as low-income students are enrolled in college preparatory classes, and low-income students are substantially less likely to be placed in such classes than wealthy students with similar academic records.[34]

For parents who can afford the tuition, there's always the option of using private schools. About a tenth of the nation's schoolchildren attend private schools, and these tend to be much whiter in their enrollments than their public counterparts.[35] Numerous studies have shown that white parents become more likely to send their children to a private school as the black enrollment of their local public school grows. Many parents also appear unwilling to have their children educated around large numbers of immigrants. An analysis of census data from 132 different metropolitan areas found that for every four immigrant students who enroll in a public high school, one native-born student switches from that public school to a private one, and white students account for nearly all of those who leave.[36] Both Catholic schools, which enroll about 48 percent of private-school students, and nonsectarian private schools, which enroll nearly 16 percent, are substantially more integrated than they were a few decades ago. But Catholic schools, especially in the Southeast and the Great Lakes region, tend to be either overwhelmingly white or mostly black, reflecting the composition of their parishes, and about half of nonsectarian private schools have enrollments that are less than 5 percent black.[37]

Many parents who enroll their children in private schools say they do so only to secure them a good education. Indeed, the U.S. Education Department has found that private high schools typically have more demanding graduation requirements than public high schools, and their students perform better on standardized achievement tests and are more likely to complete advanced courses. Among students who were in eighth grade in 1988, those in private schools were twice as likely as those in public schools to have earned a bachelor's degree or higher by their mid-20s.[38] On average, students at independent private high schools post SAT scores about 5 percent higher than those at religious schools, and nearly 10 percent higher than those at publics. There is considerable debate in the education field, however, over whether such statistics reflect the quality of private schools or the advantages that their better-off students bring to school with them. With annual tuition and fees now exceeding $3,200 at the average Catholic school, $10,000 at the average nonsectarian private school, and $25,000 at many elite private boarding schools, there is a correlation between the academic reputations of most private schools and the family incomes of the students enrolled in them.[39]

Given how much of a school's educational quality seems tied to the income and education levels of the parents of its students, it is worth exploring what separates wealthy home environments from poor ones. Class begins shaping children's fates in the womb. Wealthier mothers are not only able to afford better prenatal care but are less likely to be pregnant at a young age, and research has found that being born prematurely or with a low birth weight greatly reduces a child's chances of keeping up in school.[40] Low-income children are more likely than those from wealthier families to be raised by single mothers and to be moved from school to school, and less likely to receive decent health care or to be enrolled in a preschool.[41] Their parents talk to them less, read to them less, and are much less likely to take them to educationally enriching environments such as museums or libraries.[42] One recent study found that 85 percent of children from the wealthiest fifth of society enter kindergarten able to recognize the letters of the alphabet, compared to 64 percent of children from the middle and 39 percent of children from the bottom fifth. Class accounts for nearly all of the gaps between racial and ethnic groups at this age.[43]

Social scientists disagree on the question of whether it is the income level of wealthy parents that actually makes the difference for their children, or whether the personal attributes that enable parents to make good money play a bigger role. Clearly it is important for parents to at least have enough money to provide their children with food, shelter, and decent medical care. But among those families that can meet their children's basic needs, the relationship between parental income and the development of children becomes harder to pin down. When parents get stressed out or depressed over a lack of money, is it the lack of family money or having a distracted or irritable parent that most harms the children? While wealthier parents are more likely than poor ones to take their children to museums, is money the issue when entry to the museum is free? Might many of the character traits that make people valuable employees—such as reliability—be the same traits that make them good parents and role models, regardless of how much they earn?[44]

Annette Lareau, a sociologist who has extensively studied class-linked differences in parenting by shadowing families, believes that parents who are middle class or above differ substantially from the less fortunate in terms of how they rear their children and interact with schools. They focus on developing their children's talents, filling their days with organized activities. They also teach their children how to interact with others on an adult level, partly by talking to them often and using reason in dealing with them. Such kids walk into school with "a robust sense of entitlement" and a high degree of comfort with authority figures, and they know how to work the system to their advantage. Their parents view educators as equals or subordinates and are not afraid to challenge or circumvent them.

Lareau says poor and working-class parents, by contrast, tend to have a let-kids-be-kids attitude, letting their children spend leisure time in unstructured ways. Even when they want their children to participate in some organized activity, they often lack money for fees or the flexible work schedule and reliable car needed to haul them around. Such parents communicate with their children much less than wealthier parents, and tend to control them by laying down the law and punishing misbehavior. They approach schools with a sense of deference to authority, and their children are not nearly as comfortable in school as their middle-class peers.

Lareau offers the caveat that her observations reflect American families at this particular point in history. Middle-class children did not live such structured lives a generation ago. Other societies—including many that America's immigrants have left—continue to regard the parenting styles she observed in poor and working-class families as more appropriate.[45]

Nonetheless, knowing the traits that the admissions departments of selective colleges look for in applicants—including heavy involvement in extracurricular activities and the ability to make a good impression in interviews—it is easy to see how the products of a middle-class upbringing have an edge.

Other research suggests that teachers look for cues as to the social status of their students and adjust their expectations accordingly. David N. Figlio, an economist at the University of Florida, took the academic records of 55,000 children in Florida schools from the fall of 1994 through 2001 and, by using birth certificates to examine which names high school dropouts were most likely to give their babies when those children were born, analyzed whether teachers treated children differently based on the social status the names conveyed. When he compared students *from the same economic backgrounds* to see how much their names influenced their academic fates, he found that children with names associated with whites fared better in school than those with names associated with blacks, but it was the class, rather than race, connoted by a child's name that played the biggest role. Figlio found that just having a name associated with higher social status made it more likely that a child would be placed in a program for the gifted, and estimated that differences in teacher expectations associated with different names accounted for 15 percent of the gap in academic achievement between black and white students.[46]

About 10 percent of white children and a third of black and Hispanic children in the United States are raised in poverty. While whites are less likely than minorities to be impoverished, they nonetheless account for the majority of the nation's poor population, and research does not suggest that growing up white and poor is any picnic. John Hartigan Jr., an anthropologist at the University of Texas at Austin, has extensively studied poor whites in cities such as Detroit and found that they have more in common with poor blacks than with white suburbanites.[47] Edward Morris, a sociologist at Ohio University in Athens, studied working-class white youth at a middle school in a large Texas city and similarly found that they felt and displayed more in common with nonwhite people in their communities than with whites in the suburbs. While their black teachers treated them better than black students, their white teachers generally held them in disdain.[48]

Asian Americans, who account for about 4.5 percent of the nation's population, are commonly stereotyped as "the model minority," and on the whole are nearly 60 percent more likely than whites to earn a college degree. Their situation varies tremendously, however, depending on their country of origin. Taiwanese, Japanese, Indians, and Sri Lankans earn more per capita than whites, but 12 other Asian or Pacific Islander ethnic groups have above-average poverty rates. About half of Hmong, Cambodian, and Laotian adults in the United States lack high school diplomas.[49] Many of the children of Asian immigrants harm their chances of getting into a selective college by helping in their parents' businesses rather than getting involved in extracurricular activities.[50]

Clearly, many factors other than discrimination can contribute to the gaps between various immigrant groups. Some immigrants were better educated in their homelands or have been in the United States longer or learned English better than others, or have simply settled in parts of the country where wages are higher. Hispanic advocates often note that theirs is the nation's least-educated major racial or ethnic group, with just 11 percent of those over the age of 25 having a bachelor's degree. However, when one considers the low educational levels of many older Hispanics who come here from Mexico and Central America—about 44 percent of all Hispanics who immigrate as adults never finished school in their native countries—it soon becomes clear that the low educational attainment of the nation's Hispanics is at least partly an immigration issue.[51]

It's also clear, however, that a disproportionate share of the nation's young Hispanics are failing to go to college. Although they account for about 18 percent of the nation's college-age population, they represent just 9.5 percent of all college students in the United States and just 6.6 percent of the enrollments at four-year colleges. Research shows that they, like blacks, are much worse off educationally if they grow up and go to school in a segregated environment.[52]

For black children especially, race plays a role independent of class. Even black mothers who are well educated and middle class are more likely to have low birth weight babies than is the norm.[53] On the whole, black children start kindergarten well behind whites and fall further behind them in nearly every skill area in the ensuing years, even within the same schools and classrooms and in affluent communities.[54] On average, the children of wealthy blacks perform on national achievement tests at about the same level as working-class white children. At least some of the disparities between blacks and whites in middle- and upper-income brackets seem attributable to the long-term effects of past racial discrimination. And within the upper middle class, black families and white families tend to differ substantially—black families generally have much less accumulated wealth and are much more likely to have both parents in the workforce.[55]

Although 9 out of 10 black and Hispanic parents expect their children to attend college—a figure in line with white parents—their children are much less likely than white ones to have a parent with college experience who can show them the ropes. Both black and Hispanic students are far less likely than whites and Asians to take the sorts of challenging courses that selective colleges like to see on transcripts, such as physics, precalculus, and classes offering Advanced Placement credit.[56] Often, such courses are offered but blacks and Hispanics either choose not to take them or are placed on different tracks.[57]

American Indians and Native Alaskans are studied much less than blacks or Hispanics, but their educational problems also are severe. They post lower scores than any other racial or ethnic group in reading, mathematics, and history and are more likely to drop out of high school. The geographic isolation of Indian reservations makes it difficult for their schools, many of which are run-down facilities with outdated instructional materials, to recruit and retain good teachers. Many of their students make a huge cultural and social leap in leaving for distant colleges where few other Native Americans can be found.

Selective colleges are so eager to enroll minority students that if black and Hispanics are realistic candidates for admission, they're substantially more likely than white students with the same economic backgrounds to be taken in.[58] The problem is the unlikelihood of substantial numbers of such students rising to the level of plausibly meeting selective colleges' standards. In breaking down the 2001 SAT results, for example, Educational Testing Service researchers found that just 1,561 blacks and 3,012 Hispanics around the nation posted scores high enough to put them in the top 10 percent of all test takers, compared to 14,250 Asian Americans and 76,065 white students.[59]

A lack of money is one of the key forces holding back blacks and Hispanics. As of 2003, the mean SAT score of all high school seniors from families earning $10,000 to $20,000 annually was about 890, while those from families earning more than $100,000 had a mean score of just over 1120, according to College Board data. Among students who scored in the top 10 percent on the SAT or ACT, just 4.8 percent came from the poorest fifth of society, while 39 percent came from the wealthiest fifth.[60] Students who come from families in which neither parent has gone to college are particularly disadvantaged; fewer than 1 in 100 graduate from high school and earn the SAT scores selective colleges say they look for.[61]

Keeping the Upper Hand

If, despite all their advantages, wealthy high school students do not seem on track to gain admission to a selective college, their parents still have a few tricks up their sleeves.

In looking at the distribution of top SAT or ACT scores by various income levels, it is important to keep in mind that many parents essentially buy their child a better score through test-preparation programs or, less commonly, by enlisting the help of a psychologist or some other specialist to secure their child a diagnosis of some disability to get extra time on the test.

The *Los Angeles Times* looked into the granting of special SAT accommodations in 2000 and concluded that "hundreds and perhaps thousands" of high school students around the nation were using questionable claims of disabilities to gain extra time on tests—typically, half again as much time as everyone else, enough to easily boost their scores by 100 points. In six years in which the number of students taking the test had risen by 16 percent, the number asking for extra time in response to diagnoses of learning disabilities had surged by 64 percent, with nearly all of the growth being among wealthy white males in private schools or public schools in prosperous suburbs. At 20 prominent private schools in the Northeast, a tenth of students taking the SAT received special accommodations. The share of students getting extra time was four times the national average at top private schools such as Rye Country Day, the Dalton School and the Spence School in New York, and Greenwich Academy in Connecticut. In California, most of the students getting extra time lived in wealthy communities such as Palo Alto, Beverly Hills, and La Jolla. Meanwhile, even though the poor are more likely to have disabilities than the wealthy—largely due to their parents' lack of money for adequate health care—not one of the more than 1,400 test takers at 10 inner-city high schools examined by the newspaper got extra time. Advocates for people with disabilities argued that the disparity stems from the greater resources that the wealthy have to get their children examined for various conditions. High school officials said they know of parents who shop around among psychologists until they find one who will write the desired diagnoses. Tutors who provide SAT preparation said they have watched parents circulate the names of psychologists who will readily declare kids learning-disabled.[62]

More commonly, parents try to secure their children an edge on the SAT simply by signing them up for test-preparation services. As of 2006, private companies were taking in roughly $690 million from SAT, PSAT, and ACT classes and tutoring, according to Tim Wiley, a senior analyst with Eduventures, a Boston-based research and consulting firm monitoring the education market. In fact, about one in seven students taking the SAT or ACT enrolls in a test-preparation program costing $500 or more. Well over half of the nation's high schools also offer at least some SAT or ACT preparation, but many, including the public ones, charge students several hundred dollars for these classes, and the classes tend to be better and more available in wealthier districts. The larger private providers, such as Kaplan and the Princeton Review, typically charge $900 to $1,000 for SAT classes. Extensive one-on-one tutoring services usually cost much more; Los Angeles - based Eureka One-on-One Review offers packages ranging from "Exam Cram," three 180-minute sessions for $900, to "Premier," twenty 90-minute sessions for $2,999.

Several big test-preparation providers offer money-back guarantees of 200-point increases in SAT scores, but how much test coaching improves scores remains a matter of debate. Once one understands how most coaching services work, it is not hard to see how they might improve performance. Students learn, for example, that guessing on multiple-choice sections pays off (especially if they can rule out an answer or two) and that the sections get harder as they go along (a useful tip in pacing themselves and knowing where they should second-guess the first answer that comes to mind). Many of the better-known programs, such as Princeton Review, encourage students to try to think like the test-makers, who load up the tougher tail ends of the multiple-choice sections with possible answers that look right—but aren't—in an attempt to trip up average students. By learning how to spot the sucker guesses, students can greatly improve their odds of guessing right.[63] The SAT, PSAT, and ACT are hardly the only tests for which preparation is available.

Virtually every widely used standardized admission test out there, including those used by law, medical, business, and engineering schools, is the focus of test-preparation programs.

The services available to those with ambition and money are not limited to test preparation. Many companies will edit, or even write, application essays. Among them is IvyLeagueAdmission.com, which boasts of being created by Ivy League graduates who have served on over 70 undergraduate and professional school admissions committees. Its Web site says it offers "a comprehensive, start-to-finish writing service for candidates who prefer to have us write their essays for them . . . an excellent choice for applicants who, for a variety of reasons, are unable to transform their own experiences into compelling essays that will succeed at the Ivy League level." If those who have supervised the applicant on campus or on the job cannot be counted on to write glowing and persuasive letters of reference for law, business, or medical school, the company is happy, for a fee, to draft a compelling letter "that conveys the maturity, tenacity, and professionalism" that admissions committees seek.

Consulting services offer guidance in turning children into top-college material, with some targeting tykes who have barely begun to walk. Some New Yorkers pay consultants up to $4,000 to advise them on how to get their children into the exclusive local preschools that are seen as feeders for the exclusive local private schools that in turn feed the Ivy League.[64] Consultants also are available to help prepare their children to ace the developmental and intelligence tests administered by exclusive kindergartens. For $300 or more per hour, the consultants sit down with the wee ones and coach them to maintain eye contact with the adults who will be interviewing them, and, when it comes time to be observed playing with others, to exhibit a take-charge attitude while also showing they know how to share.[65]

Two separate summer-camp industries focus on helping high school students impress selective colleges. One type sets up shop at elite college campuses and, at a cost of about $2,200 to $3,000 for a little over a week, puts students through an admissions-focused regimen that includes SAT preparation, essay writing, mock interviews, and campus visits.[66] The other offers, for $5,000 or more, to let kids spend weeks dabbling in fields such as law or medicine, or to haul them off to Third World countries to provide assistance to the locals (when they are not sightseeing or trekking or snorkeling) so that they can someday convince admissions officers of their worldliness and humanitarian impulses.[67] Many college admissions officers wonder if the quest to turn children into selective college material has gotten out of control, making kids miserable by putting them under intense pressure and forcing them to endure classes that are over their heads, extracurricular activities that hold little interest, and overly structured summers. Vanderbilt University's dean of undergraduate admissions, William Shain, recently lamented that, especially in the Boston-Washington corridor, college admissions has taken on "a Darwinian flavor of survival of the fittest," with parents more worried about the prestige of the institutions that accept their children than whether those colleges are a good fit.[68]

High school guidance counselors also can play a key role in determining whether students get into a selective college, but high schools are all over the map in terms of the quality of the guidance they provide. At the upper extreme, counselors at the East Coast's elite Select 16 private schools maintain incredibly cozy relations with the admissions officers at top colleges. When college admissions officers visit the schools, they often overnight so they can stick around for dinner and drinks; the school counselors, in turn, visit elite colleges to observe the admissions process and advocate for applicants. The two sides are tight enough that college admissions officers will tell counselors exactly what types of students they are shopping for that year—outstanding baseball players or cellists for the chamber orchestra—and counselors can persuade admissions officers to overlook flaws in certain applicants. The best of the counselors build thick dossiers on each student to have selling points on hand.[69]

Meanwhile, out in the nation's public schools, most guidance counselors are too swamped to even get to know many of their students, much less schmooze anyone on their behalf. A 2002 study by the Educational Testing Service found that, on average, American high schools have one certified counselor for every 285 students. The ratios tended to be much better in schools that were predominantly white or where most of the students were college bound; schools that were half to three-quarters minority had one counselor for every 323 students.[70]

Several studies have found large class-based disparities in the college guidance students receive at school and home. Low-income high school students are much less likely than wealthy ones to know what courses their state's flagship universities want them to have taken.[71] Just 42 percent of students at noncompetitive public high schools have a good idea of how early admissions plans operate, compared to 88 percent at highly competitive publics and 94 percent at highly competitive privates.[72] The American Council on Education has estimated, based on federal data, that about 1.5 million college students who are eligible for need-based federal Pell Grants never apply because many simply do not know such aid is available. Researchers at Johns Hopkins University found that a fifth of low-income students who rank among the top 20 percent of high school graduates in terms of academic achievement do not go on to college, mainly because they lack guidance in planning for it or assume they cannot afford it and don't bother applying for aid.[73]

Several of the things that colleges consider when weighing applicants compound the advantages and disadvantages associated with class. In calculating grade point averages, many colleges give extra weight to Advanced Placement courses—which are more common in wealthier schools and disproportionately enroll white upper-income students—even though some research says earning AP credits does not make students any likelier to excel in college or earn a bachelor's degree.[74] The reputation of a student's high school, as often measured by the share of its students who go on to college and the selectivity of colleges that admit them, also carries a lot of weight. Colleges' desire to see past involvement in extracurricular activities works to the detriment of students who need to work. Not only have studies shown that students from higher socioeconomic backgrounds are more likely to be involved in school organizations and teams, but one analysis of 194 different high schools' yearbooks found that minority students were underrepresented in extracurricular groups as a whole and tended to be disproportionately involved in some while being largely absent from others.[75] In addition, because colleges don't like to offer admission to students who will decide to go elsewhere, many look favorably on applicants who have demonstrated interest by visiting their campus at least once, thus giving an edge to those whose parents can easily afford travel.

Of course, even if students get into a selective college, they still confront the question of how they are going to pay for their education. The federal Advisory Committee on Student Financial Assistance has estimated that every year financial considerations prompt about 170,000 qualified students from low- and moderate-income families to decide not to attend any college. In addition, college students with high unmet financial needs are only about a third as likely to graduate as those with low unmet needs and equal academic qualifications.[76] The financial pressures on low-income college students are getting worse. In the period since 1976, the tuition at four-year colleges rose about three times as much as the Consumer Price Index and similarly outpaced wage growth for most segments of society. As a rule, black, Hispanic, and low-income students are more likely than others to respond to the sticker shock brought on by a tuition increase or a decline in available financial aid by choosing to enroll in another type of institution—often a local community college—or to forgo college entirely.[77]

At the same time that students are struggling to keep up with rising tuitions, several trends in financial aid policy are causing a growing share of aid dollars to go to students who don't really need the money.

Until the early 1990s, colleges routinely met to compare how much aid they planned to give certain applicants, to bring their offers into line and avoid falling into bidding wars. When the Justice Department halted the practice as illegal price fixing, the bidding wars that colleges had warned of began. These days, most colleges engage in "tuition discounting," the practice of awarding merit-based financial aid to desirable students who don't really need it, to entice wealthy and high-achieving students to enroll. From a bottom-line perspective, it makes much less sense for a college to offer a full scholarship to a poor kid than it does to spend that money on partial scholarships to draw several wealthy kids who will pay the rest of their college costs and maybe even donate generously as alumni. As of 2005, well over a third of college presidents reported being willing to cut into their budgets for need-based financial aid to award more scholarships based on merit.[78] A study of flagship universities charted a 29 percent increase in their spending on students from families making less than $20,000—but a 186 percent increase in their spending on aid to students from families making more than $100,000—from 1995 to 2003.[79] A separate 2006 study found that just 40 percent of the financial aid being given out by public four-year colleges is going to students with documented financial need.[80]

Institutional self-interests have crept into the award of need-based financial aid as well. Many colleges have adopted an approach called "merit within need," under which the more sought-after students are given grants, while less-attractive prospects are offered loans that must be repaid.[81] Because most private colleges' internal funds for financial aid come from tuition, the best way for them to come up with more aid for some is to charge the rest more.[82] Toward the end of the admissions cycle, when their annual budgets for financial aid are tapped out, many colleges choose only those applicants who can pay their own way. Some colleges with ostensibly "need-blind" admissions policies intentionally withhold financial aid from needy but undesirable students—mainly those who are low-income—to discourage them from enrolling. The practice of deliberately giving students less aid than they need to cover college costs is called "gapping," and it appears to be on the rise. "That students are rejected on the basis of income is one of the most closely held secrets in admissions; enrollment managers say the practice is far more prevalent than schools let on," the *Atlantic Monthly* reported in a 2005 story on college financial-aid policies.[83]

Many state governments are getting stingier with their spending on need-based aid, especially during economic downturns, and as a result aid has failed to keep up with inflation. Although need-based programs still accounted for more than 70 percent of all state college aid spending in the 2004–2005 academic year, more than two-thirds of need-based aid was being distributed by just eight large states—California, Illinois, Indiana, New Jersey, New York, Ohio, Pennsylvania, and Texas—and many others had small need-based aid programs or none at all, according to the National Association of State Student Grant and Aid Programs.

Meanwhile, state spending on merit-based scholarship programs has more than quadrupled in a decade, as merit-based scholarship programs financed through lotteries or legalized gambling have become the primary source of student aid in many states.[84] Georgia, which kicked off the trend by establishing its lottery-financed HOPE scholarship program in 1993, distributed $457-million in merit-based aid and just $1.5-million in need-based aid in the 2004–2005 academic year. Studies of its HOPE program have concluded that 90 percent of its scholarship money is handed to students who would have gone to college regardless of aid, which may help explain why the program is wildly popular among those with above-average incomes.[85] The program has been so successful in enticing wealthier kids to remain in the state for college that many students at the University of Georgia in Athens jokingly refer to their institution as "the University of Marietta," after the prosperous and conservative Atlanta suburb that served as Newt Gingrich's power base. Among other states with similar merit-based scholarship programs, Louisiana handed out about $116.7 million in merit-based aid and $1.5 million in grants based on need. A January 2007 report by Eduventures, an education-consulting company, found that from 1994 to 2004 students from the top family income quartile received three times as much financial aid than students in the lowest quartile.[86]

The federal government has been shifting away from need-based grants as well. It began giving out a large share of aid dollars in the form of loans during the Reagan administration, and then adopted tuition tax credits, which primarily benefit middle- and upper-middle-class families, under Clinton. Today, under President George W. Bush, just 20 percent of federal student aid dollars is given out in the form of need-based grants, while about 70 percent is disbursed as loans, 9 percent as education tax breaks, and the remaining 1 percent as payments to students through federal work-study programs. Meanwhile, spending on the chief federal program providing need-based aid, the Pell Grant program, has not risen fast enough to keep up with tuition inflation, so that such grants now cover just 36 percent of the total cost of attending a four-year public college.

For families and students without a considerable amount of equity to fall back on, borrowing for college can be a scary proposition. About a fifth of students who borrow for college eventually drop out, and the long-term financial consequences of borrowing for college and then failing to earn a degree can be severe. Nearly a fourth of students who drop out after borrowing end up defaulting on their student loans within six years, with one result being that they are saddled with bad credit ratings. Several of the things that low-income students routinely do to try to pay for their education—such as deferring college entry, going to college part time, or working full time while enrolled—have been shown to substantially reduce their chances of graduating.[87]

Even the way in which the federal government determines aid eligibility works to the detriment of low-income students. For the sake of preventing families from gaming the system, the federal government makes it extremely difficult for aid applicants to declare themselves independent and thus exclude their parents' income in calculating how much money they have available—even when their parents truly won't be giving them a dime. When students work long hours to pay their college bills, the money that they earn is counted as part of their financial resources, rendering some ineligible for aid and reducing how much others receive.[88] Meanwhile, an entire segment of the financial-planning industry has evolved to help wealthier families hide their money from the federal government when filling out financial aid applications. Among the advice they offer: Put money into annuities where it does not have to be reported on aid applications, spend down children's trust funds to make them look needier, and defer bonuses to keep reported income artificially low.[89]

Looking at the picture broadly, it seems that poor and working-class kids must traverse a daunting obstacle course to get to a selective college while rich kids stroll along a moving sidewalk.

Nearly all of the obstacles that have been put in front of the less fortunate have been assigned some justification. Federal officials say that their financial aid policies help them stretch federal tax dollars to help as many students as possible. State backers of merit-based student aid argue that tying aid to grades encourages many students to push themselves harder. Colleges say that their definition of academic merit—and their consideration of SAT and ACT scores and school quality in measuring it—is based on their best judgment of which students are most likely to succeed.

But some researchers who have looked into college admissions and financial aid policies take a darker view. Among them, David Karen, a sociologist at Bryn Mawr College, and Kevin J. Dougherty, a higher education professor at Columbia University's Teachers College, have argued that decisions as to who deserves admission or financial aid "are not politically innocent, in either origin or consequences." How colleges define merit is shaped by the values and self-interests of the definers. The colleges decide who they want to serve and see get ahead, and then set their admissions standards accordingly.[90] To borrow from George Orwell's *Animal Farm,* if pigs were to decide who was fit to rule the barnyard, their criteria for leadership almost certainly would include a snout, a curly tail, and hooves.

Colleges adopted affirmative action for the sake of helping certain segments of society transcend the barriers placed before them by racial and class segregation. But, upon close examination, it is clear that rather than rethinking their old definition of merit, colleges simply carved out new exceptions to it based on race and ethnicity. Rather than offering true equal opportunity, they decided to create the appearance of it, by giving the members of certain minority groups the same sort of special treatment they were giving the well connected. They appeased those who were threatening to tear down their walls by letting some of them through the gate.

Chapter 3

Putting Out Fires

The Origins of College Affirmative Action

I have never witnessed the birth of a college affirmative action policy, but I was around at the conception of one, and I don't recall there being much love.

In March 1987 student protests erupted at the University of Michigan at Ann Arbor, and the Detroit bureau of the Associated Press sent me, one of its reporters, to cover events unfolding there. There had been growing unrest on the campus since the previous fall, when black student leaders first began pushing the administration to do something about racism on campus and the university's declining black enrollment. In the intervening months, tensions had been heightened by several incidents. Someone had slipped a flier declaring open hunting season on "porch monkeys" under the door of a dormitory student lounge occupied by a group of young black women. A campus radio station had aired a series of calls from listeners telling racist jokes. And unseen vandals had repeatedly toppled a wooden shanty erected on campus to protest Apartheid in South Africa. Earlier in March, at public hearings held on campus, black state lawmakers had heard from minority students enough complaints of racism and racial isolation that they threatened to try to withhold tax dollars from the university unless it took steps to show it cared about anyone other than rich white kids from the suburbs.

I arrived on campus to find several hundred of the university's roughly 39,000 students marching outside the Fleming Administration Building. Most were black or Hispanic, but they included a smattering of Asians and dozens of whites, many of whom advertised their political leanings by displaying slogans such as "Stop Rape," "Free South Africa," or "U.S. Out of El Salvador" on their jackets and backpacks. Anthony Henderson, a black graduate student, clenched a microphone and declared, "When you have 500 students marching around saying 'black power,' the university has failed you!" Later that day, as protesters arrived with pillows, blankets, books, sodas, and bags of cookies and chips to begin an overnight sit-in on the first floor of the main administration building, one of their leaders told me, "We may have to shut the whole university down."

Over the next few days, protesters would disrupt a meeting of the university's Board of Regents, badger regents and administrators as they walked the campus, and summon Jesse Jackson to Ann Arbor to draw attention to their cause and negotiate on their behalf. The unrest ended when the university's president, Harold Shapiro, announced a series of new initiatives responding to their demands. Speaking to about 4,000 students in an auditorium, Shapiro said, "The single most important thing we have agreed on is that it is in the interest of the university to increase the representation of blacks, proportionate to their numbers in the population"—an ambitious goal considering that blacks accounted for 5.3 percent of the university's enrollment and about 13 percent of Michigan's residents. Shapiro also pledged that the university would increase funding for black student groups, name a senior black administrator in its Office of Affirmative Action, recruit more black faculty members and administrators, and adopt policies aimed at squelching bigotry.[1] The Michigan administration's efforts to make good on Shapiro's promises would eventually result in the admissions preferences challenged before the Supreme Court 16 years later.

Jackson praised Shapiro's plan and the campus returned to calm. But Sarah Goddard Power, a university regent with 12 years of service on the board and a long history of human rights advocacy, remained bothered by the racial tensions on campus and deeply hurt by the chants of protesters who had hounded her on a trip across campus, her friends later said. The day after Shapiro's speech, she made her way to the eighth floor of the university's Burton Memorial Tower, sat on a window ledge, and pushed herself free of the edifice, to her death.[2]

A current college freshman—someone born well after the emergence of punk rock, too young to remember the Berlin Wall—might be forgiven for thinking that colleges adopted race-conscious admissions policies purely for educational reasons, as if their administrators were swayed by research showing that all students, including white ones, would learn better. This, after all, is the justification for racial preferences that Michigan and other colleges presented to the Supreme Court in 2003 and continue to espouse today.

But if I had asked those young protesters back in 1987 if their objective was to enhance the learning experience of white kids, I would have gotten confused or dirty looks. Few people in the Michigan administration seemed to be talking about the educational benefits of diversity then. For that matter, they had not said much about such benefits back in 1975, when a group calling itself the Black United Front unsuccessfully demanded control over 25 percent of the university's budget; or back in 1970, when black students held a campus strike and detonated a tear-gas bomb at an honors convocation to get administrators to promise to increase black enrollment to 10 percent; or in 1968, when more than 100 black students responded to the assassination of Dr. Martin Luther King Jr. by locking themselves inside an administration building until the university pledged to recruit more black students and professors.[3]

Colleges initially adopted affirmative action in the 1960s for the sake of becoming racially integrated and keeping the peace at a time when the nation's campuses were in turmoil and many of its major cities were on fire. Such policies were very much the product of black rage and white fear. When the U.S. Commission on Civil Rights issued a statement of support for such programs in 1977, it noted, looking back, that they had been developed for two fundamental reasons: to provide redress for past discrimination by the colleges and to offer opportunities to people who might not get them otherwise.[4]

What enabled blacks—and, to some extent, women—to make inroads into selective colleges was a combination of political agitation and real and threatened litigation. No similar gains were made by other segments of society that were marginalized but failed to mobilize, such as poor and working-class whites, or Jews, Catholics, Poles, and Italians.[5] Native Americans, due to their small share of most colleges' enrollments and most states' electorates, have had mixed success in getting colleges to meet their needs—today one of America's most racially segregated public college systems is

South Dakota's, where two public four-year colleges are predominantly Native American, the other six, overwhelmingly white. Hispanics have been successful in getting colleges' attention in states where they are numerous enough to elect lawmakers who champion their cause, but elsewhere they often have remained off the radar screen. Although some selective colleges gave preferences to Asian American applicants early on, by the 1980s, Asian Americans received little extra consideration from admissions offices and, at some colleges, complained they were the victims of the same sort of admissions bias that Jews had suffered a half century earlier.[6]

By the early 1970s, the federal government was promoting the use of racial preferences in employment and contracting, and federal bureaucrats' decisions as to who should benefit from affirmative action would help shape the policies of academe.[7] By the mid-1970s, colleges came to see being committed to recruiting and educating minority students as a way to attract financial support from business, philanthropies, and federal agencies.

Colleges were not completely oblivious to the idea that diversity on campus had educational benefits. As far back as 1950, in *Sweatt v. Painter,* one of two landmark rulings that year calling for the desegregation of public colleges, the Supreme Court declared: "Few students, and no one who has practiced law, would choose to study in an academic vacuum, removed from the interplay of ideas and the exchange of views with which law is concerned." But the diversity rationale for affirmative action would be just one of several—and hardly the primary one—espoused by colleges that rallied behind the use of racial quotas in the first full-blown Supreme Court battle over college affirmative action, the *Regents of the University of California v. Bakke* case of 1978. When colleges first adopted racial preferences in admissions—as well as in hiring and contracting—they did so mainly for the simple reason that *they believed it was the right thing to do.*

As a starting point for understanding what motivated colleges, it is useful to keep in mind that slave labor was used to help build the nation's first public higher education institution, later known as the University of Virginia. At the same time the university's father, Thomas Jefferson, was expressing hopes that an intellectually talented "natural aristocracy" would lead his fledgling nation, most southern states prohibited the teaching of slaves, while many Northerners who sought to educate blacks were harassed, their schools burned down.[8] Although Oberlin College adopted a race-blind admissions policy as far back as 1835, with Antioch College and Berea College following close behind, only 28 black Americans earned baccalaureates in the 30 years leading up to the Civil War.[9]

Among the private Northern universities that prohibited or restricted the admission of black students well into the twentieth century were Columbia, Rutgers, Northwestern, the University of Chicago, and, as late as 1932, Holy Cross and Notre Dame.[10] Princeton University remained racially segregated until the end of World War II.[11] As a result of Jim Crow laws adopted in the late 1800s and the separate-but-equal doctrine enshrined by the Supreme Court's infamous 1896 *Plessy v. Ferguson* decision, public education remained segregated in the Old South, the District of Columbia, and six border states—Delaware, Kentucky, Maryland, Missouri, Oklahoma, and West Virginia—through the 1940s. Four other states—Arizona, Indiana, Kansas, and New Mexico—gave local school systems the option of operating segregated elementary and secondary schools.[12]

Blacks are not the only group that has suffered discrimination in education. Among the others, Native Americans often were denied the schools and teachers promised them in treaties and were barred by the federal government from receiving instruction in their native language. Both California and Texas allowed the operation of separate public schools for Mexican Americans, and California had separate public schools for Chinese, Mongolians, and Japanese until the Supreme Court forced it to stop in 1945. School districts routinely denied special language instruction to the non-English-speaking children of immigrants until the U.S. Supreme Court ruled the practice discriminatory in 1974.[13]

African Americans finally began making headway into previously all-white public colleges in the 1930s, as a result of a series of federal and state court decisions requiring such institutions to admit black students if nothing else was available to them.[14] And in the 1940s, as public school systems in the South came under legal pressure to take seriously the "equal" in "separate but equal," the gap between their spending on black and white schools narrowed considerably. As the forties began, Georgia was spending about 30 cents on each black student for every dollar it spent on a white one; by 1952, it was spending 70 cents.[15]

The Supreme Court's 1950 rulings striking down the segregation of public higher education came in two cases dealing with professional schools. In *Sweatt v. Painter,* Texas had gone so far as to establish a separate minority law school to avoid enrolling a black applicant at the University of

Texas's. In the other, the University of Oklahoma's graduate program had admitted a black student but forced him to sit in a designated "colored" seat. The Supreme Court declared both universities to be violating the Fourteenth Amendment's guarantee of equal protection under the law.

In its landmark 1954 *Brown v. Board of Education* decision striking down the racial segregation of public elementary and secondary schools, the Supreme Court repudiated its 1896 *Plessy* ruling by declaring separate educational facilities to be inherently unequal. In a follow-up *Brown* decision a year later, the Supreme Court ordered school systems to desegregate with "all deliberate speed." The South, however, was in no hurry and generally resisted, at times fiercely; the white unrest that followed a black man's efforts to enroll in the University of Mississippi in 1962 resulted in two deaths and 160 injuries. Meanwhile, federal officials began seeing racial integration as partly a national security concern as the Soviet Union's cold war propagandists publicized the ill treatment of blacks in the United States to win over people in Africa and elsewhere in the third world.

What jump-started the actual desegregation of American education was the Civil Rights Act of 1964, which called on the federal government to take a host of steps to eliminate racial and ethnic discrimination in education and employment, including withholding federal funds from any college or school system that discriminated. Although civil rights leaders heralded that measure's passage as a great victory, they were coming to realize that merely outlawing segregation would not begin to bring about integration and equality, especially given the prevalence of racism in American society and the impoverished conditions of many blacks. The severity of America's lingering racial problems would become apparent on July 18, 1964, just 16 days after the Civil Rights Act's passage, when tensions between black Harlem residents and New York's police sparked one of hundreds of riots that would devastate the nation's cities over the next several years.[16]

Even before then, a few selective colleges were working hard to take in black students. Harvard, for example, had been struggling to increase its black enrollment since the 1950s. In 1962 Yale hired a recruiter specifically for black students and joined the seven other Ivy League colleges and the elite women's colleges known as the Seven Sisters that year in forming a cooperative to share contacts and strategies to aid such efforts. It soon became apparent, however, that merely having color-blind admissions policies and increasing recruitment would only get colleges so far, especially given the low number of black high school graduates around the nation with solid SAT scores.

In the 1965–1966 academic year, Yale's admissions office took a revolutionary step that would help usher in a new era in college admissions and set the stage for today's affirmative action debate. Believing that the low SAT scores of many black applicants reflected cultural deprivation rather than a lack of talent, it adopted the practice of giving extra consideration to those with scores below its usual standards. The following fall, blacks accounted for 3.4 percent of its entering freshman class, up from less than 2 percent two years before. However, in another development serving as harbinger of what was to come, many black freshmen found adjusting to Yale difficult, and more than a third did not return as sophomores.[17] Other selective colleges around the nation began experimenting with similar policies. The University of California at Berkeley roughly doubled its minority enrollments from 1966 to 1967 through a new program combining aggressive recruitment and generous financial aid offers with a policy of letting minority students qualify for an exemption from academic standards that was previously reserved for athletes.[18]

As 1967 rolled around, the civil unrest in the nation's cities intensified. Detroit's riot left 43 people dead and block after block turned into charred wastelands.[19] In many ways, that city has never recovered. A federal commission convened by President Lyndon Johnson to investigate several of that year's biggest urban uprisings concluded that the typical rioter was a young unemployed or underemployed black male who felt extreme hostility toward both whites and middle-class blacks, distrusted the political system, and had become fed up with problems such as police brutality, a lack of work, and poor public services in his neighborhood. Better access to higher education was not a primary concern for the rioters, the commission found, but in 18 of the 24 civil disturbances it examined, many of the best-educated and better-off black residents of the affected communities had walked the streets urging people to calm down. "Apparently, high levels of education and income not only prevent rioting but are more likely to lead to active, responsible opposition to rioting," the panel concluded. Most of its recommendations focused on alleviating urban poverty, but they included a call for increased federal assistance to help the disadvantaged afford college.[20]

Among the leaders of the nation's elite colleges, there was a belief that their institutions could defuse tensions in America's cities—or at least help prevent their long-term escalation—by helping to usher more blacks into the nation's elite. Jerome Karabel notes that the dominant theme in Harvard, Princeton, and Yale internal memos calling for increased black enrollments "was neither diversity nor compensation for past injustices, but rather the need for 'Negro leadership.'" They felt compelled to act quickly based on a "sense that a fateful struggle for the soul of the nation's black population was being waged," pitting advocates of nonviolence and integration such as Martin Luther King Jr. against militant "black power" advocates such as Stokely Carmichael and Malcolm X, whose followings had grown substantially.[21]

In assembling its entering freshman class of 1968, Princeton accepted 53 percent of black applicants, almost twice the share admitted the year before.[22] Although the federal government had not yet adopted racial preferences on its own, U.S. Commissioner of Education Harold Howe II nonetheless urged college leaders to take the past disadvantages of black applicants into account in evaluating admissions test scores. As selective colleges began to recruit black students more aggressively and to bend academic standards to admit more, they began enrolling more students who otherwise would have gone to historically black colleges or predominantly white institutions with less prestige. S. A. Kendrick, an executive at the College Board, expressed fears that higher education was seeing the beginning of "an all-out recruiting war" for "a very limited number of Negro youth of moderate to high ability."[23]

By the spring of 1968, it was clear that college campuses would not be immune to the civil disorder still roiling the nation's cities. Within a period of just a few weeks, black students had seized control of buildings at Howard University and Virginia Union University and held trustees of Tuskegee Institute captive in one of its guesthouses. When Martin Luther King Jr. was assassinated outside a Memphis hotel on April 4, 1968, college campuses throughout the nation exploded. Black militants clashed with National Guardsmen at Shaw University in North Carolina and shot at police at Florida A&M. At Colgate University, about 500 demonstrators occupied an administration building for five days to protest racial discrimination by campus fraternities. In an effort to quell the unrest, colleges promised to redouble their efforts to recruit black students and to pump money into minority scholarship programs.[24] Officials at Harvard University resisted demands that they adopt minority enrollment quotas but seized on the idea of enrolling a "critical mass" of black students, loosely defined as enough to ensure that such students would not feel racially isolated and would have enough black peers around for support.[25]

Colleges may have been hoping to peacefully assimilate black students into their student bodies to help them eventually become part of the ruling elite, but many black students, alienated by their experiences on campus, had different ideas. James E. Cheek, the president of predominantly black Shaw University, told of letters "seething with hatred" written by Shaw students who had gone to Harvard as part of an exchange program and had fallen in with black militants there.[26] In May 1968, black students seized control of the business office of Northwestern University, abandoning it only after administrators agreed to establish separate black dormitory wings and to concede in writing that Northwestern has been "a university of the white establishment."[27] Over the next few years, the nation would witness weeks of severe racial violence at San Francisco State University, the takeover of Cornell University's student center by gun-brandishing black militants, and—just 10 days after the Kent State massacre—the killing of two black youths at Mississippi's Jackson State College by police summoned to quell a campus riot.[28] College officials felt they had no choice but to heed the demands of black students if they wanted to restore order.

Colleges established more than 200 black studies programs in the year after Reverend King died.[29] Predominantly white colleges scrambled to hire more black professors, prompting white applicants for such positions to allege "reverse discrimination" and the leaders of historically black colleges to complain that their faculties were being raided to the detriment of their students.[30] At the 1969 annual conference of the National Association for College Admission Counseling, its governing assembly passed a resolution calling for member colleges to increase their minority enrollments to at least 10 percent, to stop relying on admissions test scores in evaluating minority applicants, and to make sure at least half of the minority students they enrolled were "high risk" and appeared unlikely to succeed based on normal admission criteria.[31] That same month Logan Wilson, the president of higher education's umbrella organization, the American Council on Education, gave a speech warning that academe's proponents of meritocracy and egalitarianism were on a collision course and their demands eventually would become "irreconcilable."[32]

By 1970, the nation's colleges were enrolling twice as many black students as they had six years earlier. Blacks accounted for about 5.8 percent of all college students—a figure still well short of their 11.5 percent share of the overall population, but impressive nonetheless considering where they had stood just a few years before.[33] About a fourth of colleges were offering financial aid specifically for black students while about half were offering black students extra academic help.[34]

Colleges also embarked on efforts to recruit and assist Hispanics and Native Americans, with the expansion of college affirmative action beyond blacks being especially evident at medical schools. In a 1969 memo, the Association of American Medical Colleges had called on its members to aim for enrollments that were 12 percent black; a year later, it said medical colleges could count Mexican Americans, mainland Puerto Ricans, or Native Americans toward that 12 percent goal. Despite past discrimination against them, Asian Americans generally were denied affirmative action in higher education. In a 1970 report, the Carnegie Commission on Higher Education advised colleges against providing affirmative action for Japanese Americans and Chinese Americans because both groups "are well represented in higher education and are not educationally disadvantaged."[35] About the only higher education institutions that gave Asian American applicants an edge for long were law schools, and their perceived need for such preferences declined in subsequent decades as the children of Asian immigrants proved more willing than their parents to go into fields other than the hard sciences.

In its willingness to adopt quotas and dual standards for minorities, higher education was a few steps ahead of the federal government, which did not get into the business of granting minorities preferences until 1969. Presidents John F. Kennedy and Lyndon Johnson had both pushed racial integration, but neither had been willing to endorse the use of racial preferences to bring it about. When Kennedy issued a 1961 executive order directing that federal contractors take "affirmative action" to make sure none of their facilities discriminated, his intent was to enforce color-blindness, not to give any minority group an advantage. Advocates of racial preferences often cite the logic Johnson used in delivering the 1965 commencement address at Howard University. Asserting that the civil rights movement was reaching a stage at which Americans would demand "not just equality as a right and a theory but equality as a fact and equality as a result," Johnson said: "You do not take a person who, for years, has been hobbled by chains and liberate him, bring him up to the starting line of a race and then say, 'you are free to compete with the others,' and still justly believe that you have been completely fair." However, Johnson's speech made no direct references to racial preferences, calling instead for people to have jobs, decent homes, adequate health care, and "an equal chance to learn."

Both Johnson and Kennedy feared that such preferences would threaten the Democratic Party's New Deal coalition by pitting blacks against Jews, Catholics, and labor unions.[36] The first president to call for black job applicants to get preferences over white ones was Richard M. Nixon, and a fair amount of historical research, along with the memoir of one of his top cabinet members, suggests that he did so mainly to create just the wedge in the Democratic Party that Kennedy and Johnson had feared.

Nixon's decision to favor racial preferences in employment arose in the context of the federal government's troubled efforts to integrate the construction unions in Philadelphia, where most well-paying trades were dominated by tightly knit white ethnic groups that made sure their relatives and friends got first dibs on available jobs.[37] The Nixon administration attacked the problem by requiring unions working under federal contract to set numerical goals and timetables for racially integrating their ranks, putting them in the position of having no choice but to select black applicants over whites with better qualifications or more seniority.[38] Nixon emphasized the plan's value as a wedge issue in a December 22, 1969, meeting with Republican congressional leaders.[39] His assistant for domestic affairs, John Ehrlichman, would later write in a memoir: "The NAACP wanted a tougher requirement; the unions hated the whole thing. Before long, the AFL-CIO and the NAACP were locked in combat over one of the passionate issues of the day and the Nixon administration was located in the sweet and reasonable middle."[40]

Nixon would not stick to that position for long, however. By the time the 1972 presidential election rolled around, he was campaigning as an opponent of racial quotas, and the Democratic Party had moved from being skeptical of quotas to using them to select delegates for its national convention.[41]

Despite Nixon's about-face, the federal government continued to adopt policies giving preferences to certain racial and ethnic groups, determining who should qualify as it went along. In his book *The Minority Rights Revolution,* sociologist John David Skrentny writes that the federal government came to see it as "a cheap, easy, and available way to appeal to and appease" minority groups. Federal officials "never spelled out what were the necessary and sufficient conditions or qualities for minorityhood" but "classified groups just the same." Hispanics gained minority status largely through the intervention of Mexican Americans in key positions in Congress and by virtue of their status as a constituency that could swing Texas in a tight presidential race. Representatives of some white ethnic populations that had experienced discrimination, such as Jews, Poles, and Italians, lobbied hard for minority status but were denied it by federal officials who cited practical problems such as the difficulty of determining whites' ethnicity. The federal government classified some Asian groups from the Far East as minorities, but not those from the Middle East or Central Asia.[42]

Higher education's leaders, in crafting their own affirmative action policies, would be influenced by the federal government's determination of who was worthy. Over the following decades, they set up large networks of offices, programs, and organizations designed to recruit minority students, help them prepare for college, and provide them with the support that they would need to complete their degrees and, ideally, go on to graduate or professional schools. The new administrators overseeing such initiatives would join admissions officers, minority students, and faculty members in becoming a powerful internal constituency demanding yet more affirmative action. State and federal lawmakers, as well as some regional accreditors of higher education institutions, also pressured colleges to have more minority students and employees.

By the mid-1990s, the University of Michigan had set up over 100 diversity programs. As of the 1997–1998 academic year, blacks, Hispanics, and Native Americans were getting more than 31 percent of its need-based grant money and nearly 36 percent of the merit-based scholarship aid it awarded, despite accounting for only about 14 percent of its enrollment. Detroit-area high school counselors told me of watching Michigan give merit-based scholarships to black students with much worse academic records than white students who got nothing. Among the Michigan students that I interviewed for *The Chronicle of Higher Education* during a fall 1998 reporting trip to Ann Arbor was a senior who seemed incredulous that she had received a full-tuition scholarship. Both her parents were physicians, and although her father was black and her mother of Arab descent, she had grown up in the posh, overwhelmingly white suburb of Bloomfield Hills. "I got a full-tuition scholarship, and I didn't need it. I didn't even apply for it," she said.

Many selective colleges elsewhere became similarly generous with their financial aid and other inducements as they vied for the limited number of black students who could meet their minimum qualifications. Carnegie Mellon University began dispatching fleets of luxury motor coaches to Northeastern cities to pick up prospective black students for visitation weekends.[43] As of 2003, about a third of colleges were considering race or ethnicity in admissions decisions, more than two-fifths had set up programs to help minority students get through college, nearly half employed multicultural recruitment staff, two-thirds had commitments to racial and ethnic diversity in their mission statements, and nearly three-fourths engaged in recruitment activities intended to increase minority enrollments, according to a survey by the national admissions counselors' group.[44] As a rule, colleges are reluctant to discuss how much they spend on their diversity efforts, mainly because they fear giving ammunition to critics of affirmative action. One of the few to attempt to give a thorough accounting of such expenditures—the University of Colorado at Boulder, which had been pressured to open its books by the Independence Institute, a libertarian think tank based in Golden—acknowledged in early 2007 that it was spending well over $21 million annually on its efforts to promote diversity on campus.

In many ways, however, colleges' efforts to take in more black students have remained an uphill struggle. Almost from the time colleges first adopted affirmative action, various forces swirling around them would hinder their efforts to take in black students and would undermine black gains.

As far back as 1970, many higher education institutions had concluded that their own efforts to take in more black students had gone too far and had resulted in the admission of many from low-income backgrounds who lacked the preparation to handle the academic demands that would be made of them. Harvard's dean of admissions wrote in a report issued that year that officials there had learned "that we cannot accept the victims of social disaster however deserving of promise they might have been, or however romantically or emotionally an advocate (or a society) might plead for them." As of 1969, when Harvard's efforts to recruit blacks from the inner cities were at their peak, nearly 40 percent of its black students came from lower-income backgrounds. By 1973, fewer than 25 percent did. Other colleges similarly scaled back their efforts to recruit black students from poor urban environments.[45]

Many black and Hispanic students from middle-class families also ended up having difficulty in college. Faced with this fact and realizing their own limitations in helping those from poor backgrounds, higher education leaders changed how they talked about disadvantage. Instead of operating on the assumption that poverty was what left many black, Hispanic, and Native American students disadvantaged, they began to base policies on the belief that just being a member of one of those minority groups was a disadvantage in itself.[46]

Colleges' affirmative action efforts may have been more successful—or seen as less necessary—if the nation had made more progress in racially integrating its elementary and secondary schools in the half century after the *Brown* decision. Almost from the outset, however, white flight undermined desegregation. The schools of Louisville and surrounding Jefferson County, Kentucky, for example, lost 23,000, or 21 percent, of their white students in the three years after federal courts ordered their desegregation.[47] Overwhelmingly white, no-frills Christian fundamentalist schools popped up all over the South, where they continue to educate more than half of the white students in many rural counties of Alabama, Georgia, and Mississippi and to account for about 40 percent of all school segregation in that region. In many metropolitan areas of the South, more whites found themselves able to afford more expensive private schools as local economies boomed.[48]

The biggest wall hit by school desegregation, however, was a 1974 Supreme Court decision involving the Detroit school system and 53 neighboring districts—many of the schools that send the University of Michigan a large share of its students. In *Milliken v. Bradley,* the court ruled that school systems cannot be compelled to remedy racial segregation that has not been proven to be the result of their own policies. The effect was to shield many suburban school districts from court-ordered inclusion in metropolitan desegregation plans.

By the mid-1990s, school desegregation plans throughout the nation appeared headed for extinction, due mainly to a 1992 Supreme Court decision involving the DeKalb County, Georgia, school system. DeKalb had achieved a substantial level of school desegregation back in 1969, when its black population was so small and evenly distributed that all district officials needed to do was to stop parents from sending their children long distances to predominantly black or white schools and to require them to put their kids in schools near their homes. In the intervening decades, however, middle- and upper-income blacks flocked to the southern part of the county, leaving the district with some schools that were 98 percent black, others that were more than 90 percent white. The Supreme Court held that the school system's good-faith efforts to achieve racial balance had been good enough, and that it bore no obligation to keep up with demographic changes. This ruling—combined with a Supreme Court decision a year earlier holding that the Oklahoma City school system needed only to eliminate the vestiges of its past segregation "to the extent practicable"—left school systems everywhere arguing that they had done the work of desegregation and should be released from court oversight. Even at that time, the segregation of the nation's schools had reverted to 1970 levels.[49]

Since the mid-1990s, the racial isolation of black students has become substantially worse, especially in communities where blacks and whites live apart and court-ordered desegregation plans had been the only thing keeping schools racially balanced, or where schools have become overwhelmingly minority as a result of influxes of nonwhite students.[50] As civil rights lawyers gathered in 1994 to commemorate the fortieth anniversary of the *Brown* decision, they were pessimistic about the prospects of much more racial progress at the hands of the federal courts: "At least in the short run, a generation of black children is going to be educated in racially isolated schools in many of the urban centers of the country," lamented U.S. District Court judge Robert L. Carter, who had helped argue the *Brown* case as an NAACP lawyer.[51] In a survey of urban school officials, a third said their districts' enrollments were so overwhelmingly minority that desegregation efforts were immaterial, and two-thirds expressed the belief that it is possible, given enough resources, to provide minority students a high-quality education in a racially segregated setting.[52] The big unanswered question was whether enough resources would ever be forthcoming.

Although education researchers disagree on the explanation, there is no question that the educational gaps between black and white Americans closed quickly during school desegregation's heyday in the 1960s and 1970s. As of the late 1980s, however, blacks had stopped making progress, even as white achievement had continued to rise. Why the gap stopped narrowing remains a mystery. People have pointed fingers at school resegregation, wage stagnation, a sharp rise in the number of black single mothers, cuts in spending on federal programs for the poor, the crack epidemic, and the emergence of rap music and hip-hop culture. But education researchers have been able to poke holes in just about every explanation offered so far; they suggest that either a bunch of different forces are working in tandem or the real reasons have yet to be discovered.[53]

The black-white gap in college-going rates stopped closing a full decade before black progress in elementary and second education stalled. The growth of black enrollments had slowed at the nation's law schools and leveled off entirely at medical schools by 1974.[54] Blacks' share of total college enrollment peaked at about 9.4 percent from 1976 to 1978, but then declined.[55] There would be another black enrollment surge in the late 1980s, as colleges stepped up their affirmative action efforts in response to a wave of student protests over racial incidents and the stalled progress of affirmative action. Once colleges realized they needed to reach out to prospective minority students below the high-school level, and to help ensure those in elementary and middle schools were getting adequate academic preparation, they were able to take additional steps to substantially widen their minority applicant pools. For the most part, however, blacks would never make gains like those experienced in affirmative action's first five years.

Why did blacks stop making gains in terms of access to higher education even before their progress in elementary and secondary schools stalled? For starters, the legal landscape had begun to change. The first major challenge to race-conscious admissions policies arose in 1971, just a few years after most of these policies came into being, in the form of a lawsuit against the University of Washington law school by Marco DeFunis, a white student it had twice rejected. The dispute made it all the way to the Supreme Court, which in 1974 ducked the questions presented by ruling the case moot because DeFunis, who had been ordered admitted into the law school while the matter was pending, was just a few months from graduation. The U.S. Commission on Civil Rights later observed that the case nonetheless left law and medical schools skittish about using race-conscious admissions.[56] Four years later, in the case *Regents of the University of California v. Bakke,* involving a white student rejected by a medical school, the Supreme Court struck down the use of racial quotas.

As the *DeFunis* and *Bakke* cases were working their way through the courts, the nation was undergoing profound economic and political changes that would build support for fiscal conservatism and greatly slow government spending on student aid. Increased competition from abroad, inflation driven by skyrocketing oil prices, and a mounting federal deficit had left the economy in shambles and Washington under pressure to be austere. The federal government put the breaks on spending on need-based aid even before Ronald Reagan won the presidency with a campaign attacking "tax-and-

spend liberalism." Jimmy Carter initiated a sea change in the federal government's approach to student aid by signing a measure providing assistance
to middle-income families in the form of loans; the size of need-based federal Pell Grants, accounting for inflation, would never again be as high as it
was in 1976. In the next decade, a growing share of Pell Grant recipients
would be unable to afford anything but community college. In passing the
tax-cutting ballot measure Proposition 13 in the summer of 1978, Californians helped give rise to a national tax revolt that would limit the amount
of money available for higher education and student aid down the road.

Beginning in the 1970s, efforts to increase black enrollments at selective
colleges were complicated by the long-term effects of what had been three
key civil rights victories: the opening of previously all-male colleges to
women; the passage of the Immigration and Nationality Act of 1965, and a
1967 Supreme Court decision striking down all state bans on interracial
marriage.

As of 1960, women had accounted for just 22.5 percent of the enrollment in the Ivy League and less than 27 percent of the enrollment at prestigious colleges other than the all-female Seven Sisters.[57] But admissions
policies excluding them were about the only things keeping them out. "Female Yalies, Princetonians, and Harvardians were, after all, the daughters,
sisters, and neighbors of the men who had historically attended the Big
Three, and only their gender had prevented them from enrolling," Jerome
Karabel notes in *The Chosen*. "Once the doors were opened, they were
deemed to possess no less 'merit' than their brothers."[58] Today, women are
overrepresented at the vast majority of colleges and in nearly every field of
study other than math, science, and engineering. Because two out of three
black students at selective colleges are female, it is likely that blacks might
be even more underrepresented at such institutions if not for coeducation.
Yet, there is no question that by doubling the size of the population eligible
for admissions to many colleges, the shift to coeducation greatly increased
the competition for each available seat.

The 1965 immigration act would result in huge influxes from Asia,
Latin America, and other regions of the world that had not been a major
part of the nation's immigrant stream, profoundly changing the nation's ethnic makeup, putting considerable burdens on public schools, and leaving selective colleges' affirmative action offices struggling with how to
accommodate new populations without alienating the old ones.

Researchers have found that as more immigrants enter a given high school, the proportion of native-born minority students who earn their diplomas and go on to college declines.[59] Although researchers have not yet reached consensus on an explanation for this phenomenon, many believe that it is because schools are forced to shift resources away from the native-born English speakers to support programs that bring children with limited English proficiency up to speed. Changes in the composition of the peer groups of native-born students also may play a role. In some cities with large immigrant populations, advocates for immigrant children and advocates for native-born black children have clashed over access to educational resources. In San Francisco, for example, advocates for Chinese American children filed a lawsuit challenging the district's policy of trying to keep the city's elite Lowell High School integrated by letting it hold different applicants to different standards. Chinese Americans had the hardest time getting in, blacks and Hispanics the easiest. In my visit there to cover the case, I found Chinese American activists were bitterly divided over the wisdom of challenging racial preferences, I heard a prominent local black activist denounce the Chinese Americans behind the lawsuit as greedy, and I met white Lowell parents who had gamed the system by scouring their family histories for the tiniest hint of black or Hispanic blood.[60]

Higher education experienced similar controversies as Asian Americans accused selective colleges of discriminating against them and filed bias complaints with the Education Department's Office for Civil Rights. Statistically there was enough smoke around to look for fire. Beginning in the 1970s, Asian Americans' share of selective-college enrollments had not grown nearly as rapidly as their share of the college-aged population, and although there had been no drop in their scholastic achievement, their chances of being admitted, relative to whites, had sharply declined.[61] Brown University's Asian American Students Association noted that that institution had gone from accepting 44 percent of Asian American applicants to just 14 percent in the matter of a few years.[62] In 1984, Brown's Committee on Minority Affairs acknowledged that the "cultural bias and stereotypes which prevail in the Admissions Office" had resulted in some Asian American applicants receiving unjustifiably low ratings in nonacademic areas.[63] The chancellor of the University of California at Berkeley subsequently issued a public apology for the "disadvantaging" of Asians in the selection process, and an in-house review at Stanford found "unconscious bias."[64] The Office for Civil Rights ordered the University of California at Los Angeles to admit five Asian Americans that it judged to have been unfairly excluded from its graduate program in mathematics, but cleared Harvard after accepting its argument that Asian Americans fared relatively poorly against whites in its admissions process because they were less likely to be legacies and tended to have unimpressive records of involvement in extracurricular activities in high school.[65] The debate over whether selective colleges are biased against Asian American applicants heated up again in late 2006, when a Chinese American student filed a federal discrimination complaint against Princeton University, which rejected him despite his near-flawless academic record.

For the most part, colleges have shown themselves to be much more eager to enroll Hispanics, even if the task of defining which ones deserved preferences has sometimes proved challenging. "Hispanic" is a term coined in the 1970s by federal bureaucrats who wanted a broader label than "Chicano," "Puerto Rican," or "Cuban" to apply to people with linguistic or cultural ties to Spain. Aside from the fact that "Hispanic" also refers to people from Portuguese-speaking Brazil, the term is so loose and broad that it covers members of every racial and ethnic group—about half of Hispanics think of themselves as white—and many populations that have not been the victims of oppression and discrimination in the United States, such as the well-educated middle-class South Americans who have been flocking to many of the nation's major cities. Some question whether colleges should be giving preferences to the children of well-educated Spaniards, Cubans who built up fortunes in Miami, Germans who spent a few decades in Argentina, or people whose sole connection to the Spanish language and culture is a last name inherited from a great-great-grandfather. Many colleges, eager to be able to boast of large Hispanic enrollments, apply the Hispanic label to anyone who wants to claim it.

In seeking to enroll more students of Mexican or Puerto Rican descent, colleges confront many of the same obstacles stemming from poverty and discrimination that they face in trying to recruit blacks—plus a few others related to language barriers and culture. Students with limited English proficiency, for example, tend to earn SAT scores that understate how well they actually will perform in colleges. And because Hispanic families have a culture-based tendency to want to keep their young adults close to home, it is difficult for colleges—and especially graduate and professional schools and specialized programs—to recruit large numbers of Hispanic Americans from distant states. Partly as a result of such characteristics, Hispanics have the lowest rate of graduate school enrollment of any major racial and ethnic group, and earn only about 4 percent of doctorates awarded by colleges.

Immigration has further muddied the waters by raising such questions as whether people from abroad should get preference over the U.S.-born and whether they have any moral claim to benefits initially intended for the victims of past oppression here. During the 1990s, the nation's black population from sub-Saharan Africa nearly tripled, to more than 600,000, while its black population from Caribbean nations grew by more than 60 percent, to 1.5 million. Both groups are, on average, much wealthier and better educated than American-born blacks and Hispanics. The average African living here has had at least 14 years of education—an attainment level higher than that of whites and Asians, suggesting that those Africans who come here are either already well educated or have plans for higher education upon their arrival.[66] Likewise, the subset of Jamaicans coming into the United States is among the most class-selective of immigrant streams, consisting heavily of ambitious members of the island's skilled middle class. As of 1999, when immigrants accounted for 3 percent of the nation's black population, immigrants accounted for 9 percent—and the children of immigrants, about 25 percent—of black freshmen in one heavily studied set of 28 selective colleges. As a rule, the more selective the college, the more immigrants were overrepresented among its black students; at the four Ivy League universities in that 28-college sample—Columbia, Princeton, University of Pennsylvania, and Yale—41 percent of black students were either immigrants or immigrants' children.[67]

About 7 percent of the nation's colleges routinely send their admissions officers on recruiting trips outside the United States.[68] While many of the students recruited on such trips will be classified as "foreign" or "international," it is also the case that colleges pad their minority enrollments—and help meet various industries' demands for minority workers—by recruiting in foreign nations with strong educational systems, such as Trinidad and Tobago, or from well-regarded private high schools and public colleges on the island of Puerto Rico.

When I visited the University of Medicine and Dentistry in New Jersey in 2005 to check out a summer program set up to encourage minority undergraduates to pursue careers as researchers in science and engineering, six of the program's ten Hispanic participants were from colleges in Puerto

Rico, while a seventh had been born and raised in Peru. Of the five black students in the program, two were born in Africa while two others had Jamaican parents. One of the program's participants was a white kid who routinely identified himself as African American on applications solely because his father had lived several years in Egypt.

Hugh Davis Graham, a historian and political scientist at Vanderbilt University, has observed that civil rights groups that support both affirmative action and liberal immigration policies "are anxious to avoid discussing their linkages."[69] In recent years, however, some conservative pundits have noted with considerable ire that college affirmative action programs are giving some illegal aliens preference over white and Asian U.S. citizens.

Marriages between members of different races are further complicating colleges' efforts to classify students and determine which ones merit preferences. The 2000 U.S. census counted 1.46 million interracial marriages in the United States, nearly 100 times as many as there had been 40 years before. More than half of the children of many Asian and Hispanic immigrant populations are marrying members of another ethnicity or race—usually, non-Hispanic whites. As a result of changes in the U.S. census that allow people to check off more than one box for race, it is now possible for Americans to identify themselves in 126 different ways.[70] Such trends appear to be having an even bigger impact on the composition of college enrollments than on society as a whole. Researchers have found that students that selective colleges classify as black are about three times as likely to identify themselves as being of mixed race as might be expected given the percent of the nation's blacks who marry whites.[71] Young people whose parents both identify themselves as black are not making as much progress gaining access to selective colleges as the institutions' enrollment figures may suggest.

The upshot is that more than five decades after the Supreme Court struck down segregation in education and more than four decades after academe adopted affirmative action, blacks, Hispanics, and Native Americans are less than half as prevalent on the campuses of selective colleges as they are in society.

A 2003 study concluded that since the advent of affirmative action on campuses, blacks and Hispanics have actually fallen further behind whites in terms of their college-going rates. Larger absolute numbers and percentages of blacks and Hispanics are going on to college, but the number and percentage of whites doing so has been rising much faster. Among the factors the study blamed were admissions policies that tend to give an edge to certain white applicants such as legacies and the children of donors; state prepaid tuition plans, which benefit only those families with substantial savings; and the recent movement among many public colleges to tighten their admissions standards and stop offering remedial programs. The author of the study, K. Edward Renner, a psychology professor at the University of Pennsylvania, argued that "affirmative action, largely as preferential admissions, has failed."[72]

Many civil rights and higher education leaders strongly disagree with such assessments. Regardless of its impact, affirmative action remains something that they are willing to fight tooth-and-nail to defend. Leaders in business, law, medicine, and other fields have similarly become staunch supporters of race-conscious college admissions policies. Having been born out of black rage, white fear, and a desire by our society's leaders to appease those demanding profound change, affirmative action is now, rightly or wrongly, one of the chief tools that the establishment uses to try to keep the peace between the races and maintain the status quo.

Chapter 4

The Golden Pipeline
Profiting from Preferences

As much as the black power movement played a key role in pressuring colleges to adopt affirmative action, it was mainly the white power structure that got higher education to keep minority programs and racial and ethnic preferences in place.

In the late sixties, at about the same time black activists were pushing America's selective colleges to increase their minority enrollments, many of the nation's big corporations, as well as the legal and medical professions, began working hard to diversify their ranks. Employers became so focused on hiring minorities that some of their recruiters visiting college campuses refused to meet with anyone but students of color. College career centers began hosting "minority job fairs" solely for nonwhite students and those hoping to hire them. Large companies joined professional associations, the federal government, and several of the nation's largest philanthropies in pumping money into programs designed to increase the share of the black population completing college and earning advanced degrees.

Had blacks' demand for selective-college access not been accompanied by demands from the white establishment for black employees with solid academic credentials—had the push at one end of the higher education process not been matched by a pull at the other—colleges might not be using affirmative action today, at least not to the same extent. After all, the civil rights and black power movements lost steam decades ago. Race-conscious admissions policies offend a large share of the population and are susceptible to legal challenge. It's expensive for colleges to operate programs to build and sustain minority enrollments, and after four decades of affirmative action they are nowhere close to their goal of graduating black, Hispanic, and Native American students in numbers reflective of American society. Left on their own, colleges might have been tempted to abandon affirmative action programs as unpopular, unaffordable, unworkable, and unworthy of the hassle.

Outside support for college affirmative action programs changed the equation, however, transforming them from drains on colleges' budgets into fonts of revenue. It did not matter that black activism had waned or that the American public was badly split on racial preferences, because college affirmative action efforts had acquired the backing of much of the nation's power structure, from the American Bar Association to the American Medical Association, Wall Street to Silicon Valley, Washington, D.C., to Hollywood-LA.

Colleges went well beyond merely trying to provide the blacks who knock on their doors with an education that would help them pursue their dreams, whatever they may be. Colleges became key players in the field of employee recruitment, searching high schools for talented black or Hispanic kids who could be shepherded into a career working for high-tech firm A or investment brokerage B. Academe no longer saw itself simply as a destination for talented minority kids who could make their own career choices, but as a pipeline channeling them into the companies that helped finance colleges' diversity efforts.

In 2000, as dozens of big companies came to the defense of the University of Michigan's race-conscious admissions policies, I set out to write a *Chronicle of Higher Education* story examining what had inspired so much of controversy-averse corporate America to jump into the affirmative action fray. I was amazed to learn how closely businesses and colleges were working together in training minority students for specific jobs at specific companies. Businesses were not just donating money to colleges that produced large numbers of minority graduates. They were offering promising minority students the whole package: scholarships, internships, mentors, and a job down the road. Higher education institutions saw such arrangements as a way to cut costs by making it possible for them to recruit and educate many minority students without having to give them much, if any, financial aid. Colleges and universities had only to provide the necessary classes and academic-support programs, many of which also were subsidized by corporate donations.

Intel Corporation, a large company with a scholarship program for female and minority students, reported that about 70 percent of the program's beneficiaries eventually ended up on its payroll. Procter & Gamble was annually donating $200,000 to the University of Michigan and sending its managers to Ann Arbor to recruit minority students. "It is important to understand that diversity is really a critical piece of our overall business strategy," said Bob Jerich, a spokesman for Lucent Technologies. "As a global company, we really feel that our employee body needs to reflect the diversity of our markets and customers." Bernard J. Milano, the president of an education-supporting philanthropy established by the consulting and accounting firm KPMG, said: "The ultimate end game is for corporations to be able to have the diversity we need to function. The university itself becomes a tool to that end."

Several large nonprofit organizations also were helping minority students through the pipeline. They included Inroads, a St. Louis–based organization that matches minority students who are pursuing degrees in business, management, or technical fields and have met certain academic standards with companies providing mentors, paid summer internships, and promises of jobs. As of the 2004–2005 fiscal year, Inroads had an annual budget of about $22 million and had counseled and trained more than 5,000 students. The Consortium for Graduate Study in Management, consisting of universities with well-regarded business schools, offered minority students scholarships jointly funded by colleges and companies. As of the 2004–2005 fiscal year, it had a $13 million budget and had served more than 400 students, about 95 percent of whom eventually took jobs at the companies putting up their scholarship money. Francis Aguilar, the executive director of the Management Education Alliance, a nonprofit organization established six years earlier to link businesses to business schools with large minority enrollments, said companies initially joined his organization "primarily from a social-responsibility position," but "most of the companies that have joined us recently have joined because of the recruiting opportunities." He said they had discovered that acquiring minority employees in this manner was much more cost efficient than bidding for them in the labor market, and that it helped avoid the risks associated with hiring people they did not know.

Officials at the University of Michigan acknowledged that corporate interest in their diversity programs was part of why they were defending affirmative

action so strongly. "We, and all colleges, are under pressure by industry to increase diversity," said Stephen W. Director, the dean of Michigan's College of
Engineering, which was taking in $800,000 a year in direct corporate sup-
port for its minority scholarships and minority programs, and credited its
track record of producing minority graduates for much of the additional $4.8
million in corporate support it annually received. The university's administrators were afraid that being precluded from considering race in admissions
would cause Michigan to lose many of its corporate benefactors, who might
choose to take their money to other institutions, such as historically black
colleges, where minority students are more plentiful. B. Joseph White, the
dean of Michigan's business school, said, "Our best corporate friends are
telling us that the diversity of our student body is absolutely essential to their
attachment to the school."

How serious companies are about such demands was made apparent recently when Alcoa, General Motors, and the Green Bay division of Procter
& Gamble all cited a lack of diversity at the University of Wisconsin at
Madison as the reason they were halting recruitment at its engineering
school, at least temporarily. Other companies, frustrated with the small
number of potential minority employees coming out of Wisconsin's flagship
public university, were threatening similar moves. UW-Madison serves an
overwhelmingly white state and finds its efforts to recruit qualified minority
students hindered by the poor quality of public schools in Milwaukee and
by its own reputation among blacks as an unwelcoming place.[1]

The reasons why corporations put such a high priority on hiring large
numbers of minority employees have changed over time. Businesses initially
undertook such efforts back in the late 1960s in response to black unrest. In
some cases, they were trying to build up good will in the local black communities in hopes that their stores or factories would be spared if destructive
riots occurred. In other cases, businesses were trying to comply with court orders or to offset bad publicity resulting from discrimination lawsuits, or were
facing well-organized boycotts if they did not hire more minority employees.

During the 1980s and 1990s there was a profound change in how the
nation's major employers characterized their efforts to hire and promote minorities and women. Seeking to distance themselves from the whole affirmative action controversy, they no longer talked about helping the victims
of past discrimination, but instead characterized their consideration of employees' race, ethnicity, and gender in purely self-interested terms, saying
that they needed diversity to adjust to changes in the workforce, broaden

their perspectives, and better position themselves to compete in a global economy and tap into minority markets.[2] Critics of affirmative action have argued that assertions that companies need black employees to market to black customers have no more moral weight than the protestations of Jim Crow–era businesses that hiring black employees would drive white customers away. But such criticisms have fallen upon deaf ears among business leaders preoccupied with global competition.

The nation's leading medical and legal associations, in initially adopting affirmative action, shared the desire of business leaders to bring peace to the nation's cities. But from the outset they had an additional, practical concern: There were certain jobs—such as providing medical care to poor or rural communities or legal representation to the indigent—that many white people in their professions were simply unwilling to do. In calling on colleges to produce black doctors to care for black patients or Hispanic lawyers to represent Hispanic clients, the professional associations took racial segregation as a given.

The shortage of physicians willing to work with certain populations has remained acute, keeping medical schools under pressure to take in more minority students. Many white medical school graduates come from wealthy families or emerge from school laden with huge debt—either way, they have shown that they are not eager to put down roots in poor urban or rural communities where there is less money to be made. Proposals to link medical school admission or financial aid eligibility to students' willingness to work in underserved areas have generally been opposed by groups such as the Association of American Medical Colleges (AAMC), which resist the idea of interfering with the market forces that largely determine who works where.

Medical schools' assumption that blacks, Hispanics, and Native Americans would tend to members of their own population has been backed over time by several studies showing that these groups not only are more willing to work with the underserved but appear to do a better job of it, by, for example, paying more attention to what minority patients have to say.[3] Among these studies is a 1996 AAMC survey that found two-thirds of minority students and just 16 percent of all other students want to locate in areas characterized by socioeconomic deprivation.[4] So much stock has been put in the statistical link between race or ethnicity and willingness to serve the underserved that some medical schools have been shown to give more weight to applicants' skin color than applicants' expressed views as to what populations they aspire to serve. A 2001 legislative audit of admissions at Utah's public medical schools found that the list of (normally fatal) flaws that selection committees had overlooked in some black and Hispanic applicants included self-centeredness and a lack of concern for the less fortunate.

In embracing affirmative action, law schools shared medical schools' desire to remedy past discrimination and graduate more students willing to tend to the underserved. In addition, as a key gateway to positions of power in our society, law schools see themselves as having a vital role to play in the ascension of blacks to the nation's elite. Although they have emerged among academe's strongest proponents of the idea that diverse enrollments produce educational benefits, their affirmative action programs have retained their focus on just one group: blacks. Law schools give three times as much scholarship aid to black students as those of other races and ethnicities. Hispanics, who tend to be financially needier, get much less aid.[5]

Research suggests that racial preferences are used by nearly all law schools, regardless of their prestige, largely as a result of what college admissions experts call "the cascade effect." It works like this. Top-20 law schools, which would have enrollments that are 1 or 2 percent black in the absence of racial preferences, bend their admissions standards to take in more minority applicants and in doing so recruit such students away from middle-tier institutions. The middle-tier law schools then find themselves with a shortage of qualified minority students and bend their standards to take in those who otherwise would enroll in lower-tier law schools, which then feel forced to bend their standards to take in students who otherwise would not get into any law school at all. Any law school that attempted to take in more black students by simply lowering its admissions standards for all applicants, regardless of race or ethnicity, would experience a decline in its reputation and, consequently, its black enrollments, as other law schools that had retained their prestige snatched its black applicants away.[6]

In early 2003, as the Supreme Court was deliberating the University of Michigan cases, Derek Bok, Harvard's president from 1971 to 1991, made clear how much the rationale for affirmative action had evolved over time. He wrote: "Law firms and major hospitals and corporations are not interested exclusively or even primarily in recruiting minorities from disadvantaged backgrounds. What they want above all is minorities with the best possible professional qualifications." Because the higher education institutions seeking to graduate qualified minority employees are responding to such pragmatic concerns, there was no basis, Bok said, for the accusation that they "are merely engaging in some form of social engineering to promote their own private vision of a just society."[7]

The problem, however, is that ignoring injustice does not make it or its effects go away. And no matter how much pragmatism has gone into the construction of the education pipeline, the hard truth is that many minority students are having trouble getting through it. In virtually every field of study, black, Hispanic, and Native American students have higher dropout rates, lower scores on admissions tests for graduate and professional school, and lower passage rates on certification and licensure tests.[8] The observation holds true even for those whose parents are wealthy and well educated, and is not simply a reflection of the disproportionate representation of minority students among two other academically troubled subsets of the population—people from low-income families and people whose parents never went to college.

L. Scott Miller, executive director of the National Task Force on Early Childhood Education for Hispanics, has spent more than two decades making a personal crusade of trying to call attention to the low academic achievement of minority students in higher education. One recent study typical of his work found that black, Hispanic, and Native American students are underrepresented among selective colleges' top performers and overrepresented at the bottom on "virtually all traditional measures of achievement including grade point average, class rank, and academic honors." At most of the institutions he examined, they were only a third or fourth as likely as white students to earn GPAs above 3.5. Miller argues that as a result of the academic problems he documents, few such minority students "are fully competitive for admissions to top professional schools and graduate programs" in medicine, law, economics, computer science, and many other fields. As a long-term consequence, they're underrepresented in professional and executive leadership positions.[9] Miller lays much of the blame for the minority underachievement problem on higher education institutions, nearly all of which, he says, focus simply on keeping such students around long enough to graduate and do little to develop or replicate programs to ensure these students perform at high levels.

Miller says his message is one that a lot of people in higher education don't seem to want to hear, that his studies have often been met with "indifference at best, and very angry denials of their importance at worst." The problem he faces is that critics of affirmative action often seize upon evidence that minority students are struggling to make the case that racial preferences play a huge role in admissions, place minority students in educational settings where they are over their heads, and should be junked as harmful to everyone involved. College administrators fear that by even discussing minority underachievement, they provide the critics of affirmative action with ammunition and risk airing numbers that will be misused to stigmatize all black, Hispanic, and Native American students—including those who are excelling academically—as low achievers. They also argue that how well minority students do in college is irrelevant because grades do not matter nearly as much as degrees in determining how far one goes in life. In *The Shape of the River,* the authors observe that selective colleges' race-conscious admissions policies have promoted the upward mobility of blacks and Hispanics simply by giving them a chance to earn prestigious academic credentials that opened doors.[10]

Complicating the discussion is the paradoxical finding that minority students and people from disadvantaged backgrounds have higher graduation rates at selective colleges than at institutions with lower standards, regardless of whether they received special consideration in admissions. They may be less likely than other students in their classes to graduate, but their chances are better than at an institution with less prestige. Why is unclear. It might be because selective colleges hear from enough applicants to be able to choose among the best at each SAT score level, or because they generally have the resources to offer extensive academic support, or because of the educational benefits of studying alongside smart, driven students. But research shows that even students with low SAT scores have a better chance of graduating from a selective college than from one with lower admissions standards.[11] It is actually harder to flunk out of Harvard than Humble State U.

In a widely cited 1997 study, Linda Wightman, formerly vice president for testing, operations, and research at the Law School Admissions Council, examined data on students entering law schools in 1991 and concluded that all of the schools' minority enrollments would drop sharply in the absence of race-conscious admissions. She also determined that minority students who would not have been accepted into their law schools without race-conscious admissions were about as likely as minority students who were accepted outright to graduate and pass the bar exam.[12] But in 2004 Richard Sander, an economist and law professor at the University of California at Los Angeles, took the same data used by Wightman and drew the controversial and counterintuitive conclusion that "the annual production of new black lawyers would probably increase if racial preferences were abolished tomorrow." While acknowledging that black students are much less likely to drop out of elite law schools than law schools with lower admissions standards, Sander argues that grades matter and that the end result of affirmative action's cascade effect is that most black students end up at law schools where they struggle academically and thus learn less. The long-term result is that black law students are more than twice as likely as whites to never graduate, about four times as likely not to pass the bar on their first attempt, and nearly six times as likely to be unable to pass the bar despite multiple attempts. Sander concedes that about 14 percent of the black students would not have gotten into *any* law school without race-conscious admissions, but he says that a large number of them are unable to graduate or pass the bar anyway. The more important thing, he says, is that race-blind admissions policies would channel black students into law schools that are the right academic fit, where they could master the material, and the end result would be a significant net increase in the supply of new black lawyers. While those black students who go to elite law schools may benefit in the job market from the prestige associated with their institutions, Sander says many of those who attend middle- and lower-tier law schools find that the price they pay for earning poor grades outweighs any benefit associated with their institution's name.[13]

Given his personal history as a civil rights advocate and a community organizer on Chicago's South Side, Sander is hard to dismiss as just another right-wing affirmative action critic. Nonetheless, he and his findings were roundly attacked. Critics said his study wrongly assumed that blacks admitted under race-neutral criteria would perform as well as their white peers, overstated the correlation between law students' grades and their chances of passing the bar, and failed to recognize that many blacks might choose not to attend any law school at all if they cannot get into a prestigious one. Others in the field cheered his work, and he has engaged his critics in a debate that still rages.[14] Sander's basic argument echoes a controversial 2003 book that blamed race-conscious college admissions policies for much of the shortage of minority professors, based on the reasoning that such policies place students in undergraduate programs where they struggle academically and often either cannot earn the grades needed to get into advanced degree programs or simply lose their confidence in their abilities.[15]

In 2006, Sander again poked a stick into a beehive by arguing that although black and Hispanic law school graduates are much more likely than equally qualified whites and Asians to be hired by corporate law firms, they generally are not trusted by the firms with as much work or given as much opportunity to rise through the ranks, because their bosses care about law school grades and the skill levels associated with them.[16] Critics accused him of severely underestimating the role that racism plays in thwarting black lawyers' ambitions.[17]

Whatever the explanation, minorities are severely underrepresented in the upper ranks of business, government, and nearly every professional field. A 1995 report by a federal commission examining the glass ceiling in workplaces found that 97 percent of the male and 95 percent of the female top executives of Fortune 1500 companies were white. Moreover, the commission and other researchers in the field have found that the blacks and Hispanics who make it to the top tend to be lighter-skinned than the average member of their racial or ethnic group.[18] The federal commission concluded that "too often, minorities and women find themselves channeled into staff positions that provide little access and visibility to corporate decision-makers, and removed from strategic business decisions."[19] In many cases, companies route their minority executives into positions in which they are asked to work with minority employees, or market to minority customers, or serve as liaisons to minority communities.[20]

Richard Zweigenhaft of Guilford College and G. William Domhoff of the University of California at Santa Cruz have devoted much of their careers in psychology and sociology to researching who rises to positions of power in America. In examining corporate boards of directors, they found that minorities were severely underrepresented, and that most of the blacks in boardrooms did not rise through the corporate elite, but were outsiders who had previously made their names as lawyers, management consultants, college presidents or deans, or proprietors of their own businesses. Most of the Hispanics in the corporate elite are Cubans from wealthy families, while most of the Asian Americans are either Japanese or from well-educated families that came over from China, Taiwan, or Hong Kong.

Minorities who have ascended to positions of power generally share the same values and "sense of hard-earned class privilege" as the whites already there, and have "found ways to signal that they are willing to join the game as it has always been played," Zweigenhaft and Domhoff concluded. Few can be called liberals, and fewer still can be called crusaders. When presented with a dispute pitting their employers against their own racial or ethnic group, they almost inevitably sided with their employers. "Diversity has given the power elite buffers, ambassadors, tokens, and legitimacy."[21]

Such research suggests that college affirmative action policies have largely failed to fulfill their original purpose—giving the nation's downtrodden access to the elite and a voice in its affairs. It is worth asking, then, What exactly are such policies accomplishing? Are the benefits they provide—on campus and in society—worth their costs?

Chapter 5

Collegiate Divisions

The Volatile Mix on Campuses

Satan would take pride in much that transpires at the home of the Blue Devils.

People at Duke University may not have sold their souls, but the university's administration has acquired a national reputation for essentially selling admission to applicants tied to donors who can help build Duke's endowment. The university's willingness to accept mediocrity in the moneyed has been extensively chronicled by former Duke admissions officer Rachel Toor and, more recently, in a series of newspaper articles that helped win Daniel Golden of the *Wall Street Journal* a Pulitzer Prize. Duke also has shown a willingness to give admissions breaks to promising athletes; in 2003, for example, it took in a star lacrosse player who had been rejected elsewhere because of his involvement in a major SAT cheating scandal.[1] Although Duke's academic profile has risen substantially in recent decades, its campus remains known to many as a playground for expensively dressed frat boys who would rather tap a keg than crack a book.

Duke also has a national reputation as an institution tormented by the evils of racism. In this respect, few colleges have done more penance for past transgressions and yet so often stand accused of new sins. Having not admitted any black students until 1963, Duke eventually undertook exceptionally

aggressive minority recruitment efforts, and in 2004 enrolled a freshman class
that was 11.5 percent black, a feat unmatched that year by any other top-
ranked American university.[2] Duke also has worked hard to hire more black
professors and has more on the tenure track than most other private universities in its class.[3] "As many black people like to say, 'They are walking the
walk as well as talking the talk,'" the *Journal of Blacks in Higher Education*
proclaimed in 2000.[4] Nonetheless, Princeton Review often rates Duke as one
of the nation's colleges with the least interaction between its students of different races and backgrounds. Most of Duke's black students choose to live
on its Central Campus, while most of its white students prefer to live on its
West Campus, where black students complain of feeling unwelcome.[5]

Several members of Duke's lacrosse team were accused in 2006 of rap-
ing a young black single mother who, in the course of working for an escort
service while attending nearby North Carolina State University, had been
dispatched to their house to perform a striptease at a party. As of April 2007
the criminal charges had been dropped, but no one disputed the following
revelations about Duke's lacrosse team emerging from the scandal: Many of
the team members felt no compunction about routinely pissing all over
Durham and waking their neighbors with drunken shouts and blared
stereos. In the days after the party incident, another Duke lacrosse player—
not one of the accused—sent his teammates an e-mail in which he joked
about inviting over more strippers, "killing the bitches," and then skinning
them. Several at the party had hurled racial slurs at the woman who later alleged rape because she did not perform her striptease to their satisfaction. As
she left the house, someone yelled, "Thank your grandpa for my nice cot-
ton shirt."[6] The whole episode exposed racial tensions between the campus
and surrounding Durham, which is about 44 percent black. Local residents
were so incensed that Duke officials worried about their students' safety.

Few other colleges have ever been at the center of such an ugly scandal, and few outside the South have such an overtly racist past. But, truth
be told, Duke has more in common with other selective colleges than
many realize.

Let's start by considering Duke's aggressive efforts to acquire a reputation for diversity. Nothing unusual there. Selective colleges around the nation seek to depict themselves as places that bring together students of every
stripe. Doing so helps them solicit outside support and assure prospective
minority students they will be comfortable, and it makes their institution

more appealing to white parents who wish to expose their children to people of color.

Sometimes colleges are so bent on portraying diversity they resort to dishonesty. In the fall of 2000, a black senior at the University of Wisconsin at Madison glimpsed the cover of a university brochure and found his own smiling face in a photograph of people at a football game—a game that he had not attended. After he complained, the university apologized for pasting his face into the image so the crowd depicted would not look so lily-white.[7] Although it is rare for colleges to engage in such acts of photographic trickery—especially after they saw how badly Wisconsin's public relations attempt backfired—it remains quite common for their photographers to artificially stage scenes of racial diversity and harmony by rounding up students of different races and asking them to gather and smile.[8] In a 2005 report, researchers involved with the Campus Diversity Initiative—a $29 million, foundation-funded effort to help 28 private California colleges build up minority enrollments—said they had heard many black and Hispanic students "describe the disorientation they experienced when they arrived on campus and discovered far fewer students of color—particularly sharing their own racial/ethnic background—than were indicated through admissions materials, campus tours, and minority student recruitment events." Part of the problem lies with a practice of many colleges of classifying those students whose race is unknown as "multiracial"—and, by extension, as "students of color"—when, in fact, most students who don't state their race on college applications are white.[9]

Duke also is hardly unusual in having a reputation as a haven for economically privileged kids with little understanding of how the other half lives. The same can be said for the overwhelming majority of selective colleges in the United States. When I visited the University of Michigan for *The Chronicle* in 1998, just as federal courts were about to take up the lawsuits challenging its admission policies, administrators there estimated that more than 80 percent of the university's white students, and well over two-thirds of its Asian and Hispanic students, came from predominantly white high schools and neighborhoods. Of its black students, about 42 percent came from high schools that were mostly black or Hispanic. Surveys conducted a year later found similar patterns in the backgrounds of students at the law schools of both the University of Michigan and Harvard University. It determined that about 45 percent of the Michigan law students and 40 percent of the Harvard law students had little or no contact with people of other racial or ethnic backgrounds while growing up, and nearly a fifth had little or no such contact as undergraduates. When the figures were broken down by race, it turned out that nearly all of the students who had been raised in racially homogeneous settings were white.[10]

I asked University of Michigan for a school-by-school breakdown of where its entering freshmen came from in 1997, the year it rejected two of the three plaintiffs in the lawsuits against it. Its numbers made vividly clear why so many of its students had so little interracial exposure. Of the 5,719 in-state applicants it had admitted, more than a fifth came from schools in seven affluent and overwhelmingly white suburbs in Oakland County, north of Detroit. Another 130 came from Grosse Pointe, an exclusive community east of the city. Large delegations also came from Okemos, a well-to-do suburb of the state capital, Lansing, and Ann Arbor, where many of the university's employees live. Some schools in upscale Detroit suburbs had watched more than half of their graduating seniors get the nod to become Wolverines. Meanwhile, the guidance counselors at high schools in blue-collar Detroit suburbs told me that Michigan seldom accepted more than a few of their graduates and sometimes turned down their salutatorians and valedictorians. Among the black students admitted, a large percentage were either the children of black professionals living in wealthy suburbs or the products of the competitive, open-enrollment high schools that are the jewels of many urban school systems. Michigan had admitted 96 students—or about 15 percent of the graduating class—from Detroit's well-regarded Cass Technical High School while taking in less than a half dozen students from most ordinary high schools in the Motor City.

After the Supreme Court's 2003 affirmative action rulings, I looked at Michigan's fall 2004 admissions statistics to see if anything had changed. The university had accepted a smaller share of the graduates of some public schools in wealthy communities, but the overall patterns were still the same. For example, it admitted 61 students, or roughly a fourth of the graduating class, from Andover High School in Bloomfield Hills, a community where the median annual income was nearly $190,000, about three times the state average. (Just 1 percent of Andover's students had family incomes low enough to qualify for federally subsidized lunches, compared with 36 percent of all children in Michigan.) Expensive private schools were well represented in the university's incoming class; it admitted about 40 percent of students graduating from the Cranbrook-Kingswood School, a Bloomfield Hills institution where the annual tuition is $22,900 for day students, $31,900 for boarders.[11] Michigan's out-of-state students were especially likely to have been silver-spoon fed. Sizable delegations came from Beverly Hills and Rolling Hills Estates in California, upscale suburbs of New York and Chicago, prestigious old New England boarding schools such as Phillips Exeter, and exclusive Washington, D.C., prep schools.

While the working class and poor are underrepresented among all racial and ethnic groups at selective colleges, the skew toward wealth is especially severe among white students. On most campuses, white kids from humble origins are rare.[12] Many people from working-class or poor backgrounds complain of feeling they don't belong on college campuses, or of encountering professors who cannot understand how some students need to hold outside jobs.

Meanwhile, the privileged kids who dominate such campuses seem to be fitting in well enough not to miss out on any fun. Fourteen states' flagship public universities made the 2007 Princeton Review list of the nation's 20 best "party schools" based on student responses to survey questions dealing with drug and alcohol consumption, Greek life, and time spent studying. And prestigious private colleges such as Bard, Colorado, Oberlin, Sarah Lawrence, and Skidmore were well represented on the list of the 20 best places for smokers of marijuana.

For the book *The Source of the River,* four University of Pennsylvania researchers extensively surveyed students at 28 selective colleges to find out their backgrounds. They concluded that these colleges' admissions policies "operate to produce a freshman class composed of two very distinct populations." One is white or Asian, the other, black or Hispanic.

The chief thing the whites and Asians surveyed had in common is socioeconomic privilege. Almost all had fathers who had college degrees, and overwhelming majorities said both parents were employed in upper management or the professions. Four out of five came from families in which both parents were present. Only 4 percent came from families that had ever received welfare.

The black and Hispanic students surveyed, by contrast, exhibited tremendous variation in their socioeconomic backgrounds. While just over a third of the Hispanics and a fourth of the blacks came from families that were upper-middle class or above, it was also the case that 12 percent of

Hispanic and 17 percent of the black respondents had been on welfare at some point. More than a third of Hispanic students' fathers and 40 percent of the black students' fathers lacked a college degree. Nearly half of the blacks and 40 percent of the Hispanics grew up without a father around.

Based on such statistics, the authors concluded that many white and Asian students at selective colleges experience not just one but two kinds of culture shock in their first interactions with their black and Hispanic peers. Not only have they had little or no past interaction with other races, they also have had little or no interaction with people from lower-income backgrounds. Because lower-income white and Asian students are so rare on campus, they are likely to be stereotyped as privileged, leaving those who aren't feeling cut off from both their race and their class.

Picking a black student at random, it is hard to make an accurate guess of her background, the *Source of the River* notes. She could be the heir to a sizable fortune or the child of a single welfare mother, so any assumptions about her background based on her race would likely be wrong, and acting on them may give offense. The economic diversity of the black and Hispanic populations on selective college campuses is such that it "creates considerable potential for conflict" among their own members. "For many black and Latino freshmen from segregated inner cities, it will be the first time they have ever encountered rich minority members who may not share the same linguistic or cultural styles. For others coming from affluent, integrated settings, college will be their first chance to move through black and Latino worlds (in theme dorms and student organizations)."

Many of the black freshmen surveyed harbored "considerable class resentment" that got in the way of their adjustment to life on a wealthy campus. They felt kinship with poor Hispanics and blacks and severe alienation toward rich whites and Asians, and they stood out among all the groups on campus in terms of how negatively they felt toward rich people of their own race.[13]

The presence of large numbers of immigrants in the black population further complicates relations, and black students may notice a double standard in how they are treated, depending on where they hail from. Whites have a much higher comfort level with black immigrants than with those who were raised here, according to a separate study by three of the book's authors. "To white observers, black immigrants seem more polite, less hostile, more solicitous, and generally 'easier to get along with,'" they concluded.[14]

At a fall 2003 reunion of Harvard's black alumni, law professor Lani Guinier caused a furor when she noted during a public forum that a majority of the university's black students are immigrants, the children of immigrants, or, to a lesser extent, the children of biracial couples, and called diversity there "a question of aesthetics." Some administrators at selective colleges applauded her decision to take note of how badly such colleges are doing at enrolling students descended from blacks brought to the United States during the nation's long period of slavery. Others, however, argued that the origins of black students are irrelevant in admissions and urged that the matter be dropped.[15]

Among black students at selective colleges, women outnumber men two to one. The long-term consequence is that much of the black elite will consist of women who are single, or married to black men with lesser educations, or married to nonblack men.[16] The tensions arising from the shortage of black males boiled to the surface at Brown University in October 1995, when several black women threw the campus into an uproar by creating a "Wall of Shame" listing black men who were dating women of another race. The men on the list as well as several multiracial students took offense, but Brown's administration declined to treat the matter as a possible violation of its student conduct code.[17]

In teasing out their findings for other groups, the *Source of the River* researchers found that 49 percent of Hispanic students characterized themselves as "white/Latino," 3 percent simply as white, 13 percent as "black/Latino," and 28 percent as mixed race. The presence of such a rich racial mix within the Hispanic population may help explain why, compared to others, it has been found to be better at dealing with diversity and more willing to get to know students from other racial and ethnic backgrounds.[18]

Asian Americans, being greatly overrepresented at selective colleges vis-à-vis their share of the overall U.S. population, often end up saddled with the "model minority" stereotype on these campuses. As a result, the colleges often fail to provide struggling segments of their population, such as students from Southeast Asia, the academic support services they need. While most Asian American college students say they are happy and feel accepted on campus, it is not unheard of for them to suffer racially motivated assaults, and sizable numbers complain of being the victims of racial slurs by students and discrimination by faculty members and administrators. In focus group interviews conducted in the early 1990s, David Wellman, a sociologist at the

University of California at Santa Cruz, found that many white students' advocacy of admissions policies based strictly on grades and test scores evaporated as soon as they were asked how Asian American applicants should be judged. Suddenly, they didn't think applicants' SAT scores were nearly as important as whether or not they were "well rounded."

Perhaps because of their status as both the victims of bias and the chief beneficiaries of admissions standards based solely on academic merit, Asian Americans are more conflicted in their views of affirmative action than any other group on campuses.[19] Only black students are more likely to support affirmative action in principle, and only white students are more likely to object to it as practiced. A study of Asian American students at a large public university in the Midwest found that those who viewed the racial climate on campus negatively were the most supportive of affirmative action measures. Its author contemplated whether colleges should let the racial climate on their campuses deteriorate for the sake of building support for affirmative action, but concluded that doing so would be a mistake given the likelihood of negative consequences such as increases in the black dropout rate.[20]

Some research suggests that Native Americans are among the most marginalized populations on campus. For example, they are the least likely to forge close friendships with whites or Asians and among the least likely to befriend Hispanics, even though they are likelier than most other students to get to know blacks.[21] They are such a small presence at most selective colleges that they have not been extensively studied. About the only times their concerns get much public attention is in the context of controversies over American Indian–themed team mascots, such as the "Chief Illiniwek" figure who until early 2007 entertained football and basketball fans at the University of Illinois at Urbana-Champaign.

It is a rarity to walk into a public college's cafeteria and find students of different races and ethnicities sitting together with any regularity. Almost always, there are white tables interspersed with black, Asian, and Hispanic tables. Mixed tables are few and far between. The pattern repeats itself all over campus. Walk through nearly any university's student union building and you will find dozens of organizations for members of specific racial and ethnic groups. Many colleges set aside dormitory wings or floors for one minority group or another. As a University of Michigan student once observed to me, "You'll go into parties, and there will be only one race there. They'll be completely black, completely Asian, completely Jewish, completely Indian. With the exception of one or two people, everyone will be like that." The separation is not always voluntary. Many minority organizations on campuses either ban white students from joining or preclude them from holding leadership positions. Meanwhile, at some universities, black students say they stay away from parties at white fraternities for fear of being beaten up.

If you look at the enrollments of selective colleges purely in mathematical terms, it appears that whites should have an easy time keeping to themselves, while minority students have little choice but to get to know people who look different. After all, if a biology class section has seven white students, one black, one Hispanic, and one Asian, it is possible for six of the white students—but none of the minority students—to have a lab partner from their own racial or ethnic group. Numerous studies have found, however, that white students are actually much likelier to reach out to people of other races and ethnicities than black students, a sizable share of whom have little interest at all in getting to know the white students around them. A report on students at the University of California at Berkeley attributed part of the separation between groups on campuses to differences in how blacks and whites defined racism. Most white students tended to see racism—or its absence—in terms of personal interactions, and thus saw themselves as free of prejudice so long as they were friendly to minority students. Most black students looked for racism in people's views, and thus were inclined to see the white student who extended his hand in friendship while being opposed to affirmative action as not worth their time. White students tended to think the best way to promote interracial understanding was through informal socialization. But most black students were inclined to refuse their invitations, instead favoring the promotion of interracial understanding through formal activities such as sensitivity training—an idea that most whites found unappealing.[22]

Many college professors and administrators are not bothered by the self-segregation that takes place among college students. Troy Duster, the director of the University of California's Institute for the Study of Social Change, has suggested that it is a mistake to think that the only two roads open to minority students on campus are either assimilation or separation. There's a third route, he says, in which minority students spend time with members of their own race or ethnicity as a way of making themselves stronger when they interact with other groups.[23] Beverly Daniel Tatum, the president of historically black Spelman College and a professor of psychology, similarly argues that the clustering of black students among members of their own race is a natural, positive coping strategy in dealing with racism on campus.[24]

Certainly, racist acts such as spoken, spray-painted, or e-mailed slurs happen with some regularity on college campuses. At least a few times each year, white kids at one college or another somehow decide it would be a good idea to be photographed in blackface or to have a theme party based on racist stereotypes, inevitably triggering an uproar that results in disciplinary proceedings against them. Over the past decade, though, hate crime hoaxes have become a feature of college life as well. In April 2005, Trinity College in Illinois evacuated its entire campus after several black and Hispanic students received hate-filled e-mails, one of which mentioned a gun. The sender turned out to be a black student who wanted to create the impression the campus was unsafe so her parents would let her transfer out.[25] Earlier, hundreds of students at Claremont McKenna College marched in support of a psychology professor who, after speaking out at a forum on hate crimes, filed a police report saying her window had been smashed, her tires slashed, and her car spray-painted with the words "whore," "nigger lover," and "bitch." A jury later convicted her of attempted insurance fraud and filing a false report after witnesses recounted seeing her do the damage herself.[26]

Complicating the picture is the fact that one person's hate speech may be another's free expression. In one of my visits to the University of Michigan, I met black students who were upset that the administration had not taken disciplinary action against several conservative students who had pulled the now-cliché "affirmative action bake sale" stunt, in which critics of race-conscious admissions dramatize their objections by setting up a table of goodies that they offer to blacks and Hispanics at a lower price. Some higher education institutions have shut down such demonstrations and, in at least a few cases, sought to discipline the students involved, but it is understandable that the University of Michigan was reluctant to do so. Following the 1987 black student protests on its campus, the school had adopted a speech code broadly prohibiting any remark that created a "hostile or demeaning environment," only to find itself being slapped down by a federal court which held that it was violating students' First Amendment rights. Similar speech codes have been struck down at Stanford University and the University of Wisconsin.

Seeking to avoid any open discussion of race-conscious admissions preferences has been one of the ways colleges have sought to avoid racial tensions on campus and to make minority students feel more comfortable. As Colin Diver, president of Reed College in Oregon, noted in a 2003 speech at the University of Illinois, many educators have believed "a lack of candor" on the subject is appropriate to avoid stigmatizing the minority students who benefit from preferential admissions. If college administrators acknowledge giving any consideration to race, they generally say they do so only as a "tie-breaker" or "thumb on the scale"—until, that is, someone uses a lawsuit or state open records laws to extract from them information that proves otherwise. One college professor I interviewed recalled that, as an admissions committee member at a large Midwestern public university in the 1980s, he was specifically instructed to grant acceptance to a few white students with admissions test scores so abysmally low they stood little chance of graduating. The point was to lower the average admissions test score for all white students to statistically obscure the gap between them and the black students admitted.

In refusing to provide details on their affirmative action efforts, colleges say they fear critics of race-conscious policies will misrepresent them to inflame existing tensions on campus. Major controversies erupted at the law schools of Georgetown University in 1991 and of the University of Miami in 1995 as a result of students obtaining access to records showing the differences between the LSAT scores and grade point averages of entering white and minority students. The University of Miami suppressed publication of the information and formally reprimanded the student journalist, who had been leaked the records, for the honor code violations of "engaging in conduct which causes serious doubt on his fitness to be an attorney" and "interfering with the rights of students to pursue their education free from any real or perceived need to justify their existence."[27] The student said the punishment was undeserved and disputed the assertion that his actions violated the ethics code for lawyers. During a fall 2004 visit to Texas A&M, which had explicitly forbid its admissions office from considering applicants' race, I encountered black and Hispanic students who were relieved to be on a campus where their fellow students had no reason to question whether they belonged.

Colleges may have a sound educational reason for discouraging open discussions of the differences between the races in terms of their academic

qualification and performance. A fair amount of research shows that a sizable share of minority students perform worse academically if they feel negatively stereotyped. For example, Douglas Massey and Margarita Mooney
have found that minority students who internalize negative stereotypes
about their group's intellectual ability reduce the number of hours they
study, which then enables them to shrug off bad grades by telling themselves they did not work very hard anyway.[28] Claude Steele, a social psychologist at Stanford, has constructed laboratory experiments proving the
existence of a phenomenon called "stereotype threat": If you convince students that they will confirm a negative stereotype of people like themselves
by performing poorly on a test, at least a few of them will choke and perform much worse on the test than they would have otherwise. In one study
examining the effects of stereotype threat, Massey and Mooney reached the
paradoxical conclusion that when colleges give big admissions breaks to
black and Hispanic applicants, it is not the students getting the breaks but
other blacks and Hispanics who run into academic trouble. The students
who got the biggest admissions breaks actually did fine—refuting the argument that race-conscious admissions decisions inevitably set students up
for failure—but, nonetheless, the colleges that put the most weight on race
or ethnicity in admissions had the lowest average black and Hispanic grade
point averages and graduation rates, suggesting that stereotype threat looms
large on such campuses.[29]

An unresolved question is whether colleges' use of race-conscious admissions policies helps or hurts race relations on campuses or out in the
world beyond, where both the people who graduated from such colleges and
those who never got in end up living out their lives.

One study from the early 1990s took two groups of whites with similar
backgrounds, mentioned the phrase "affirmative action" to one but not the
other, and then asked them several questions about blacks. Those to whom
affirmative action had been mentioned were much more likely to express a
belief in negative stereotypes of black people, by, for example, agreeing with
the assertion that they are lazy.[30]

When I visited the University of Michigan in 1998, administrators there
showed me a study that found that, after four years at the university, 35 percent of the black students and 56 percent of white students said that Michigan's efforts to increase diversity actually promoted racial division more than
they fostered racial understanding. Although all students had grown slightly

more supportive of affirmative action over time, they remained racially polarized in their views, with 6 percent of blacks but nearly two-thirds of whites agreeing that "students of color are given advantages that discriminate against other students at colleges and universities." The likelihood of students being good friends with members of other races actually declined every year they were on campus.

Forty percent of whites over the age of 18 believe that they or someone they know will be rejected by college due to an unqualified minority applicant being admitted, according to one analysis of 2000 national survey data. The authors of that study argued that such a perception has little basis in reality, as the number of white students rejected by a selective college in any particular year is many, many times the number of students whose race or ethnicity plays a role in their admission.[31] But given how many highly talented students get rejected by colleges every year, and how much institutions deny or downplay those admissions preferences that have nothing to do with affirmative action, I can understand how many whites and Asians leap to the conclusion that race-conscious admissions have kept them or their children out of a prestigious college.

Truth be told, colleges probably benefit from such false assumptions. After all, if well-qualified whites or Asians are angry because they believe they were rejected in favor of blacks, Hispanics, or Native Americans, colleges can try to claim the moral high ground by accusing them of being racially insensitive, failing to understand the educational value of diversity, or refusing to own up to our nation's racist past. If, on the other hand, people are angry because they believe they were rejected in favor of applicants with more money or better connections, about all they can be accused of is being too naïve to realize that money talks, it isn't what you know but who you know that matters, and life just isn't fair.

Chapter 6

Assault from the Right

Affirmative Action Under Attack

If you wanted to launch a crusade to reform the admissions policies of selective higher education institutions, it would be hard to find better "poster children" than Jennifer Gratz and Barbara Grutter.

The application that Gratz submitted to the University of Michigan at Ann Arbor in 1995 could best be summarized as: "Bright, well-rounded, nice kid with charisma and leadership ability. Has done exceptionally well given her circumstances." She had grown up in a modest home in a section of working-class Detroit suburbs known as "Downriver," where smokestacks obscure the horizon. Neither her father, a police officer, nor her mother, a hospital lab worker, had graduated from college, yet she had a 3.8 grade point average and ranked thirteenth in her class of 298 at Southgate Anderson High School. Although her ACT score had been a less-than-stellar 25, putting her in the eighty-third percentile, she had been a cheerleader, had won election as class vice president and homecoming queen, and had cared enough about the world around her to volunteer to tutor other kids, work with the elderly, and organize a blood drive.

Barbara Grutter was a 43-year-old mother of two who had been operating her own health care consulting business out of her Plymouth, Michigan, home for several years when she made a midcareer decision to study health care law. She had graduated from Michigan State University with a 3.81 grade point average back in 1978, and thought she had what it took to become part of the University of Michigan Law School's entering class of 1997. Granted, her LSAT score, 161 out of a possible 180 points, was a bit low for the school, where the average LSAT score among the white students admitted was 167. But she believed her extensive work experience should count for something, and she figured that Michigan's law school would see how its classroom discussions would benefit from the presence of someone who had spent nearly two decades out in the real world.

The University of Michigan rejected Grutter outright and sent Gratz a letter telling her she had missed the first cut but was welcome to put herself on a waiting list with such long odds that she would be wise to look elsewhere. Neither of the two welcomed such news. Michigan had accepted plenty of other white applicants with lower grades and test scores, but Gratz and Grutter did not fret over the possibility that they had been elbowed aside by people connected to alumni, donors, prominent politicians, or university employees. Neither argued that the admissions tests they had taken were poor measures of their true abilities, and Gratz took no umbrage at Michigan's tendency to look down on applicants from Downriver high schools. Both knew of black and Hispanic applicants with lower scores and grades who had gotten into the university, and both concluded that their own white skin had played a decisive role in keeping them out. Both, indeed, became "poster children," lending themselves to the cause of forcing colleges to abandon racial and ethnic preferences in admissions.

Along with Patrick Hamacher, a young man whom the university had denied entry as a freshman in the fall of 1997, Gratz was recruited to become the lead plaintiff and the public face of a class action lawsuit challenging the race-conscious admissions policies of Michigan's chief undergraduate program, its College of Literature, Science, and the Arts.[1] Grutter took on the same role in a lawsuit challenging the consideration of applicants' race and ethnicity by Michigan's law school.

As the lawsuits were gearing up, I traveled to Michigan for *The Chronicle of Higher Education* and interviewed state Senator David Jaye, one of several Republican legislators who helped organize the lawsuit by recruiting and screening plaintiffs and putting them in touch with lawyers from the Center for Individual Rights, a libertarian-leaning, Washington-based legal advocacy group. Jaye told me that affirmative action was "the number one economic and social issue" in the working-class, overwhelmingly white, Macomb County suburbs he represented, where just about everyone knew someone "who has suffered a loss due to minority preferences."

The story of the war on college affirmative action is very much the story of how Republican politicians—as well as conservative advocacy groups and the broader conservative movement—tapped into the resentments of people like Gratz and Grutter to promote agendas that often went well beyond protecting anyone from discrimination.

I have no reason to doubt that those leading the fight against race-conscious college admissions were convinced that such polices are immoral and unconstitutional, and for that reason far more objectionable than any other preference colleges may give. But in rebelling against affirmative action, ordinary working- and middle-class Americans ended up—sometimes wittingly, sometimes not—lending their support to a long list of other causes. These included getting Republicans elected to office; fighting the cultural left on college campuses; curtailing civil rights enforcement and school desegregation; pressuring immigrants and minority groups to assimilate into the dominant U.S. culture; and reducing the tax burden on the nation's wealthy.

Ward Connerly, a Sacramento businessman and one of the most prominent leaders of the movement to end racial preferences, has acknowledged: "Organizations drive this debate on both sides. This is all a war in the trenches between organizations, and individuals are just selected to further the aims of the organizations. That is the reality."

By strengthening the hand of fiscal conservatives, many of those enlisting in the fight against race-conscious admissions actually may have hurt their own children's chances of attending a selective college. As the government has reined in spending on public schools, colleges, and student financial aid, the nation's colleges have responded by capping enrollments, raising tuition and fees, and seeking more applicants who can pay their own way. These trends have made it harder for all but the wealthiest to gain admission and cover the cost of earning a degree.

The popular backlash against affirmative action began well before the creation of the chief organizations now fighting it. As far back as the early 1960s, trade unions were complaining of "reverse discrimination" in response to President Kennedy's demands that government contractors integrate their workforces.[2] On the whole, many middle- and working-class

whites felt they were being unfairly asked to shoulder most of the burden associated with affirmative action, busing for school desegregation, and other
liberal remedies to the problems of black America. Robert J. Hoy, a leader
of the 1970s white populist backlash against such policies, would later sum-
marize the resentments of blue-collar whites in Boston and other cities by
noting that "no Kennedy has ever had to experience the horrors of having
himself or his children bused into the ghetto." He protested that white,
working-class Americans "have been expected to welcome the social and
racial experimentation which bodes only disaster for themselves and their
communities," administered at the hands of "do-gooder politicians who
consider them expendable."[3]

Back in 1964, George C. Wallace Jr. campaigned for the Democratic
nomination for president by railing against school busing and other liberal
policies aimed primarily at helping blacks. And although he failed in his bid
to get on the ticket, he nonetheless convincingly demonstrated how a national candidate could win over both Southerners and blue-collar voters in
the North by appealing to whites who felt unfairly burdened by integration
efforts. Richard M. Nixon took that lesson to heart in his 1968 presidential
campaign, using opposition to busing and a pledge to restore law and order
to the nation's riot-torn cities to narrowly defeat his Democratic opponent,
Hubert Humphrey, and to stave off Wallace's third-party bid.[4] A decade
later, Ronald Reagan proved a master at using attacks on affirmative action,
busing, and other liberal policies to persuade working-class whites to switch
over to the Republican Party and ally themselves with the big-business interests they previously had opposed.[5] The strategy would become a key part
of the Republican playbook, to be used by GOP candidates again and again
in the ensuing years. In fact, many political analysts believed it was vital to
the GOP's success in the1994 midterm elections, in which Republicans took
control of both chambers of Congress for the first time in 40 years by winning more than 62 percent of the white male vote.

In 1972, when federal officials threatened to withhold research dollars
from universities until they adopted plans to hire more women, the nascent
rebellion against affirmative action was joined by about 500 professors who
united in forming the Committee for Academic Nondiscrimination and Integrity to protest the use of racial and gender preferences by colleges. Among
them was Nathan Glazer, a Harvard sociologist who was becoming a major
figure in the emerging neoconservative movement. Three years later he

would publish a groundbreaking book, *Affirmative Discrimination: Ethnic Inequality and Public Policy,* that would help frame the right's critique of affirmative action for decades to come.[6]

The neoconservative critics of affirmative action had backgrounds that made it difficult to dismiss their objections as based on elitism, naked self-interest, or a belief in racial segregation or white supremacy. Virtually all were Northern intellectuals well removed from the racial battles of the South, and many were Jews whose own families had suffered persecution. Most of the early neoconservatives had been leftists before converting to an ideology that championed individual rights, and there remained little in their writings or mannerisms that suggested disdain for the less fortunate. The key document that they looked back upon as the basis for their critique of affirmative action—the federal Civil Rights Act of 1964—was a hallowed liberal text that many of their conservative predecessors had staunchly opposed.[7] Citing that law—as well as the words of some of the civil rights movement's own leaders, such as Martin Luther King Jr.—they argued that affirmative action was morally offensive because it violated the fundamental principle that people should be judged by the content of their character, not by the color of their skin. In his influential book, Glazer argued that the use of affirmative action to promote racial equality "has meant that we abandon the first principle of a liberal society," that the welfare and rights of individuals matter above all. "The implications of the new course," he said, "are an increasing consciousness of the significance of group membership, an increasing divisiveness on the basis of race, color, and national origin, and a spreading resentment among the disfavored groups against the favored groups."[8]

The appeal of the neoconservative philosophy would help give rise to the various advocacy groups that would take it upon themselves to fight affirmative action in the media, in the courts, and at the voting booth, sustaining the struggle over the long haul.

Ironic as it may seem, the same man who enshrined the diversity rationale for race-conscious admissions in law also helped give rise to the conservative advocacy groups that would emerge as affirmative action's chief threat. The late Justice Lewis F. Powell Jr. was still a lawyer in private practice, months shy of being nominated to the Supreme Court by Nixon, when he wrote a 1971 memorandum to the U.S. Chamber of Commerce complaining that environmental and consumer advocacy groups were being allowed to exert undue influence on the nation's affairs. What was needed, he said, was a conservative counterpart to such organizations, a nonprofit legal center that would promote the interests of business. His memo inspired the California Chamber of Commerce to create the Pacific Legal Foundation to promote individual rights, free enterprise, and property rights in that region. Businesses and conservative philanthropies showered the new organization with support, leading to the formation of similar regional groups as well as national organizations such as the Washington Legal Foundation.

The Pacific Legal Foundation would be the first of the bunch to jump into the affirmative action fight, weighing in with an *amicus curiae* (friend of the court) brief when the U.S. Supreme Court took up a legal challenge to the use of racial quotas by the medical school at the University of California at Davis. Siding with Allan Bakke, the rejected applicant who had brought the lawsuit, it argued that white people are as entitled as anyone else to the Constitution's protections against state-sponsored racial discrimination.

Among others submitting briefs in support of Bakke were the U.S. Chamber of Commerce, the American Subcontractors Association, various labor unions (including the American Federation of Teachers), and a host of groups representing Jews, Poles, Italians, Greeks, and Ukrainians—populations that saw themselves as victims, rather than perpetrators, of the sort of discrimination that they were being asked to give up college seats and job opportunities to remedy.

Even before the Supreme Court's 1978 *Bakke* ruling, as the case was rising up through the courts and it became clear that race-conscious admissions policies would remain the target of legal challenges in the long term, selective colleges began tinkering with their policies to make them more legally defensible. In 1977, the Carnegie Council on Policy Studies in Higher Education urged colleges to consider "racial experience, not race *per se*" and "experience in a non-English-language home, not heritage or surname *per se*" because not all minority applicants "have special characteristics that we believe warrant consideration." Some minority students, it noted, "have not experienced prior adverse discrimination, have not been educationally disadvantaged, have had little or no contact with a minority culture, and have no interest in special services to society."

The council recommended that colleges adopt two-stage admissions processes. In the first, they should determine which applicants of any race had met their absolute minimum academic standards, which should be set "no higher than is necessary." Considerations of race and ethnicity could then come into play in the second stage, in which colleges would pick and choose among applicants who had made that first cut.[9] Colleges everywhere adopted such two-stage admissions processes as a way to admit more minority students while being technically right in claiming not to hold them to lower standards. I have yet to encounter a college that does not claim to accept only those applicants who can do the work needed to graduate, no matter how high its dropout rate. But, as would become apparent as a result of subsequent court challenges and investigations by conservative groups, many colleges and professional schools ignored the Carnegie Council's advice to look at minority applicants as individuals; instead, they adopted policies in which any candidate from certain racial or ethnic groups automatically received extra consideration.

Nixon had made opposition to busing a litmus test for his judicial appointees. Largely as a result, when the *Bakke* case came before the Supreme Court, there were five justices, including Powell, who leaned far enough right on matters of race to strike down the medical school's use of racial quotas. That five-member court majority also rejected the medical school's contention that its racial preferences were justified by the need for more minority physicians and by the existence of broad societal discrimination. Powell, however, broke away from his conservative brethren—thereby denying them the fifth vote needed for a majority—on the point of whether the court should prohibit race-conscious admissions policies entirely. Explaining why he had sided with the four justices who wanted to keep such policies intact, he said that given the asserted educational benefits of diversity, he thought colleges were justified in considering applicants' race or ethnicity as a modest "plus factor."

Critics of affirmative action would later argue that Justice Powell erred in thinking he could prevent colleges from setting aside a predetermined share of seats for minority students simply by striking down the use of numerical quotas. As long as colleges were allowed to consider race or ethnicity, they could continue to achieve a desired student mix simply by calibrating how much weight they gave to minority status. Although Powell clearly had not envisioned them considering race as more than a small thumb on the scale, as long as they described their admissions processes as subjective or hid them from public view, no one would be the wiser. Based on his analyses of the admissions policies in place at the nation's law schools, Richard Sander of the

UCLA law school concluded that after the *Bakke* ruling, "racially separate admissions tracks were draped with fig leaves of various shapes and sizes to conceal actual practices, which changed hardly at all."[10]

There was a lull in the legal struggle over race-conscious admissions for more than a decade after the *Bakke* ruling. But in 1988 the Center for Individual Rights (CIR) arrived on the scene and took an approach to its work that would help escalate the conflict, transforming what had been a series of legal skirmishes into a multifront war. Founded by two lawyers who had worked together at the Washington Legal Foundation, Michael Greve and Michael McDonald, the CIR resembled other conservative and libertarian groups in the causes it championed: protecting individual rights, limiting the power of the federal and state governments, and defending campus conservatives who felt their free-speech rights were being trampled by the forces of political correctness. What set the CIR apart was how it advanced its agenda. Rather than weighing in on controversies through friend of the court briefs—which the courts often virtually ignore—it decided to make its mark by becoming directly involved in litigation. To stretch its resources, the CIR borrowed an approach that had been successfully used for years by liberal advocacy groups such as the American Civil Liberties Union: Instead of having a large in-house staff, the CIR relied largely on the services of private-practice lawyers who shared its views enough to be willing to work pro bono. In higher education, the CIR initially made a name for itself by defending the free speech rights of professors who believed they had been disciplined or denied promotion for espousing views that did not conform to liberal orthodoxy. It would take half a decade for the group's interest in individual rights to draw it into the fight against racial preferences.

In the meantime, Greve and McDonald's old shop, the Washington Legal Foundation, took up the representation of Daniel Podberesky, a Hispanic man who was suing the University of Maryland at College Park for denying him a scholarship reserved for black students. In a 1994 ruling, the U.S. Court of Appeals for the Fourth Circuit handed Podberesky and his lawyers a huge victory by declaring the scholarship program's race restrictions illegal. Noting that the program was awarding scholarships to black students from other states and even Jamaica—despite its stated intent of drawing black Marylanders to the College Park campus—the court held that the program was far too broad in its scope to meet the legal requirement that race-based policies be narrowly tailored to serve a compelling government interest. A long list of colleges, higher education associations, and civil rights groups filed briefs in support of the university's request that the Supreme Court overturn the Fourth Circuit decision, but the Supreme Court refused to hear the case, thereby letting the lower court's decision stand. The Education Department's Office for Civil Rights, which was then under the leadership of Clinton appointees who supported affirmative action, responded to the Fourth Circuit ruling by issuing guidelines suggesting that most race-exclusive scholarship programs remain permissible. But the office's guidelines represented only their interpretation of the law—not the law itself—and thus were widely seen as affording colleges little protection from court challenges. As confusion over how to comply with the decision reigned among higher education lawyers, most public colleges in the Fourth Circuit—which covers Maryland, North Carolina, South Carolina, Virginia, and West Virginia—quietly changed their polices to make scholarships previously reserved for black students available to members of any race. Most public colleges elsewhere kept their programs as they were.

In the meantime, the Center for Individual Rights jumped into the affirmative action fray in response to a 1993 phone call from Steven Smith, a conservative lawyer in Austin, Texas. Smith had mounted a legal challenge to the race-conscious admissions policies at the University of Texas law school and needed outside help. The lead plaintiff in the case was Cheryl Hopwood, a 26-year-old accountant with a compelling story. The wife of a member of the armed forces and the mother of a severely disabled child, Hopwood had been admitted to Princeton as an undergraduate but, coming from a blue-collar family, had decided she could not afford the tuition. She had worked part-time to put herself through community colleges and California State University at Sacramento, and had graduated with a 3.8 grade point average and earned a much higher LSAT score than many people that Texas's law school accepted. But UT had given little weight to her grades because she had not attended colleges it deemed academically competitive. Seeing a cause that clearly squared with its ideals, the CIR made the case its own and enlisted Theodore (Ted) Olson, a former top Justice Department official under Ronald Reagan, to do its pro bono work in *Hopwood v. Texas*.

Three years later, the CIR was handed a huge victory as the U.S. Court of Appeals for the Fifth Circuit struck down the Texas law school's admissions policy. In a March 1996 ruling that stunned colleges across the nation,

the court repudiated the diversity rationale articulated by Justice Powell—
which many in the field had assumed to be settled law—and held that the
law schools' policies would be acceptable only if the law school itself had
been discriminating against blacks and Hispanics, which was not the case.
The ruling applied only to those states that make up the Fifth Circuit—
Texas, Louisiana, and Mississippi—and arguably not even to all of their
public colleges, as many of those in Louisiana and Mississippi remained
under federal court orders to consider applicants' race as part of desegregation plans. Although Texas's higher education system likewise remained
under a federal desegregation order, the state's attorney general, Dan
Morales, ordered public colleges in that state to rid themselves of any policy
that considered race. When white and Asian American professors and students at the University of Texas-Austin complained that there would soon
be too few minority students there, the campus group Young Conservatives
of Texas offered them a dare: If you think there is too little diversity on campus, sign a pledge agreeing to give up your own spot.[11]

Encouraged by its victory in the *Hopwood* case, the Center for Individual Rights took the battle west. In March 1997 it filed a similar discrimination lawsuit against the University of Washington's law school on behalf of
Katuria Smith, a white woman who had been rejected despite having graduated *cum laude* from the university's business school and scoring in the
ninety-fifth percentile on the LSAT. Around that time the center began
hearing from the Michigan legislators who were trying to mount a similar
lawsuit in their state.

Although most of the groups leading the charge against affirmative action are conservative, it's unfair and just plain inaccurate to pigeonhole all
affirmative action critics as such—they can be found at points throughout
the political spectrum. Some leftists believe that racial preferences serve to
keep minority populations down by enabling the establishment to offer the
illusion of equal opportunity while cherry picking and coopting the best
black, Hispanic, and Native American minds—people who otherwise might
lead a movement to bring about real social justice. Some liberals and pro-
gressives object to race-conscious admissions policies for pragmatic reasons,
citing drawbacks such as high minority dropout rates or the stigmatization
of racial-preference recipients to argue that the policies do their intended
beneficiaries more harm than good. Some strict civil libertarians oppose
race-conscious admissions policies based on a belief that any state-sponsored

racial discrimination is offensive, no matter how noble the intent. Carl Cohen, a University of Michigan philosophy professor, falls into that last, civil libertarian camp.

A former head of the local chapter of the American Civil Liberties Union, Cohen had been a strong supporter of the civil rights movement so long as it simply advocated equal opportunity and nondiscrimination. But, due to his absolutist beliefs in individual rights, he had parted ways with civil rights organizations such as the NAACP on the issue of racial preferences. In 1995 he had become curious about how his university handled race in admissions, and he relished the role of gadfly far too much to throw up his hands when administrators told him such information was confidential. He used document requests filed under his state's Freedom of Information Act to pull the public university's admissions procedures into the daylight, and then told state lawmakers and the media what he had found.

The documents that Cohen pried loose from the university showed that its chief undergraduate program had winnowed the tens of thousands of applications it received every year using a grid system showing different combinations of grade point averages and SAT/ACT test scores. Students at one corner of the grid, with low GPAs and scores, were to be automatically rejected, those at the other, with high GPAs and scores, were to be automatically admitted, and those somewhere in the middle were sent on for further consideration. What riled Cohen was that the instructions for handling each grade-point average and test score combination varied according to race. Among applicants with a high school grade point average of 3.3 and a combined SAT score of 900, for example, blacks were automatically accepted, whites automatically rejected. A statistician from the University of Minnesota would later testify in court that, under the dual grid system, blacks generally received an advantage equivalent to having one full point added to their grade point average, so a black 2.5 was about as good as a white 3.5. Although the law school's admissions process was not nearly as formulaic, it was clear to Cohen that race was often what separated shoo-ins from long-shots. Four years after Cohen initiated his investigation, the undergraduate program would switch to a different admissions system in which it awarded applicants points for different attributes and judged them on a 150-point scale. As a practical matter, however, it still gave race about as much weight as the grid system did. Being black, Hispanic, or Native American automatically counted for 20 points, the difference between having a 3.0 GPA and a 4.0.[12]

Cohen passed his findings on to state lawmakers, who then recruited plaintiffs for the two lawsuits against the University of Michigan and turned to the Center for Individual Rights for legal help. Michael Greve described the center's involvement in the Michigan and Washington cases as "part of a larger strategy to put the consideration of race beyond the reach of the state."

At about this time, a fifth major federal lawsuit was filed against the University of Georgia over its policy of giving extra consideration to minority or male applicants. The Atlanta-based lawyer who handled that case, Lee Parks, said he and the plaintiffs acted alone and had no intentions of promoting some larger agenda. "We weren't out to change the world. We just had 12 women who wanted to be in school," he told me in a *Chronicle* interview. That case would nonetheless also strike a major blow to affirmative action, leading to a 2001 decision by the U.S. Court of Appeals for the Eleventh Circuit striking down the policy at issue.

Lawsuits were not the only avenue for trying to get racial, ethnic, and gender preferences abolished. The opponents of these policies also had the option of trying to get the law changed to explicitly ban them, leaving their illegality in no doubt. Efforts to persuade federal and state lawmakers to adopt such measures have generally faltered, but state ballot measures calling for bans on preferential treatment have yet to fail at the polls.

It probably was no accident that the movement to ban affirmative action through popular referendum arose in California. No other state is as multiethnic, and in no other state are whites being squeezed as tightly in the competition for seats at top universities and professional schools. Although the total enrollment of the University of California system grew substantially during the 1980s, there were fewer whites on its campuses at that decade's end than at its start, mainly as a result of huge increases in Asian enrollments, especially at the system's most elite campuses.[13] At the University of California at Berkeley whites accounted for 66 percent of enrollment in 1980 and just 42 percent in 1990, even though the state's population remained 58 percent white. Although Hispanics' share of Berkeley's enrollment had more than tripled to 14.4 percent, they remained even more underrepresented, considering that they accounted for more than a fourth of all Californians. Blacks accounted for 6.8 percent of the state's population and about the same share of Berkeley's enrollment, while the share of students there who were Asian American or Pacific Islander had climbed from 20.7 percent to 28.6 percent, making them three times as prevalent on that campus as they were throughout the state. Competition for a spot at Berkeley had grown so intense that about 21,300 high school graduates—5,800 of them with straight A averages—applied for 3,500 open spots every year. The campus had no choice but to turn away 2,300 applicants with perfect grades and, practically speaking, turned away many more than that to make room for less-stellar applicants who had some hook, such as a racial or ethnic background that enabled them to contribute to campus diversity. While the median GPA for white and Asian admittees was a 4.0, the median for black and Hispanic admittees was just over 3.5.[14]

Among the populations jockeying for a place on University of California campuses were people who were multiracial and did not fit easily into any classification scheme. As their numbers had grown in recent decades, they had established their own advocacy groups to promote their interests but had become divided over exactly what their goals should be. One faction wanted colleges and government agencies to place them in a distinct "multiracial" minority category and afford them the same preferences and benefits as other minority groups. Others, however, saw themselves as living testament to the need for American society to stop asking people to check such boxes, to move beyond classifying people by race.[15] In the latter camp was Ward Connerly, a Sacramento businessman whose blood is roughly equal parts French Canadian, black African, Choctaw Indian, and Irish. He was destined to become the leader of a national movement to abolish racial preferences through ballot referenda.

Although generally regarded as black—a fact of his existence that he angrily attributes to "racial ideologues" who perpetuate the "one drop rule" of the Old South where he was raised—Connerly is more politically conservative than most African Americans. He considers himself someone who has made it in life through hard work, and he expresses disdain for liberal social policies that he sees as rooted in white guilt and a black sense of entitlement based on perceived victimhood. He espouses a vision of race relations in America that is deeply assimilationist, holding that people here should be color-blind and that public colleges and government agencies encourage Balkanization and undermine the common good by categorizing people by race or ethnicity and treating them accordingly. He has written that, "Left to their own devices, Americans will merge and melt into each other."[16] He has contributed generously to the political campaigns of his old friend Pete Wilson, a Republican who was San Diego's mayor and a member of the U.S. Senate before serving as California's governor from 1991 through 1999. Wilson appointed him to the University of California's Board of Regents in 1993, and it was in that position that Connerly first became involved in the war against racial preferences.

Even before Connerly took up the cause, supporters had started to line up behind a proposed ballot initiative to amend California's constitution to ban state agencies from granting preferences based on race, ethnicity, or gender. Drafted by two academics who did not like the effects race-conscious admissions were having on academe, the measure had started getting attention and being taken seriously as of late 1994, partly through the assistance of veteran conservative strategists who had enlisted in the campaign for it. Also helping draw attention to the measure were the results from the November 1994 elections, in which Governor Wilson had come from behind to win reelection partly by aligning himself with Proposition 187, a successful ballot initiative barring illegal aliens from receiving state services. Not only had the election results demonstrated the appeal of populist conservatism, but Wilson now had his eye on the White House and made opposition to affirmative action part of the platform he hoped would get him there in 1996.[17]

Connerly has said he was moved to challenge the university system's consideration of applicants' race and ethnicity in 1994, after seeing an analysis of admissions to the medical school at the University of California at San Diego. It showed that the average admitted black or Hispanic ranked in the lowest 1 percent relative to the admitted white and Asian students, and it suggested that few if any white or Asian applicants ever got an admissions break for past disadvantage, no matter how many obstacles they had overcome.[18] He drafted two resolutions aimed at ending the use of racial, ethnic, and gender preferences throughout the University of California system and put them before the Board of Regents for a vote in July 1995. One covered hiring and contracting decisions; the other applied to admissions and included language calling for 50 to 75 percent of the university's students to be admitted based solely on academic achievement. Governor Wilson had seldom attended the regents' meetings—even though, as governor, he automatically held a board seat—but he made sure he was in the room that day. As hundreds of students demonstrated against the measures outside, the board, consisting mainly of Republican appointees, soundly approved both measures.[19] Wilson's presidential campaign fizzled within a matter of months but, with California's debate over affirmative action now all over the airwaves, the campaign for the proposed statewide racial-preference ban—known as the California Civil Rights Initiative or, eventually, as Proposition 209—was on a roll. In November 1995, Connerly became the cochairman and spokesman for the campaign for the measure that would appear on the ballot a year later.

Colleges throughout California became hotbeds of resistance to Proposition 209, with academic departments, offices, and organizations geared toward women and ethnic groups joining to denounce the measure as a threat to their very existence. In covering the pro- and anti–209 campaigns for *The Chronicle of Higher Education* in September 1996, I heard Alex Tom, a member of the governing board of the University of California Student Association, tell a crowd at a rally that the measure had been put on the ballot by a "racist, sexist, homophobic, white, elitist, heterosexual society." Students at California State University at Northridge invited David Duke, the former Ku Klux Klansman turned Louisiana politician, to campus to represent the pro–209 side in a debate. The most vocal opponents of the measure were women's groups, which issued warnings that it would leave women vulnerable to being fired for becoming pregnant or for filing sexual harassment complaints. One of the most prominent anti–209 television spots showed a woman physician being attacked by men who rip the clothes off her body.

Such warnings did little to sway most Californians. Proposition 209 passed with 54 percent of the vote. The Pacific Legal Foundation, the Center for Individual Rights, and the libertarian Institute for Justice—a group mainly associated with advocacy of school choice and school voucher plans—stepped in to defend the measure from a series of legal challenges intended to keep it from taking effect.

Encouraged by his victory, Connerly announced in January 1997 that he was forming the American Civil Rights Institute (ACRI) and its companion political-action group, the American Civil Rights Coalition, to fight racial and ethnic preferences elsewhere. He took the battle up the Pacific Coast to Washington State, where the ACRC led a successful campaign on behalf of Initiative 200, a measure that, like California's Proposition 209, banned the use of racial and gender preferences by public colleges and other state agencies. Initiative 200 fared even better than Proposition 209 did, receiving 58 percent of the vote in November 1998.

Connerly may have persuaded Governor Jeb Bush of Florida to curtail racial preferences in the Sunshine State just by threatening a campaign there. Upon hearing that Connerly intended to put such a measure on the Florida ballot in 2000—a move that could have potentially drawn blacks to the polls, creating headaches for George W. Bush in his presidential bid—Jeb, George W.'s brother and fellow Republican, decided to preempt Connerly by acting on his own. He issued a November 1999 executive order directing state agencies to stop using racial and ethnic preferences and three months later persuaded the state's public university system to abandon race-conscious admissions in favor of a plan to automatically accept young Floridians in the top 20 percent of their high school class.

The campaign against race-conscious admissions spread beyond higher education. Individual parents, as well as organizations such as the Houston-based Campaign for a Color-Blind America, cited Proposition 209 and the Fifth Circuit's *Hopwood* ruling in filing legal challenges to school system policies that considered race in assigning students to elementary and secondary schools.

As Connerly pressed for change through the voting booth and as the Center for Individual Rights fought colleges in the courts, a third key player, the Center for Equal Opportunity, undertook an aggressive effort to force public colleges around the nation to disclose information about whom they were admitting, in order to put them under public and political pressure to end race-conscious admissions policies. Like Connerly, Linda Chavez, the founder of the Center for Equal Opportunity, holds a deeply assimilationist worldview and has so little tolerance for separatist politics that she is denounced by some minority activists as a traitor to her own kind. Her father came to the United States from Mexico, and while she says she appreciates the diversity found here, she also believes that immigrants should learn English as quickly as possible, think of themselves first and foremost as Americans, and not expect special treatment. "We're one nation, and one people, and we shouldn't be divided into racial and ethnic groups," she told me in a 2003 *Chronicle of Higher Education* interview. One of the nation's most prominent critics of bilingual education, she authored a blistering attack on the Hispanic advocacy movement titled *Out of the Barrio* and served as staff director of the U.S. Commission on Civil Rights under Ronald Reagan.

Chavez established the Center for Equal Opportunity (CEO) in 1995. The following year, public colleges around the nation began getting letters from the CEO demanding, under their states' open-records laws, that they cough up the grades and standardized test scores, broken down by race and ethnicity, of the students they had recently admitted. When the University of Wisconsin and the University of Washington refused to comply, the CEO took them to court. The CEO routinely forwards the data it obtains to a Rockville, Maryland, research firm, Lerner and Nagai Quantitative Consulting, for statistical analysis. The result has been a series of reports that use comparisons of median grades and test scores to accuse colleges and professional schools of having vastly different standards for white and minority applicants. In one report, for example, the CEO alleged that as of 1999 black applicants were, in terms of odds ratios, about 730 times as likely as white applicants with similar grades to get admitted to the University of Virginia School of Law.

The colleges examined by the CEO, as well some higher education groups such as the American Association of Collegiate Registrars and Admissions Officers, have denounced the center's reports as misleading, overly simplistic, and based on the false assumption that the objective measures that the reports focus on are the best way to judge applicants. The reports also have been attacked for wrongly assuming that differences in the median grades and test scores of white and minority students can be attributed only to different admissions standards, when they may simply be a reflection of the underrepresentation of blacks and Hispanics at the top of the applicant pool. (You can have a perfectly objective admissions process, taking the 100 applicants with the best test scores, but if minority applicants account for 10 of the 50 highest scorers and 20 of the 50 others making the cut, the average white score will be higher.) The CEO-commissioned research was sound enough, however, that when George W. Bush nominated Robert Lerner, the president of Lerner and Nagai Quantitative Consulting, to the Education Department's top statistics-gathering post in late 2003, the American Educational Research Association—a leading organization of education researchers and a strong supporter of race-conscious admissions—acknowledged that it could not find any serious flaws in Lerner's methodology even if it *did* think his ideology clouded the inferences he drew from his numbers. The CEO has enough clout that it was able to persuade Virginia's attorney general to issue an April 2002 directive to colleges urging them to curtail race-conscious admissions, and some colleges, like the University of Massachusetts at Amherst, scaled back their consideration of race voluntarily after learning that the CEO had its eye on them.

The CEO's efforts to extract information from colleges have been helped by the National Association of Scholars (NAS), an organization of roughly 4,500 academics. Formed in 1987 to battle the forces of "political correctness," the association emphatically rejects the label "conservative" but holds the view that colleges have strayed from their primary academic mission as a result of their emphasis on multiculturalism and ethnic and women's studies. It opposes racial preferences in admissions because, it believes, the policy hurts the quality of the student body—putting professors under pressure to lower their demands and expectations—and fosters a climate that is racially and ethnically polarized, making it harder for students to learn from each other. In addition to helping the CEO and other groups opposed to such policies gather information, the NAS also has conducted and publicized research seeking to debunk colleges' claims that the diversity produced by race-conscious admissions policies has educational benefits.

By late 2002, the CEO and NAS had found a new line of attack: going after college scholarships, fellowships, and programs that are open only to members of certain races or ethnicities. Because most colleges prominently advertised such programs and their eligibility requirements in brochures and on Web sites, finding evidence of them generally was as easy as getting online or sending an NAS volunteer into an admissions office. The CEO's general counsel joined the ACRI's legal affairs director in sending colleges letters threatening to file federal civil rights complaints if the institutions did not open the programs up to students of any race or ethnicity. While many colleges responded that they wanted to wait for guidance from the Supreme Court in the Grutter and Gratz cases, a few, such as the Massachusetts Institute of Technology and Iowa State University, caved in after concluding they were legally vulnerable.

The Center for Equal Opportunity, American Civil Rights Institute, Center for Individual Rights, and National Association of Scholars all derived much of their financial support from the same few sources, including the right-leaning John M. Olin, Lynde and Harry Bradley, and Sarah Scaife foundations. As the campaign against race-conscious admissions gathered steam and a Supreme Court battle appeared inevitable, representatives of these groups and other leading conservative organizations began routinely working in unison. ACRI's newsletter, for example, tells of a January 2002 meeting in Washington at which those on hand "to compare notes and co-ordinate strategy" included representatives of the CIR, the CEO, and the ACRI, as well as David Horowitz (a prominent crusader against political correctness), Grover Norquist (the founder and president of Americans for Tax Reform and a prominent leader of the anti-tax movement), and Todd Gaziano (an official of the Heritage Foundation, which promotes a long list of conservative causes, including school choice and tax cuts). The Heritage Foundation also hosted weekly meetings at which leaders of several of Washington's leading conservative and libertarian organizations gathered to coor-dinate their efforts against racial preferences.

Lee Cokorinos, research director of the liberal Institute for Democracy Studies, has extensively studied the groups challenging affirmative action and characterizes them as a "well-funded, nationally based network" with the goal of "essentially trying to eliminate the gains of the civil rights movement."[20]

In an early 2003 *Chronicle of Higher Education* interview, Clint Bolick, who was involved in the fight against racial preferences as vice president of the libertarian Institute for Justice, said, "I wish there was a vast right-wing conspiracy." The truth, he said, is that the groups opposed to race-conscious college admissions policies have to split the workload for lack of financial support for their efforts. Of the three main groups in the fight, as of 2003 the CIR's annual budget was $1.7 million, the ACRI's, $1.4 million, and the CEO's, about $1 million—hardly small change, but fairly modest sums for national advocacy groups, and less than what many colleges spend on their legal affairs and public relations departments.

"Most foundations are liberal to begin with and, of those who support conservative groups, only a handful have been supportive of this issue," Bol-ick said. "Corporate America," he observed "is emphatically not interested in supporting the fight against racial preferences."

What Bolick and other opponents of race-conscious admissions did not realize at the time was just how costly the lack of corporate support for their cause would prove to be.

Chapter 7

By Any Means Necessary

Black Voices Fight to Be Heard

At 16, Agnes Aleobua already had dreams of making a name for herself as a civil rights activist. Although her father was a Nigerian immigrant with a master's degree, she felt as much a victim of America's long history of racial oppression as many black people whose families have been here for centuries. The conditions that other black Detroiters were living in angered her, as did the condition of Cass Technical High School, where she was a junior. Despite having a reputation as one of the Motor City's best high schools, Cass Tech operated in a terribly run-down building and failed to provide all of its students with books.

Agnes listened attentively when, in February 1998, one of her physics classes was interrupted for a presentation by two outside visitors, Shanta Driver and Milisa Resch, both leaders of a group called the Coalition to Defend Affirmative Action and Integration and Fight for Equality by Any Means Necessary. Driver and Resch were trying to recruit students to enlist in the effort to preserve race-conscious admissions at the University of Michigan at Ann Arbor. Aleobua jumped when they offered her a chance to become involved in one of the lawsuits against Michigan as an "intervening defendant," a representative of the minority students who might be shut out of the university if the courts ruled against it. Her goal, she later told me in a *Chronicle of Higher Education* interview, was helping "to build up a new civil rights movement."

Over the next several years, however, Aleobua and black students and activists like her would find it a struggle to have any voice at all in the debate over affirmative action in college admissions.

Although protests by minority students had played a central role in getting colleges to adopt race-conscious admissions policies back in the late 1960s and 1970s, minority students were very much relegated to the sidelines in the legal battles over college affirmative action that began in the early 1990s. As Ted Shaw, a top lawyer for the NAACP Legal Defense and Educational Fund, has observed, all of the lawsuits challenging affirmative action involved "white students suing predominantly white institutions." The key question before the courts was whether such policies are justified in light of the educational benefits they provide to *all* college students, including whites. Neither the colleges nor, for that matter, most of the nation's chief civil rights groups talked much about integrating higher education or remedying discrimination out in society. There was almost no discussion of the question of whether blacks, Hispanics, and Native Americans have a right to as much access to selective colleges as everyone else.

Any attempt to justify affirmative action policies as needed to remedy racial discrimination faced an overwhelming obstacle: Most selective colleges have never admitted to discrimination, and, moreover, they were not about to make themselves vulnerable to additional lawsuits by doing so. Outside of those Southern states that once segregated their higher education systems as a matter of law, colleges nearly always adopted race-conscious admissions policies in response to political pressure or out of a sense of *noblesse oblige,* not in response to any sort of formal admission or judicial finding of racial bias. As far back as 1977, the year the Supreme Court took up the pivotal *Bakke* affirmative action case, the U.S. Commission on Civil Rights noted that the unwillingness of colleges to discuss their own past exclusionary practices, or even the discriminatory activities of other public agencies in their states, was impeding any sort of "careful and reasoned" discussion of why race-conscious admissions policies were justified.[1]

The race-conscious admission policy that came up before the Supreme Court in the *Bakke* case was exceptional in how divorced it was from American higher education's long history of discrimination. In a country filled with selective colleges that had once declared themselves off-limits to any black applicant, the Supreme Court had managed to take up a dispute involving a medical school, at the University of California-Davis, that had existed only since 1966 and that had almost immediately adopted a policy of reserving seats for minority applicants.

The only remedial justification for affirmative action that the University of California put forward in the *Bakke* case was the broad claim that the medical school needed to use racial preferences to offset discrimination in American society. Five of the nine justices rejected that argument. Noting that many segments of the white population have themselves endured discrimination, Justice Lewis Powell said the federal courts cannot, and should not, get involved in trying to sort out which Americans had suffered enough to merit special treatment and which ones should bear the burden of making discrimination's victims whole.

A quarter century later, Gary Orfield, the codirector of the Civil Rights Project at Harvard University, observed that "the most powerful argument for affirmative action would be to show that it is remedial." Instead, he said, "We are trapped into an argument that basically dismisses the history of inequality in higher education as if it were irrelevant."

Even as far back as the *Bakke* case, colleges and minority organizations had found themselves at cross purposes over affirmative action. Minority groups had urged the University of California to refrain from taking the *Bakke* case to the Supreme Court because they thought the policy at issue— a rigid quota system adopted in the absence of any past history of institutional discrimination—was harder than most to justify, and might provoke a ruling striking down affirmative action entirely.[2]

In the *Hopwood v. Texas* case of the early 1990s two organizations representing black students at the University of Texas at Austin had sought to intervene in the lawsuit to help defend the use of race-conscious admissions by the university's law school. The federal courts rebuffed them, holding that the university's lawyers from the state attorney general's office would adequately represent the students' interest. "Texas has a history of racial discrimination, which could have been used to build a case for affirmative action. But Texas officials were not going to embarrass themselves and develop a full record on that issue," noted Ted Shaw, who blamed what he regarded as a half-hearted state defense of the law school's policy for its being struck down in 1996.[3]

Similarly, minority students represented by the American Civil Liberties Union were denied permission to intervene in a case involving the law school at the University of Washington at Seattle, based on a judge's conclusion that they would be sufficiently represented by the university. When the U.S. Court of Appeals for the Ninth Circuit upheld the law school's policies in December 2000, it did so strictly on educational diversity grounds and made no reference to any discrimination suffered by minority students. Minority students represented by the NAACP legal defense fund were allowed to intervene in a lawsuit challenging the University of Georgia's undergraduate admissions policies, but were denied permission to introduce evidence related to that state's history of racial discrimination. A federal appeals court struck down the policy in 2001.

In the lawsuit challenging the University of Michigan's race-conscious undergraduate admissions policy, *Gratz v. Bollinger,* Shaw worked with a group of Detroit-area activists called Citizens for Affirmative Action's Preservation to mount an effort to intervene on behalf of current and prospective students. He felt precluded for conflict-of-interest reasons, however, from seeking involvement in *Grutter v. Bollinger,* involving the policies of Michigan's law school, because he was a member of the faculty there. Intervention in that case was left to the Coalition to Defend Affirmative Action and Integration and Fight for Equality by Any Means Necessary. The group would tinker with its full name over time, but it would consistently go by the acronym BAMN, and it would show that it was not bluffing in its professed willingness—borrowing from the statements of Malcolm X—to use "any means necessary" to advance its cause.

Agnes Aleobua, the student recruited by BAMN at Cass Tech, would go on to gain admission to Michigan as an undergraduate through the university's Summer Bridge program, which offered weak applicants a chance to enroll if they took classes in the months before their freshman year. Once on campus, she would become a leading BAMN organizer and, on many occasions, the public face of the organization.

In dealing with the Michigan cases, BAMN and the NAACP Legal Defense and Educational Fund (NAACP-LDF) would take markedly different approaches, each deeply rooted in their respective worldviews and histories.

The NAACP-LDF is one of America's most venerable civil rights organizations. The National Association for the Advancement of Colored People set it up in 1940 (Thurgood Marshall wrote its charter), and it has been involved in key civil rights battles ever since. With the assistance of lawyers from the Mexican American Legal Defense and Education Fund and the American Civil Liberties Union, the NAACP-LDF sought to justify the University of Michigan's undergraduate admissions policy for reasons deeply rooted in history. It noted that until the 1960s, the university operated racially segregated campus housing and allowed black students to be excluded from fraternities and sororities. It alleged that blacks and Hispanics remain racially isolated on the campus and "continue to be subjected to racially hostile actions," including racist graffiti, the distribution of racist literature, and "endemic" discriminatory treatment at the hands of the university police, with one consequence being that Michigan's reputation deterred minority students from applying. Its briefs also argued that the university needed to consider race and ethnicity to offset other aspects of its admissions formula which systematically awarded points for traits that had nothing to do with academics and were disproportionately possessed by whites, such as legacy status, access to prestigious high schools and Advanced Placement Courses, and residency in overwhelmingly white Northern Michigan. The NAACP-LDF did not challenge the validity of the SAT and ACT test scores that factored into the admissions formula out of a belief that the courts were not interested in taking up the issue. In light of the Supreme Court's *Bakke* ruling of 1978, which had rejected the desire to remedy societal discrimination as a justification for race-conscious admissions policies, the group thought it was futile to try to defend such policies as necessary to promote racial justice.

The founders of BAMN were not civil rights leaders but radical leftists who had cut their teeth as advocates for the laboring class. They were members of the Detroit-based Revolutionary Workers League (RWL)—a labor rights advocacy group that followed the insurrectionist teachings of Leon Trotsky—and the National Women's Rights Organizing Coalition (NWROC), an RWL spin-off. They established the first BAMN chapter in California in 1995 to fight both the proposed Proposition 209 ban on state-sponsored racial preferences and the University of California Board of Regents' efforts to end preferences in admissions, hiring, and contracting. Both RWL and NWROC had been accused of inciting violence during a long-running, bitter strike by workers for Detroit's two major newspapers, and members of NWROC had been involved in violent counterdemonstrations against the Ku Klux Klan in Michigan and Ohio and had skirmished with

Operation Rescue in several other states. BAMN also had an edge to it; Eileen Scheff, an NWROC member who helped found it, told me, "Affirmative action was built by people taking direct militant action." At public universities in California, BAMN clashed with other protesters and police, and quickly gained a reputation for trouble from its tactic of summoning large groups of high school kids to take to the streets.[4]

The Michigan BAMN chapter, founded in 1997, made headlines that September by storming a public hearing at which state lawmakers were discussing proposed legislation to bar the University of Michigan from using racial preferences. (Police ended up clearing the room with teargas.) At Michigan, as had been the case at the University of California, BAMN quickly gained a reputation for trying to commandeer the pro–affirmative action activities of other student groups and for summoning large numbers of high school students to campus for protests that often turned disorderly. In a January 2001 letter printed in the university's chief student newspaper, Agnes Aleobua expressed hope that she could influence a Detroit federal court's deliberations of the *Grutter* case by filling the courtroom with militant students. Her letter predicted that objections to BAMN testimony by the plaintiffs' lawyers from the Center for Individual Rights "will happen far less if sitting behind them is a crowd of people who are making clear they will not be resegregated," and that the judge's orders that BAMN lawyers limit how long they speak "will be far less enforced if sitting in his gallery are black students demanding that he not deny them the opportunity to attend the University Law School."

I witnessed the strong-arm tactics of BAMN-mobilized protesters firsthand in covering a rally that the group staged in Cincinnati's Fountain Square in December 2001, as the Michigan cases were being heard in a nearby federal appeals court. When a white counterdemonstrator on a rooftop held a sign reading "Affirmative Action Poisons Equality," several young black BAMN-organized demonstrators pushed him halfway over the ledge to get him to give the sign up. A few people witnessing the scene expressed horror at how close they had just come to seeing someone seriously injured or killed, but most of the crowd below applauded as the sign was seized and torn apart.

The legal strategy used by the BAMN-organized *Grutter* intervenors seemed at least as concerned with scoring political points and asserting a moral basis for affirmative action as it was with prevailing on points of law.

When the U.S. Court of Appeals for the Sixth Circuit heard oral arguments in the Michigan cases, their lead attorney—Detroit lawyer Miranda K. S. Massie, sister of a key BAMN organizer, Luke Massie—opened her presentation by pointing to a stack of boxes containing more than 50,000 petitions calling for the preservation of race-conscious admissions. (Chief Judge Boyce Martin cut her off, saying, "I don't think petitions are what decide lawsuits.") In her briefs and in the courts, Massie challenged the validity of weighing applicants based on Law School Admission Test scores and undergraduate grades, alleging that the LSAT was racially biased and that minority students' undergraduate grades often suffer from the racial isolation they experience at college and from the poor academic preparation they received at inadequately funded elementary and secondary schools. Bringing up an argument that Justice Powell had declared irrelevant back in 1978, she contended that affirmative action was needed to offset the effects of the societal discrimination that minority students experience. "In this society, white people are systematically given unearned benefits and privileges," she told me in a *Chronicle* interview.

Like Ted Shaw, Massie argued that campuses are hostile environments for minority students. Among the expert witnesses she put on the stand in district court was Walter R. Allen, a professor of higher education at UCLA, who testified that, in general, minority students were subject to "unconscious prejudice in the grading process" and "face a daily run of slights and profiling" in which professors fail to distinguish among them, teaching assistants accuse them of cheating if they perform well, and library employees search their book bags.

When I visited U of M for the *Chronicle* in 2003, I talked with several minority students who thought discrimination was pervasive there. Nearly all recalled the same incident, the anonymous chalk-scrawling of "Only Niggers Want Affirmative Action" on a campus sidewalk. Aundrea Johnson, a senior majoring in psychology and black women's studies who served as spokeswoman for the Black Student Union, said, "You get professors who are shocked by the amount of work you do or see being very articulate as something they don't expect of you because of your color." Others expressed a belief that their professors coddled them, or seemed to call on them for "the black perspective" or "the Hispanic perspective." Several wanted U of M's administration to do more to stop white students from saying and writing things they found offensive—including criticisms of affirmative action—but the university, having already lost a federal law-suit over a speech code adopted in the late 1980s, was not about to risk treading on the First Amendment again. Its general counsel, Marvin Krislov, told me that offensive speech cannot be stopped, and probably should be expected, in a free academic environment where people from different backgrounds come together.

Agnes Aleobua, then a senior majoring in education, recalled living in a dormitory her sophomore and junior years and said racism was why people did not say hello when she walked down the hallway or stop to visit when she left her room door open. When two white women who lived in the adjacent room and had never spoken to her asked her to turn her stereo down one day, "I knew that was race related," she said. When I asked her if any professors had ever discriminated against her, she took a moment, and then recalled a psychology class that she had often skipped either because she was feeling depressed or out of sorts or because she had pro–affirmative action events to plan or attend. When her professor told her that other students in the class were missing out for not having her there, she considered it "a slap in the face" that "goes toward the way the university uses affirmative action to produce tokenism." For the most part, she added, her professors were "overwhelmingly supportive," and were willing to open up their classes to students making announcements or presentations in support of affirmative action. Several had cancelled classes and rearranged test dates so students could attend a pro–affirmative action march in Washington, D.C.

At times, Aleobua and other BAMN organizers undercut the university's defense of its admissions policies. In one pamphlet, for example, BAMN denounced the diversity rationale for race-conscious admissions as "half-honest" and said "we must defend affirmative action on its real basis." It said "affirmative action is about the fight for equality" for minority students and women, and "it is NOT fundamentally about enriching the educational experience of an otherwise segregated white student body." Noting that University of Michigan's undergraduate enrollment was about 8 percent black while the state's population was about 14 percent black, BAMN argued that the university should offer enough equality of access so that its enrollments roughly reflect the state's composition.

In my visits to the University of Michigan for *The Chronicle,* I found that many black Michigan students backed the university and its legal strategy and had little use for BAMN. In January 2001, members of the Black

Student Union and the Black Greek Association charged into a BAMN rally and proclaimed that affirmative action was *their* issue, not BAMN's. Aundrea Johnson, the BSU spokeswoman, later said of BAMN, "They always paint the issue in black and white, and that does not help our cause." Monique Luse, a black senior from the well-to-do Detroit suburb of Farmington Hills whom the university's administration routinely referred the media to for interviews, disputed BAMN's contention that the university should be equally accessible to all, regardless of race or class. "It is not your average state university," she said. "It has become a national institution and has a different idea of who it needs to be educating."

Inside the courtroom—especially at the Supreme Court level—the University of Michigan said little to challenge the assertions of the intervenors in either case, but it also made no admissions of racial bias. Judges, for their part, were skeptical of the intervenors' bias allegations. In the undergraduate case, for example, U.S. District Court Judge Patrick J. Duggan said that the racial segregation practiced by Michigan into the 1960s had no bearing on current applicants and students, and that he remained unconvinced that Michigan was using biased admissions standards or doing too little to respond to racist incidents on campus.

Both Massie and Shaw said that if the Supreme Court were to strike down race-conscious admissions entirely, they envisioned their organizations turning against Michigan and other selective colleges and mounting lawsuits that would challenge as racially discriminatory those admissions policies (such as legacy preferences) that disproportionately benefit white students. "We will have to turn up the scrutiny," Shaw told me in a *Chronicle* interview. "We are not going to sit around and allow double standards to apply in terms of who gets access to higher education."

In *amicus curiae* briefs submitted to the Supreme Court, other civil rights groups overwhelmingly sided with the University of Michigan and its diversity rationale, and said little in support of the intervenors. "The positions taken by the intervenors are important positions, but it is also kind of generally recognized that those are not the issues that the Supreme Court seems ready to take on now," observed William Taylor, a lawyer who submitted a brief on behalf of the Leadership Conference on Civil Rights, a coalition of more than 180 national civil and human rights groups. Privately, some higher education and civil rights lawyers expressed fear that the intervenors' briefs might hurt Michigan's defense of race-conscious admissions by making it clear that there were alternatives, such as revising admissions policies that generally favored white applicants.

When it came time to hear oral arguments in the *Grutter* and *Gratz* cases, the Supreme Court refused to take the unusual step of extending the time allotted for each case by 10 minutes to let the intervenors have their say. The University of Michigan's lawyers, who had shared their allotted argument time with the intervenors in the lower courts, had the option of sharing it again in the Supreme Court but refused. Godfrey Dillard, a lawyer for the *Gratz* intervenors, complained that he felt Michigan's lawyers had betrayed him. "They led us to believe they were going to give us time, and at the last minute they pulled the rug out from under us," he said. "They are supposed to be representing us, and now the black man is up in the damn gallery again."[5]

Chapter 8

Breaching Walls

The Uprising of the Excluded

Texas A&M University is not an institution one expects to find on the cutting edge of higher education's efforts to increase minority enrollments. Until 1963, it was a military-training college that completely refused to admit blacks and women. Its College Station campus remains a distinctly conservative place, home to the George H. W. Bush presidential library and museum, George Bush Drive, and a student body that generally seems to delight in Republican politics and clean-cut conformity. It does not award minority students an edge in admissions, even though its lawyers have given it the green light to do so.

Yet, at a time when many colleges with race-conscious admissions policies are experiencing flat or declining minority enrollments, this fairly selective university has been boasting of impressive gains. From 2003 to 2006, the number of black students entering Texas A&M as freshmen rose by 77 percent, the number of Hispanics, by 59 percent. About a fourth of its students are members of the first generation of their family to attend college. Although Texas A&M's student body remains whiter than many other colleges'—and much, much whiter than the population of Texas as a whole—most selective higher education institutions would kill to match its recent progress in diversifying.

What has made the difference there? Texas A&M has undertaken sweeping efforts to recruit minority and low-income students and to ensure that those accepted get whatever financial aid they need. It stations recruiters in big cities like Dallas and Houston and in the heavily Hispanic Brazos and Rio Grande Valleys. It dispatches financial aid officers to sit down with families at their kitchen tables and walk them through the process of applying for grants—a huge help for Hispanic parents with poor English skills, as well as for families with little experience in dealing with higher education. It annually awards more than 600 scholarships to students from modest backgrounds whose parents never went to college and has an additional scholarship pool for students at Texas high schools that typical send few graduates its way. It refuses to grant preference to applicants tied to alumni, and about half of its students gain admission through a law by which Texas guarantees its young residents a spot at any of its public universities as long as they are in the top tenth of their high school class.

Falling under the jurisdiction of the U.S. Court of Appeals for the Fifth Circuit, Texas A&M was initially forced to abandon race-conscious admissions as a result of that court's 1996 *Hopwood v. Texas* ruling. When the Supreme Court effectively voided the *Hopwood* decision with its 2003 rulings involving the University of Michigan, Texas A&M passed up the opportunity to revert to considering ethnicity and race. Its president, Robert Gates, declared that students there "should be admitted as individuals, on personal merit—and no other basis." Minority lawmakers and civil rights groups were outraged, but Gates insists his institution made the right call.

When I visited College Station in October 2004 to interview Gates for the *Chronicle of Higher Education,* he told me that he thought reinstituting affirmative action in admissions would have been the easy way out, enabling him to tell the world he was doing everything possible to increase minority enrollments and then throw up his hands when the numbers remained flat or declined. By making the controversial decision to stick with race-blind admissions, he put himself under the gun to make darned sure those numbers actually rose if he wanted to keep his job.

It is worth noting that Texas A&M's medical school decided to go back to using race-conscious admissions after concluding it could not take in enough minority students any other way. And there is no escaping the fact that, in states where such policies have been banned, black and Hispanic enrollments initially plunged—and have been slow to rebound—at the most selective public colleges and at many law and medical schools.

But the elimination of race-conscious admissions policies has put in motion other developments that have brought comfort to the disadvantaged. No longer able to offset society's inequities by using double standards to judge those competing for admission, colleges have been forced to confront those inequities and to take steps to make the contest fairer. Public colleges, as well as the state leaders who regulate and finance them, have had to try to figure out—and deal with—whatever was keeping a disproportionate share of minority students out of the pool of applicants eligible for admission based on academic merit. That has meant doing something about vast wealth-based disparities in the quality of public schools, taking a critical look at admissions and financial aid policies that favor students from moneyed backgrounds, and paying much more attention to the role that parents' income and education play in determining college access.

When the *Chronicle* recently ranked elite public universities with endowments of over $500 million based on the share of their enrollments that was financially needy, those in states where race-conscious admissions had been banned generally fared better than others. Among them, the University of California at Los Angeles ranked second, with more than 37 percent of its students on need-based Pell Grants as of the 2004–2005 academic year. Also high on the list were the University of Washington and the University of Florida. The University of Michigan at Ann Arbor, which had successfully fought to preserve its race-conscious admissions policies, ranked 28 of the 31 institutions examined, with just 13.5 percent of its students on Pell Grants.[1]

The bottom line is that the assault on affirmative action has forced people to grapple with a subject that many Americans have long treated as taboo: class. Those concerned about maintaining racial diversity at selective colleges have found themselves talking about the obstacles faced by poor people of any color—including poor *white* people, a population that for the most part had been completely off their radar screens.

It has been decades since the leaders of government, civil rights organizations, and academe paid as much attention to the educational disadvantages of all poor Americans, regardless of race or ethnicity. There had been a fleeting moment in 1968 when Martin Luther King Jr. appeared poised to try to blend the causes of racial and economic equality by launching a "Poor

People's Campaign." But King was assassinated before the campaign could get off the ground, and the loss of his integrationist leadership left the black civil rights movement increasingly dominated by those focused on advocating black power. The winner of that year's presidential election, Richard Nixon, not only used affirmative action as a wedge issue to politically divide blacks and working-class whites, but also sought to cut and run from Lyndon Johnson's War on Poverty.[2] In the decades since Nixon's presidency, the nation's electorate and political leadership has become steadily more fiscally conservative and hesitant to spend tax dollars on higher education and other social needs. Back in the 1960s, a majority of Americans believed that most of the costs of a college education should be borne by the government; today, about two-thirds subscribe to the view that the costs should be paid primarily by students and their families.[3] It is telling that the most liberal president of the last quarter century, Bill Clinton, promoted and signed a change in federal welfare law that forced most aid recipients who were in college pursuing baccalaureate degrees to quit school and take whatever jobs they could find.

It is not as if our federal and state officials have spent the last four decades completely oblivious to concerns about access to college. But, for the most part, their focus has been on getting more people to go on to *any* college, to help ensure they have the minimum training to meet the nation's workforce needs. Getting more people from lower-income backgrounds into *selective* colleges did not emerge as much of a priority anywhere until the mid-1990s, when race-conscious admissions policies came under attack.[4] With many higher education experts predicting that black enrollments would drop by three-fourths or more at any selective college that dropped affirmative action and evaluated applicants based solely on grades and admissions test scores, people began to seriously deliberate how to deal with the societal inequities hindering minority students' college access.

In striking the first major blow against race-conscious admissions, the University of California Board of Regents seemed mindful of the broader issues it would now need to grapple with. Its 1995 resolution banning the use of racial and ethnic preferences throughout the UC system included provisions calling for the creation of new outreach and academic preparation programs to help increase the number of qualified minority students applying from the state's high schools. When Californians voted the following year to approve Proposition 209—banning the use of racial, ethnic, and gender preferences by all state and local agencies, including public colleges—state officials joined those at the University of California in being under pressure to find new ways to make selective higher education more accessible. One step they quickly agreed on was doing more to ensure that all of the state's public high schools offer the advanced courses that selective colleges look for on transcripts.

The California regents' resolution barring racial and ethnic preferences—and the pleas for fairness used to justify it—caused other admissions preferences used by the system to come under a microscope. The *Los Angeles Times* exposed how the state's public officials had for several years been using their influence to get the University of California at Los Angeles to admit applicants who clearly were poorly qualified and, in some cases, had already been rejected. After hearing UCLA administrators argue that only a handful of students in each entering class had benefited from such intervention, the regents chose not to completely abolish such VIP admissions, but instead adopted a policy requiring campus chancellors to inform system officials and get the approval of the university's Academic Senate every time they planned to consider an applicant's connections as grounds for giving him or her a break. The regents also adopted a policy forbidding the system's campuses from giving extra consideration to the children of employees.[5]

In the ensuing years, often in response to pressure from civil rights groups and black and Hispanic state lawmakers, the regents instituted a number of other major changes aimed at redefining the concept of merit and bringing in a wider mix of students. In 1999, the regents adopted a policy guaranteeing young Californians who graduated in the top 4 percent of their high school classes a spot on a campus somewhere in the University of California system, helping to bring about a one-year increase of 17 percent in the number of underrepresented minority students entering it as freshmen. In 2000 the board adopted a policy offering a second chance to students who did not quite make the cut for admission as freshmen; as long as the rejected applicants ranked in the top 12.5 percent of their high school class, they could transfer into the system after successfully completing a two-year course of study at a community college. In 2001, the regents adopted a policy requiring the more selective campuses to subject all applications that met the system's minimum standards to a "comprehensive review"—basically, a thorough reading that looked for evidence that the applicant had overcome socioeconomic disadvantage or some other form of hardship. That new policy resulted in an increase in the share of entering students from rural areas, low-performing schools, and families that were low-income or had no college experience.[6]

Maintaining diversity in the university system's professional schools proved a much bigger challenge, in part because the schools drew from private and public colleges all over the country, making it impractical for them to establish outreach programs at every possible feeder institution. The Boalt Hall School of Law at Berkeley took a small step to at least draw students from a wider range of schools in 1997, by ditching its practice of automatically adjusting upward the GPAs of students from elite undergraduate institutions such as Harvard. That same year, the law school at UCLA undertook a bold experiment with class-based affirmative action, automatically awarding extra points to applicants for various traits indicating economic disadvantage. The new admissions policy produced a fourfold increase in the number of students from poor backgrounds enrolled at the school, and an entering class that more closely resembled the nation's population in terms of economic status than its predecessors. But, although such consideration of class disproportionately benefited minority students, they were insufficient to keep black and American Indian students' numbers as high as they had been when the race and ethnicity of applicants was considered.[7] As a result, the law school abandoned the policy within a year, opting instead to draw in more minority students by setting up a new academic program, Critical Race Studies, with lower admissions standards than the rest of the law school.

At the same time California was dealing with the effects of the regents' preference ban and Proposition 209, Texas was scrambling to find ways to offset the effects of the Fifth Circuit courts' *Hopwood* decision, which was causing black and Hispanic enrollments to plunge. None of the new admissions policies adopted in California were as groundbreaking in how they redefined merit as the Ten Percent Plan passed by the Texas legislature in 1997. It would serve as a model for both the percent plan adopted by the California regents in 1999 and a sweeping percent plan implemented in Florida the following year.

The Texas Ten Percent Plan was the brainchild of a task force assembled by Democratic state lawmakers and consisting mainly of university faculty members and representatives of the Mexican American Legal Defense and Educational Fund. Looking around them at a state where only a fourth of high school seniors attended class in truly integrated settings, the plan's authors had an insight: By creaming the top of high schools that were overwhelmingly white, overwhelmingly black, or overwhelmingly Hispanic, colleges could turn K–12 segregation into a source of collegiate diversity. The legislation that they came up with guaranteed young Texans in the top tenth of their high school classes admission to the state university of their choice, regardless of their SAT or ACT scores. Given Texas's populist inclinations, the idea was heralded as a political stroke of genius. Among those who got behind it was the state's governor, George W. Bush. In signing the measure into law, Bush said, "This legislation says to Texas high school students, if you work and study hard enough to rank in the top ten percent of your high school class, you can earn the right to go to college." He added, "We want our universities to reach out to students from all walks of life, and this legislation gives them the flexibility to do just that."

As a practical matter, the main public colleges affected by the plan were the University of Texas-Austin and, to a much lesser extent, Texas A&M. Many of the students admitted through the plan would have gotten into one of those institutions anyway, but the plan had the effect of putting those flagships in the sights of high school students who previously never would have thought of them as an option. In 1996, the last year under the old admissions policy, just 64 Texas high schools, mainly from wealthy suburbs, accounted for more than half of Austin's enrollment. As of 2000, after three years under the Ten Percent Plan, the grip these schools had on seats at the Austin campus had loosened significantly. The total number of Texas high schools sending students to UT-Austin had increased by more than a fourth, and most of the new feeders were either large urban high schools with predominantly minority enrollments or small rural schools that served mostly white students from modest backgrounds.[8]

Among the plan's authors was David Montejano, then an associate professor at the University of Texas at Austin. He says that his analyses of enrollment numbers show that most of the racial diversity that Austin achieved under the Ten Percent Plan was not from low-performing high schools, but from "a second tier of very good schools that were being squeezed out" under the old admissions criteria. In keeping with other research showing that high school class rank in itself is a reliable predictor of future college success, one study of Austin's students found that those admitted under the Ten Percent Plan were outperforming their fellow students, in many cases earning the same grade point averages as non–Ten Percenters with SAT scores 200 or 300 points higher. Moreover, less than 1 percent needed any sort of remedial work.[9]

A separate analysis of school attendance patterns found evidence that the Ten Percent Plan was influencing some families' housing and school choices. The desire to ensure that their children were in the top 10 percent of their high school classes motivated some to stay put to keep their children in schools where they ranked high and others to move where their children could be in schools that posed less competition.[10]

The Ten Percent Plan was hardly the only new strategy adopted to promote diversity at Texas colleges. Both UT-Austin and Texas A&M pumped money into scholarships for the Ten Percenters from high schools that had previously sent few graduates their way. For its part, the multicampus University of Texas system created a program aimed at expanding access to Advanced Placement classes, which previously had been offered in only half of the state's high schools. Along with operating a summer program to train high school teachers in providing AP courses, it persuaded state officials to create a bounty system offering public schools a $100 bonus every time one of their students passed an AP exam. Within a few years, the total number of Texas students taking AP classes increased by more than half and the share of minority students taking such classes increased by nearly three-fourths, according to College Board data.

Like California, Texas had an especially difficult time bringing the minority enrollments in advanced degree programs back up to where they had been under affirmative action. In an attempt to revive these enrollments at public law and medical schools, Texas lawmakers voted in 2001 to prohibit such schools from rejecting applicants based primarily on their scores on standardized admissions tests. Under the new state law, if applicants' admissions test scores were to be considered at all, they had to be compared only with those of other applicants from similar economic backgrounds.

In February 2000, Florida's governor, Jeb Bush, appeared to one-up his brother George by persuading the governing board of his state's university system to dump race-conscious admissions in favor of a "Talented 20" policy guaranteeing Florida high school students in the top 20 percent of their graduating classes admission to at least one of the ten universities in the system (although not necessarily the university of their choice). The impact of the decision was less than met the eye, however, because nearly every public university in the state had modest enough academic standards to achieve diversity without giving extra consideration to minority applicants and already accepted nearly all applicants in the top fifth of their high school classes.[11] The University of Florida was the only member of the system giving much weight to the race or ethnicity of applicants for undergraduate admission.

Administrators at the University of Florida turned to the University of Texas and the University of California for advice. Based on what they learned, University of Florida officials pumped money into efforts to take in students from areas of the state that it had not served well before and worked to improve race relations on its Gainesville campus to bolster its reputation in minority communities.[12] The university's College of Education established partnerships with troubled, predominantly minority high schools to try to improve the quality of their instruction so that more of their students would graduate and be eligible to become Florida Gators. In 2002, it adopted a percent plan of its own, guaranteeing students in the top 5 percent of their high school graduating class admission to its campus.

Florida managed to sustain its minority enrollments at the undergraduate level, but civil rights organizations would later argue that the Talented 20 plan deserved no credit because the state never actually did away with affirmative action in higher education. While prohibited from considering race in admissions, Florida's public universities remained free to consider it in a host of other areas, including recruitment, outreach, and financial aid.[13]

All three of the states that adopted percent plans were among the nation's most racially and ethnically diverse, and all three had large numbers of high schools with predominantly minority enrollments. Whether percent plans would work elsewhere remained unclear. They probably held promise for Southern states with large black populations, high levels of residential segregation, and large public university systems. But it seemed doubtful they would bring much diversity to overwhelmingly white states or to states in New England where a huge share of top students enrolled in private colleges that the plans wouldn't cover. Betraying how far affirmative action had strayed from its origins as a response to the problems of urban blacks, Jonathan Alger, the University of Michigan's general counsel, protested in a 2003 interview that a class-rank plan would force his institution to take most of its African American students from Detroit, where a large share of the state's black population lives, rather than selecting the best from high schools across the country.[14]

Of all the flaws ascribed to percent plans, the one that is potentially the most fatal is their alleged legal vulnerability. Texas A&M bumped up against the legal limits of such plans in 2002, when it considered adopting a policy of automatically admitting the top 20 percent of students from 250 low-performing, heavily minority high schools around the state. The proposal immediately came under fire from people who asserted that it amounted to a backdoor return to race-based admissions, and it was dropped.[15] Critics of the plans on both the left and the right argue that all of the plans are susceptible to legal challenge as a result of the racial objectives underlying them. Moreover, all of those adopted so far have been accompanied by a host of outreach, recruitment, student support, and financial aid programs that venture into legally treacherous waters by focusing heavily on ethnicity and race.[16]

Not every public university that has been precluded from considering race in admissions has turned to percent plans. The University of Georgia, for example, opted to take other steps such as ending preferences for the children of alumni, increasing its minority recruitment efforts, and putting more money into need-based financial aid after losing a federal lawsuit challenging its policies in 2001. The University of Washington decided to reach out to community colleges and try to increase the number of transfer students it took in.

Especially because percent plans are not seen as workable in every state, on the national level much of the discussion of alternatives to affirmative action has focused on broader subjects, such as whether colleges need to rethink how they define merit. The alliances forged among the various key players in the war over race-conscious admissions have become strained as the discussion has turned to proposals to adopt class-based affirmative action, abolish legacy preferences, or rethink how much weight colleges and professional schools assign to standardized admissions tests. Perhaps no discussion has divided advocates of affirmative action more than the question of how colleges should use the SAT.

Criticism of the SAT is nothing new. Since the 1970s, the test has been the subject of scathing journalistic exposés and has come under attack from civil rights leaders and consumer advocates. Although many in higher education view the SAT as a decent measure of reasoning ability and a fairly accurate predictor of freshman grades, education researchers and psychologists have found that there are many types of intelligence and talent that the SAT does not measure.

Many of the objections to the SAT stem from the tendency of blacks, Hispanics, and Native Americans to score lower than whites, even when compared to people at the same income level. When students' scores on the math and verbal portions of the SAT are combined, the average white score is about 200 points above the average black score. The average Hispanic score hovers somewhere in the middle, while Asian Americans, on average, post the highest scores of all.

Many of the SAT's critics have alleged that it is culturally biased, but the Educational Testing Service (ETS) and researchers elsewhere have produced studies consistently finding that the test actually *overpredicts* the performance of black students in college, that black freshmen generally get worse grades than white freshmen with identical SAT scores.[17] Another common line of criticism has been that with the proliferation of test-preparation programs, the test has come to measure the ability of parents to write checks to Kaplan or Princeton Review more than the academic potential of their children. The College Board, which owns the test, and the ETS, which administered it until recently, initially denied that test-preparation programs have any impact at all on scores and continue to maintain that the impact of these programs is small. But a growing body of research places the edge most students gain from enrolling in SAT test-preparation programs at well over 100 points on the 1600-point scale for the verbal and math portions, enough to transform many selective college applicants from clear rejects into sought-after additions to entering classes.

Criticism of the SAT intensified in the mid-1990s, as attacks on affirmative action focused attention on the barriers that minority applicants faced when colleges were precluded from considering race. The Education Department's Office for Civil Rights jumped into the debate in early 1999 and, for a few months anyway, seemed poised to adopt new guidelines that would put the SAT in grave danger.

At the time, the civil rights office was under the leadership of Norma Cantu, a Clinton appointee who had earlier spent 14 years as a top lawyer for the Mexican American Legal Defense and Educational Fund and was widely known as an aggressive advocate of the rights of minorities and women. She had her staff draft guidelines on the use of the SAT based heavily on the "disparate impact" theory of discrimination, which holds suspect any policy or practice that disproportionately harms some race, ethnicity, or gender—no matter how racially neutral it may seem on its face. It appeared to many that the civil rights office was about to begin accusing colleges of discrimination unless they could prove that their reliance on the SAT was educationally necessary and no better options were available. Although most higher education institutions and associations had a good relationship with the Clinton administration, they were not about to accept a federally man-dated overhaul of their admissions policies. So strongly did they oppose the guidelines proposed by Cantu's office that they turned for help to leading Republicans in Congress, who were happy to oblige them by hauling Cantu before an oversight committee and accusing her of exceeding her authority. In the end, the civil rights office backed down and agreed to let colleges con-tinue to use the SAT and other standardized tests much as they had in the past.[18] But, with affirmative action under attack in the federal courts, many in higher education believed that the reprieve granted the SAT test may only be temporary.

By the mid-1990s, even officials at ETS had resigned themselves to the idea that the SAT's days may be numbered. Anthony Carnevale, who joined the Educational Testing Service as its vice president for public lead-ership in 1994, says developments such as the *Hopwood* ruling in Texas left ETS officials certain that the Supreme Court would eventually abolish race-conscious admissions. When that happened, they believed, the SAT would come to be seen as an even bigger obstacle to black and Hispanic access to top colleges than it had been before. Civil rights organizations would launch an all-out effort to challenge the SAT as discriminatory, and enough questions had already been raised about the SAT's validity that it was un-likely to withstand such an assault.

The people at ETS weren't the only ones worried at the time about how America's war over affirmative action would play out. The Democratic Party's leadership also was struggling with how to deal politically with the whole issue and was trying desperately to find a way to make the controversy go away. President Clinton already knew Carnevale, having appointed him as chairman of an independent National Commission for Employment Policy in 1993. When Clinton established a task force to review federal af-firmative action, Carnevale was one of the people that Christopher Edley Jr., a prominent Harvard law professor on leave to head up the panel, turned to for advice.

The son of working-class parents, Carnevale has retained an outsider's perspective on elite higher education. He believes that, as much as selective colleges' administrators and faculty members may espouse liberalism, the institutions themselves are at heart "profoundly conservative" and "fundamentally elitist," and see their role as sorting out who should be at the top of our society and who should be somewhere below.

Carnevale came up with an idea that had potential to defuse both opposition to the SAT and the broader debate over affirmative action in college admissions. It promised to offer his employer a way to save the test that had been its bread and butter while offering the Clinton administration a possible way out of a political bind. His notion was to devise a new way to read SAT scores, one that took into account whatever disadvantages students had faced and gave a leg up to those who had overcome major challenges. Because black, Hispanic, and American Indian students were disproportionately represented among college applicants who had encountered obstacles growing up, it seemed likely that such an admissions process might result in every bit as much diversity on campus as admissions policies that considered ethnicity and race. Carnevale's bosses at ETS signed off on his research effort, which soon came be known as "the Striver Study."

The political winds seemed to be in Carnevale's favor as his research got underway. The broader concept of class-based affirmative action already was gaining currency among policy wonks, partly as a result of the 1996 publication of the book *The Remedy,* in which Richard Kahlenberg, then a Fellow at the Center for National Policy, persuasively argued that class-based admissions preferences offered colleges a principled way out of the affirmative action impasse.[19] Polls were showing that the concept of class-based affirmative action had broad popular support, given how neatly it fit into the American belief in upward mobility as a reward for hard work. Most of the alternatives to race-conscious admissions being tried out in California and Texas were, to at least some extent, attempts to use socioeconomic disadvantage as a proxy for race.

From the very beginning, however, the advocates of class-based affirmative action encountered skeptics and detractors on both ends of the political spectrum. On the right, some conservative critics of racial and ethnic preferences said they would look skeptically upon, and might legally challenge, any class-based affirmative action program that seemed to have as its real purpose giving an edge to minority applicants. At least a few prominent conservative thinkers argued that class-based affirmative action, in itself, was a dangerous idea. Abigail Thernstrom, a senior fellow at the right-leaning

Manhattan Institute, expressed fear that class-based affirmative action threatened the very social fabric of the nation. Most Americans, she noted, think of themselves as belonging to the middle class and have little use for political campaigns that seek to pit the classes against each other. But, she said, "preferential policies that reward low-income status would encourage citizens to shed their middle class 'illusions' and adopt the language of oppression," polarizing the electorate along class lines.[20]

On the left, advocacy groups representing minority members and women had greeted President Clinton's creation of a panel on affirmative action by putting him on notice that they did not believe there were any viable alternatives to preferences based on race, ethnicity, and gender. No alternative would be acceptable to them unless it caused the numbers of black, Hispanic, and women in a particular college or career field to remain stable or rise. Thus their test of whether a class-based policy met their approval precisely mirrored conservatives' standard for judging whether such a policy was suspect. Their skepticism was heightened by their awareness that the idea of class-based affirmative action had been publicly endorsed by some prominent conservative Republicans, including then Speaker of the House Newt Gingrich and Jack Kemp, the GOP's 1996 vice presidential nominee.

Class-based affirmative action also lacked the support of many of the businesses and industries that were helping to cover the costs of colleges' race-based affirmative action programs. With *race*-based affirmative action, colleges can focus directly on recruiting as many minority students as possible and seek to enroll the most academically qualified, which, due to the strong correlation between educational achievement and socioeconomic status, generally means enrolling the most privileged. With *class*-based affirmative action, colleges must cast a wider net and admit students of all races and ethnicities, diluting the minority representation among the students they haul in and straining their financial aid budgets. Because the poor generally experience educational deprivation, the minority students that colleges admit through class-based affirmative action will not, on average, be as academically qualified as those given an edge based solely on race. The colleges themselves might see potential academic benefits in taking in students who, having coped with poverty, might have an interesting real-world perspective to contribute to classroom discussions. But class-based affirmative action programs distract colleges and professional schools from the goal that the major employers in their regions want them focused on: producing as many highly qualified minority graduates as they can.[21]

Carnevale soon discovered that the political threats to his "striver" research were not all outside ETS. Some co-workers were calling him "the new Manning," a reference to Winton Manning, an ETS expert on the measurement of mental ability who attempted to develop a similar admissions formula back in 1990. Manning's proposed system for processing the test worked fairly simply. It calculated the average SAT score one might expect of students from certain backgrounds (as defined by their parents' income and education level) and adjusted test takers' actual scores upward or downward based on whether they had exceeded or failed to meet expectations. Once scores were recalculated through such a process, much of the difference in the scores of different races and ethnicities vanished. ETS officials had serious reservations about Manning's approach, however. Along with alleging that his proposed system had technical flaws, they argued that adjusting students' SAT scores would raise questions about the legitimacy of the test. They were also mindful of the immense political pressure ETS would come under if it began to systematically adjust downward the scores of the children of the nation's wealthy and well educated.[22] Just as Manning was beginning to talk to others in the field about his work, higher-ups at ETS told him to cease his efforts, and like a good company man he complied.

Being a vice president at ETS and having its president's approval for his work, Carnevale felt secure in his job. Moreover, his approach differed from Manning's in one key respect that made it seem less politically volatile: He was not seeking to adjust students' SAT scores; he was simply trying to find a way to identify those who had posted much higher scores than might be expected of them given their life circumstances. In determining who deserved the "striver" label, Carnevale took into account the quality of each student's high school, whether that school was rural, suburban, or urban, and whether English was a student's native language. Whereas Manning's primary goal had not been finding an alternative to racial and gender preferences, Carnevale and his colleagues repeatedly tweaked their admissions formula to try to make sure it was yielding enough diversity among those it identified as promising.

In the summer of 1999, his research group finally came up with what he had been looking for, a way to maintain or increase ethnic and racial diversity on college campuses without giving any consideration to applicants' ethnicity or race. The trick was to have their formula take into account how much wealth each applicant's family had accumulated—a measure of advantage that favors blacks because, at the median income level, their families have less than a third as much accumulated wealth as whites. Carnevale ran student profiles through a version of their formula that had been revised to take into account one key indicator of wealth—how much any given student's family had saved for college—and found that black and Hispanic enrollments would actually be higher than they had been under affirmative action with racial preferences. The striver researchers regarded family college savings as an imperfect variable for several reasons, its chief problem being that such information is self-reported. But they were optimistic that they could develop a workable system if they crunched their student data through versions of the formula that considered other family-wealth measures. Then they would be able to submit their findings through a peer review process and make them public.

In hindsight, Carnevale badly underestimated how unpopular his approach would be with the two most important constituencies ETS dealt with, the colleges that relied on the SAT and the College Board. When the *Wall Street Journal* ran a story suggesting that colleges might begin using striver study formulas within the year, all hell broke loose. Gaston Caperton, who had just recently been named the College Board's new president, was blind-sided by the news and responded by telling college officials there is no new system, "only research," and he would make sure such a system was never used.[23] Newspapers and magazines published letters from parents protesting that the system would be unfair to their high-scoring children. Nearly a dozen colleges threatened to drop their membership in the College Board if the research went forward. The ETS let the striver researchers forge ahead behind the scenes but, out of deference to the College Board, kept their work out of the public eye. By that point, however, the odds were stacked against the project.

In a world where affirmative action was not in dispute, striver formulas, percent plans, and other race-neutral alternatives to affirmative action probably would be hailed by educators and minority advocates as clever ways to bring more diversity to colleges and open doors to underserved populations. In the United States at the dawn of the new millennium, the situation was different. It was clear that the Supreme Court would be taking up the debate over race-conscious admissions sometime soon, and critics of such policies—including George W. Bush, then a Republican candidate for president—were signaling their intent to argue that race-based affirmative action was no longer necessary. On the other side of the issue, many advocates for minority students had come to regard class-based affirmative action as "a nefarious distraction because it can so easily be characterized as an effective alternative to race-sensitive policies," recalls Christopher Edley, who was still working closely with civil rights groups at the time. Noting that low-income whites vastly outnumber low-income blacks and Hispanics, Edley argues that class-based affirmative action will not maintain racial and ethnic diversity on campus in most demographic contexts.

In March 2000 in Washington, D.C., Carnevale and other ETS officials met with key stakeholders in the affirmative action debate. Among those on hand were Elaine R. Jones, then president of the NAACP Legal Defense and Educational Fund, and Ted Shaw and Norman Chachkin, two of the fund's top lawyers; University of Michigan education professor Michael T. Nettles; Sarita Brown, executive director of the White House Initiative on Hispanic Education and Excellence; Jules LaPidus, president of the Council of Graduate Schools; Gary Orfield of the Harvard Civil Rights Project; and Michael Baer, a senior vice president of the American Council on Education. Many at the meeting were concerned that the Supreme Court would be more likely to call for an end to race-conscious admissions if it got word of the alternative that the striver research offered. Carnevale and Nancy Cole, then the president of ETS, assured them that they would be consulted before any public release of new findings from the research.

Carnevale and his colleagues continued to work behind the scenes. But Cole retired as ETS president and was replaced by Kurt M. Landgraf, former chairman and chief executive officer of DuPont Pharmaceuticals. Landgraf proved much less willing than Cole to support the controversial striver study, which ETS's biggest customer, the College Board, still opposed. The research encountered resistance within ETS and fizzled out over the following year. Officials at ETS have said the study was killed off simply because it was bad research, but at least one well-respected researcher outside ETS has produced findings similar to those of Carnevale and his colleagues.[24]

Three years later, as the Supreme Court weighed the *Grutter* and *Gratz* cases, the College Board submitted a brief to the court arguing that race-conscious admissions policies should be preserved because "the evidence on race-neutral alternatives is uneven and incomplete."

In March 2003, Carnevale joined Stephen J. Rose, another economist, in releasing a report commissioned by the Century Foundation that showed how selective colleges could make their campuses much more socioeconomically diverse by adopting a class-based affirmative action formula that considered parents' education and income. They recommended that colleges also continue to use race-based affirmative action, however, because they said that there was no way to maintain current levels of racial and ethnic diversity on campus using the formula described in their report. Carnevale knew he was not giving the world the whole story, that by tweaking the formula he and Rose were describing—and taking accumulated family wealth into account—colleges could in fact use class-based affirmative action to maintain their current levels of racial and ethnic diversity. But he could not discuss such tweaks without bringing up the suppressed findings of his striver research, which would cause him to run afoul of his bosses at ETS.

Getting large populations of low-income students into and through college generally requires substantial increases in expenditures on outreach, financial aid, and student support services. With Washington dominated by fiscal conservatives and many state legislatures limiting their higher education spending in response to a severe economic downturn, it seemed doubtful that public dollars would be poured into such efforts any time soon. Richard Kahlenberg says the Bush administration turned to him for advice in preparing to try to sell the Supreme Court on class-based affirmative action, and he made a point of reminding the officials present that such policies can be financially costly. "There wasn't a big response of 'here is the money.' So it was kind of a strange political situation," he says.

The only alternatives to affirmative action that seemed to have much political momentum behind them were proposals by a few leading Democrats in Congress to pressure colleges to end early admissions policies and legacy preferences. The idea of going after such policies was largely the brainchild of Michael Dannenberg, a lawyer working in the office of Senator Edward Kennedy, then chairman of the Senate education committee. As it had become clear to Dannenberg that a Supreme Court showdown over affirmative action was inevitable, it occurred to him that Democrats could justify the need for race-conscious admissions policies and score political points with middle- and working-class Americans by attacking those admissions preferences that favored the white and wealthy. Looking ahead to the 2004 elections, he also saw a public campaign against legacy preferences as a way to stick it to George W. Bush, a mediocre student who had gotten into Yale on his father's and grandfather's coattails.

Dannenberg's opposition to legacy and early decision policies was not just the result of some political calculation. The product of a modest up-bringing, he sees such policies as unfair and harmful to both campus diversity and college quality, and he expresses little patience for the argument that colleges need legacy preferences as a tool for maintaining good relations with financially supportive alumni. "If a university wants to use college admissions as a fund-raising tool, it would be fairer and more efficient to auction acceptance letters off on eBay than it is to have the legacy preference. You could raise more money and everyone could participate," he says.

When it became clear that Democratic U.S. Senator John Edwards of North Carolina would seek the presidency, Dannenberg persuaded an Edwards aide of the worthiness of taking on the antilegacy cause as a campaign plank. Because Edwards is the son of a mill worker, attacking legacy preferences played perfectly into the personal narrative he was trying to present to voters—someone who had risen from humble origins and would look out for the common man. In a November 2002 speech, Edwards, who had not yet formally announced his candidacy, railed against legacy preferences as "a birthright out of eighteenth-century British aristocracy, not twenty-first-century American democracy."

Edwards continued to beat the antilegacy drum as 2003 rolled around and his campaign became official. Meanwhile, Dannenberg and other members of Kennedy's staff mulled over the idea of trying to insert some sort of antilegacy and anti–early-decision provision into a key federal law providing financing to colleges and student aid programs. And lawyers for the NAACP Legal Defense and Educational Fund were making it clear that if the Supreme Court were to strike down race-conscious college admissions, they planned to challenge legacy preferences as illegally biased against the minority populations that are underrepresented among selective colleges' alumni.

For their part, college officials expressed exasperation that legacies had even become an issue, and began putting pressure on Kennedy's staff, which generally had good relations with them in the past, to abandon its antilegacy efforts. Higher education leaders argued that legacy preferences are essential to their fund-raising efforts, contribute to a sense of tradition on campus, and simply are not going away. In an essay written for *The Chronicle of Higher Education,* two public relations officials at Rice University argued that legacy preferences are defensible because, when it comes to college admissions, "objective merit and fairness are attractive concepts with no basis in reality."[25]

It was clear that colleges were not just fighting to preserve affirmative action, they were fighting to preserve the status quo. Regardless of how the Supreme Court ruled on preferences for various minority groups, colleges were not about to relinquish their preferences for the privileged any time soon.

Chapter 9

The Diversity Dodge

Fuzzy Research to the Rescue

The educational benefits of diversity were not a big concern for the college leaders who first embraced affirmative action in the late 1960s and early 1970s. But, when affirmative action came under attack three decades later, these benefits were the only rationale for race-conscious admissions policies that the higher education establishment professed to care about.

A lot had changed since the days when affirmative action was adopted as a means of promoting social justice and trying to offer black people enough hope to end urban rioting and calm campus unrest. Most importantly, colleges and universities were operating in a completely different legal environment. Beginning with the Supreme Court's 1978 ruling in *Regents of the University of California v. Bakke,* the federal judiciary had made it clear that the argument that diversity improved education was the sole acceptable justification for race-conscious admissions available to most colleges. The only higher education institutions that were allowed to continue using such policies as a remedy for discrimination were those covered by federal desegregation orders.

Even the educational-benefits justification for race-conscious admissions appeared to be on increasingly shaky ground by the 1990s. Some federal judges had begun questioning the assumption that racially and ethnically diverse college enrollments yielded true diversity of opinion or measurably improved learning. Even more significantly, judges were doubting whether any such educational benefits offset the harm being done to those white and Asian Americans whose rights to equal protection under the law were being trampled by colleges that rejected their applications based on their race.

By the late 1990s, it seemed inevitable that the Supreme Court would soon take another hard look at race-conscious college admissions. And higher education's leaders and lawyers had concluded that, given recent shifts in the legal landscape, it would no longer be enough for them to assert the educational benefits of diversity as an article of faith. They would need to convince the Supreme Court that there was a factual basis for their claims that racial diversity improved learning for all students.

Initially, higher education's supporters of race-conscious admissions policies made a good faith effort to find empirical evidence that racial diversity yielded educational benefits. The problem, however, was that such evidence proved elusive. The harder some researchers tried to prove the point, the more vulnerable they were to allegations their research was biased. And those studies that seemed truly scientific and objective yielded findings that were fuzzy or inconclusive or, worse yet, suggested that race-conscious admissions policies might even cause harm.

Unable to come up with solid evidence to back its claims that affirmative action yielded educational benefits, the higher education establishment settled on an alternate plan: It would make such assertions anyway, and use spin, exaggeration, and a false sense of certainty in its assertions to pull the wool over the justices' eyes.

The stratagem paid off magnificently when the Supreme Court took up the University of Michigan cases. A majority of the justices accepted the diversity rationale for race-conscious admissions without question in the court's 2003 rulings.

In the long term, however, the ploy would leave race-conscious admissions policies resting on a foundation of sand. Until the claim that diversity offers educational benefits can be shored up with solid, unbiased research, such policies remain in danger of being washed away by judicial skepticism.

Part of what makes the educational diversity rationale for race-conscious admissions policies so vulnerable is the fact that colleges came up with it after the fact, well after the policies were already in place. Although leftist thinkers had been praising racially diverse classrooms as intellectually stimulating as far back as the late 1960s, their assessment of diversity's value was not a motivating factor for the college administrators who, at about that time, first in-

structed admissions offices to give minority applicants extra consideration.[1]
The educational benefits of diversity had not even been discussed in the first
dispute over college affirmative action that came before the Supreme Court,
the lawsuit that the rejected white applicant Marco DeFunis filed against the
University of Washington's law school in 1971. Had the justices actually decided DeFunis's case, rather than declaring it moot because a lower court had
already ordered the law school to admit him, the entire debate over affirmative action might have been framed in starkly different terms.

As of the mid-1970s, when selective colleges' leaders expressed concern
about the level of racial and ethnic diversity on their campuses, they did so not
for educational reasons, but because they saw their minority enrollment numbers as measures of how well they were doing in promoting social justice, social mobility, and racial integration. When the California Supreme Court took
up Allan Bakke's lawsuit challenging racial quotas at the medical school of the
University of California at Davis, the university's lawyers devoted little time to
asserting that diversity yielded educational benefits. In its 1976 decision striking down the medical school's admissions policy, the California court concluded that the educational benefits of diversity are irrelevant. In appealing
that decision to the U.S. Supreme Court, the university system again said little about whether such policies contributed to learning, characterizing them
instead as necessary to provide minority students with educational opportunities that they otherwise would be denied as a result of societal discrimination.

When the Supreme Court took up the *Bakke* case in 1977, the educational diversity rationale for race-conscious admissions entered into its deliberations mainly in the context of the friend-of-the-court briefs that
colleges and higher education associations had filed in an all-out effort to
buttress the California system's defense of its racial quotas. The Association
of American Law Schools, for example, asserted in its brief that having few
or no minority students at its member institutions "would significantly de-
tract from the educational experience of the student body." The American
Association of University Professors filed a brief saying the presence of minority and disadvantaged students in medical schools plays an important
role in socializing all students to better serve the poor.

The most pivotal brief in the *Bakke* case, however, turned out to be the
one jointly submitted by Columbia, Harvard, Stanford, and the University
of Pennsylvania. It argued that diversity "makes the university a better learning environment" for both students and faculty members, and that many
faculty members report "that the insights provided by the participation of

minority students enrich the curriculum, broaden the teachers' scholarly interests, and protect them from insensitivity to minority perspectives."

None of the briefs by colleges or higher education associations offered any empirical evidence to back their claims that racial diversity produces educational benefits. Nonetheless, their arguments were good enough for Justice Lewis Powell, who was looking for a way out of a bind. Powell was too conservative in his temperament to go along with the four justices on the court who thought colleges should be completely barred from considering race. At the same time, he was too conservative in his political ideology to join the four liberal justices who argued that colleges should be allowed to use racial preferences to remedy societal discrimination. By seizing upon the idea that racial diversity has educational benefits, Powell was able to allow the continued survival of race-conscious admissions policies without giving colleges license to engage in social engineering. None of the other eight members of the court shared Justice Powell's belief in diversity's educational benefits. But by splitting the difference between the court's four-member factions—agreeing with the liberal wing that some consideration of race was allowable, while sharing the conservative wing's view that the quotas used by the medical school amounted to illegal discrimination—Powell ended up casting the deciding vote in the case and writing what was widely regarded as the court's controlling opinion.

Powell devoted much of his opinion to singing the praises of Harvard's admissions policy. He spoke approvingly of how it considers race and ethnicity as among the many "plus" factors that it takes into account in trying to assemble broadly diverse classes, where young artists study alongside athletes, Bostonians alongside farm boys from Idaho. He held that the government had a compelling interest in allowing colleges to consider applicants' race because a racially diverse student body helps ensure a diversity of viewpoints on campus, creating an atmosphere "conducive to speculation, experiment, and creation." He stressed, however, that colleges should not maintain separate admission processes for minority students or give race any more weight than other factors in trying to assemble a diverse class. He conceived of a situation where an Italian American applicant might be judged as more likely to contribute to viewpoint diversity than a black applicant and thus would be viewed as the stronger candidate for admission.

Powell's opinion was criticized from all sides of the affirmative action debate. Advocates for minority students protested that he seemed to ignore both history and reality in holding that colleges should consider being black as just another "plus" factor, no more important than traits such as the ability to run with a football or play the oboe. Academics pointed out that excellent educations are offered by many institutions with little diversity, such as historically black, Jewish, Catholic, and women's colleges. Administrators who championed affirmative action expressed fear that by declaring the social justice and social mobility rationales for race-conscious admissions policies no longer applicable, Powell had stripped the policies of much of their moral justification. Many affirmative action supporters found it distasteful that race-conscious admissions were now being conceived as a mechanism for bringing minority students on campus to contribute to the edification of whites.

Critics of affirmative action expressed fear that colleges would simply give lip service to diversity as a way of justifying discrimination against white students. Harvard University law professor Alan M. Dershowitz and former college admissions counselor Laura Hanft published an essay noting how the Harvard system that Powell held up as a model had used considerations of diversity as a pretext for discriminating against Jews. They argued that Powell had "legitimated an admissions process that is inherently capable of gross abuse."[2]

Despite such objections, Powell's opinion had a huge impact. Colleges throughout the nation rewrote their admissions policies, substituting references to the goals of remedying societal discrimination or promoting equal opportunity with boiler plate language asserting that racial diversity was worth pursuing for educational reasons. Rather than seeing the presence of racial diversity on campus as an indicator that they were fulfilling the goal of providing broad educational access, colleges began seeing such diversity as an end in itself. This shift in emphasis was a profitable one. It let colleges worry less about admitting minority applicants who came from disadvantaged backgrounds and would need financial aid, and allowed them to focus more on recruiting minority students from wealthy backgrounds, who would easily make the transition into the culture of the corporations helping to finance their minority scholarships and programs.

The term "diversity" became a buzzword in higher education, embraced by academics who were calling for the college curriculum to be transformed to accommodate movements such as multiculturalism, Afrocentrism, and feminism. As a practical matter, however, most colleges' admissions offices continued to operate after the *Bakke* decision much as they had operated before. The racial and ethnic groups that they deemed worthy of giving extra consideration for the sake of promoting educational diversity generally were the same groups that they had previously favored in their efforts to remedy societal discrimination: blacks, Hispanics, and Native Americans. It did not occur to most colleges to grant preferences to Hmong refugees from Minneapolis, Arab Americans from Detroit, or white Evangelical Christians from small towns in the South, no matter how much their experiences and perspectives differed from those of other students who were more readily admitted. Selective colleges seemed to assume that the children of white professionals had everything to learn from the children of black or Hispanic professionals, and almost nothing to learn from the children of white factory workers, shopkeepers, or farmers.

Few in higher education fretted over having diverse ideologies and political views represented on campus, or questioned whether they were hurting educational diversity by granting preferences to unexceptional legacy applicants who easily blended in. College administrators gave little serious thought to how much diversity was needed, or what kinds, for there to be any sort of educational payoffs. Most simply assumed that racial diversity had educational benefits and figured the courts would go along with the idea. Until the mid-1990s, nearly all of the educational research being done in connection with race-conscious admissions looked at either campus race relations or the achievements and needs of black and Hispanic students.

In March 1996, the U.S. Court of Appeals for the Fifth Circuit shattered the assumption that Justice Powell's opinion was binding and that federal courts would continue to accept the diversity rationale for affirmative action preferences. Ruling in *Hopwood v. Texas,* the Fifth Circuit completely rejected Powell's conclusion that racial diversity on college campuses equates to viewpoint diversity in the classroom. It said the whole notion is premised on the false assumption that a person possesses certain ideas "by virtue of being a member of a certain racial group," and it overlooks the many other personal characteristics that have far more bearing on how people see the world. The plaintiff in the case, Cheryl Hopwood, was cited by the Fifth Circuit majority as Exhibit A in proving its conclusion. The wife of a member of the armed services and the mother of a severely disabled child, she almost certainly would have brought a distinct perspective to the law school—if only it had let her in.

Over the ensuing years, the educational diversity rationale for race-conscious admissions policies would similarly be rejected by federal district court judges in cases involving the University of Georgia and the University of Michigan's law school, proving that the Fifth Circuit's decision was no fluke.

The *Hopwood* decision, combined with California's passage later that year of the anti–affirmative action ballot initiative Proposition 209, left higher education leaders stunned and scrambling to come up with a way to prevent additional setbacks. Gary Orfield, a Harvard University professor who is one of the nation's most prominent advocates of school desegregation and affirmative action, recalls in his book *Diversity Challenged* that both developments "made it clear no consensus existed on the benefits of diversity" and that "the research had not been done to prove the academic benefits and the necessity of affirmative action admissions policies."[3] A task force of the American Council on Education reviewed the research available at the time and found studies that showed minority students gained from being admitted to selective colleges through affirmative action, but nothing that showed such policies had payoffs for other students.[4]

It seemed that if race-conscious admissions policies were to stand a chance of surviving a court challenge, colleges would need to demonstrate that they enhanced the education of the student body in general, so that the number of those who substantially benefited clearly exceeded the number who were significantly harmed. But no social scientist had developed a method of empirically measuring how students learned from exposure to diversity. Although certain that such learning happened, higher education professionals could present only anecdotal evidence.[5]

Over the course of the next seven years, until the Supreme Court finally ruled on the two University of Michigan cases, Harvard and other institutions would host a series of meetings at which college officials, college lawyers, civil rights leaders, and education researchers discussed the status of research into diversity's impact on education. Again and again, education researchers who cared about scientific objectivity pointed to gaping holes in many of the studies, and higher education lawyers who cared about winning offered the same assessment: This stuff will not hold up in court as justifying racial and ethnic preferences; no skeptical judge is going to buy it.

The University of Michigan pulled together all of the key research it was going to present to the court and entered most of it into the record by the spring of 2001. I analyzed Michigan's evidence and every significant study on the educational benefits of diversity for all students, and my basic conclusion—that such benefits had yet to be proven—was affirmed by a long list of education researchers with reputations for neutrality on the issue of affirmative action, as well as by at least a few researchers who were strong affirmative action supporters.[6] In that latter camp was Alexander Astin, who, as director of the Higher Education Research Institute at the University of California at Los Angeles, headed up a long list of national studies on colleges and their students and was regarded as one of the leading scholars in the education field. When I interviewed him for *The Chronicle of Higher Education,* he expressed obvious irritation that the Supreme Court might require "some sort of incontrovertible proof" that race-conscious admissions policies yield educational benefits, which, he said, "is far beyond what is demanded of most of our standard practices" in education. Yet he admitted that the proposition that more-diverse campuses better educate their students "is yet to be convincingly demonstrated," and that "the research still needs to be done that would demonstrate the link."

Over the next two years leading up to the Supreme Court's 2003 rulings in the Michigan cases, supporters of affirmative action published additional studies purporting to show that race-conscious admissions policies had educational benefits, while critics of affirmative action countered with studies claiming that these policies caused educational harm. Typically, such studies would be released to the media with great fanfare to try to sway public opinion, and then would be summarized in briefs submitted to the courts. Inevitably, the other side in the affirmative action debate would demolish them.

The most widely cited defense of college affirmative action was *The Shape of the River* by William Bowen and Derek Bok. Based on long-term studies of more than 45,000 students who entered selective colleges in either the fall of 1976 or the fall of 1989, it found that the black students accepted through affirmative action fared much better in college and in life than they would have if those institutions had rejected them. It also found that overwhelming majorities of the black and Hispanic alumni of such institutions were satisfied with their experiences, and that majorities of the black and white students who were freshmen in 1989 felt that their college experiences contributed to their ability to work with people of different races and cultures.[7] But the Supreme Court had already made it known, beginning with the *Bakke* decision, that it was not going to allow racial preferences based solely on their benefits to the minority students that they favored. And surveys that asked students their impressions of whether they learned or gained anything from their college experiences are poor substitutes for any sort of before-and-after assessments showing whether such impressions have any factual basis.

Among the several scholars who reviewed *The Shape of the River* and challenged its findings was Terrance Sandalow, a former dean of the University of Michigan Law School. He argued that Bowen and Bok's support for affirmative action "colors their analysis at nearly every point," affecting how they looked at the data and leading them to reach conclusions that strongly supported race-conscious admissions based on data that painted a far more mixed picture.[8]

Several other studies have found support for affirmative action among the students and faculty members at selective colleges. But how people feel about affirmative action has no bearing on the question of whether race-conscious admissions policies actually produce educational benefits. Moreover, these surveys have inherent sampling biases: In polling students at selective colleges, they limit their sample to the winners of the admissions game, who generally have a vested interest in speaking favorably of the standards of the institution providing them a degree. And college faculties, while hardly ideologically monolithic, tend to consist mostly of liberals who are predisposed to speak favorably of affirmative action.

The University of Michigan's star expert witness on the educational benefits of affirmative action was Patricia Gurin, a professor of psychology and women's studies at the Ann Arbor campus. She produced studies showing that students develop valuable thinking and learning skills from various experiences generally associated with racially diverse campuses, such as taking ethnic-studies courses, participating in workshops designed to promote racial and cultural awareness, and making friends or having discussions with students from other racial or ethnic groups.

Critics of affirmative action argued that many of the educational experiences described by Gurin can take place in fairly homogeneous environments, and there is no reason to believe that they would cease in the absence of race-conscious admissions, especially if colleges found other ways to prop up their black and Hispanic enrollments. "When all other things are held equal, do you get better educational outcomes at a campus when you have more blacks and Latinos? The answer is, you don't. It doesn't make a difference," said Thomas E. Wood, the executive director of the California Association of Scholars and the coauthor of a 2001 report analyzing Michigan's evidence.

Besides seeking to pick apart pro-diversity studies, the critics of affirmative action argued that the diversity rationale for such policies was simplistic and troublingly racist because it seems to assume that most members of certain racial groups think in similar ways. Law school deans often argue that having a racially diverse enrollment helps ensure there will be black students in the classroom who are troubled by racist police tactics or by the death penalty. But why not simply look favorably upon applicants who express such views, rather than attributing them to every black student who applies?

There also was the fundamental question of whether diversity of thought really was what colleges were going for. After all, the University of Michigan previously had been found guilty of violating the First Amendment's free speech guarantee in its efforts to protect minority students from exposure to statements they might find offensive. Moreover, there have been many incidents nationally in which all copies of an issue of a college student newspaper that editorialized against race-conscious admissions policies were stolen from their drop-off points, with the administrations of those colleges often saying little to protest the thefts and doing next to nothing to catch the perpetrators. Mark Goodman, the executive director of the Student Press Law Center, a group that champions student journalists' free speech rights, observed in a November 2006 e-mail to me that student newspaper staff members complained of university administrators not taking the theft of newspapers seriously in about half of recent incidents in which the stolen papers contained articles criticized as insensitive based on race, gender, sexual orientation, or religion. Goodman said "when concerns about sensitivity to women or minority groups are at issue, college and university officials are generally less willing to come out and condemn the thieves for fear of being accused of insensitivity or outright racism/sexism/homophobia themselves." Prominent conservative intellectuals such as David Horowitz, Alan Charles Kors, Allan Bloom, and Dinesh D'Souza almost have made a cottage industry out of publishing books accusing college administrators and professors of being "politically correct" and stifling the free exchange of ideas.

To be fair, critics of affirmative action did a much better job of poking holes in the pro-diversity research than they did of coming up with empirical evidence to back their own assertions that race-conscious admissions policies hurt educational quality. For example, one of the few studies attempting to show that such policies had negative consequences asserted that those colleges with the largest black enrollments generally had the lowest levels of satisfaction with their educational environment among students, professors, and administrators. Pretty damning stuff, until one considers that the study fails to account for differences in the selectivity of the 140 institutions covered. It's probably a stretch to blame racial diversity if people at generic state colleges with no admissions standards and large black enrollments feel worse about their institutions' educational environments than people at elite private colleges with much less racial diversity.[9]

In defending its admissions policies against the foes of racial preferences, the University of Michigan not only asserted that racial diversity has educational benefits, but insisted that those benefits would largely disappear if it were prohibited from using race-conscious admissions policies to keep black and Hispanic enrollments above a certain level. Michigan was careful not to assign a number or percentage to the minimum enrollments it sought—doing so would have left it open to being accused of having illegal racial quotas. Instead, it told the courts its goal had been to maintain a "critical mass" of minority students on campus. When colleges first began talking about trying to maintain a "critical mass" of students on campus back in the late 1960s, they did so out of concern for minority students' emotional well-being. Enrolling a "critical mass" of black students essentially meant enrolling enough to ensure that those on campus did not feel so socially isolated that their academic work suffered and they were tempted to drop out. In the hands of University of Michigan lawyers fighting to preserve affirmative action three decades later, the concept of critical mass took on a whole new meaning rooted in professed concern about the education of all. The term "critical mass" was defined as, essentially, enough minority students to ensure that white students heard a variety of black and Hispanic viewpoints, and that black and Hispanic students felt free to disagree with each other and under no obligation to somehow represent their own race in classroom discussions.

A skeptic might have asked how it was that the University of Michigan concluded that a critical mass of black students need to be much larger than a critical mass of Hispanics, or why it was that Michigan's admissions officers gave extra consideration to American Indians who were so few and far between on campus that they stood absolutely no chance of achieving critical mass status any time soon. Skepticism of academe's claims about the educational benefits of diversity was largely absent from the courtroom, however.

The lawyers representing those suing the University of Michigan had made a tactical decision not to try to challenge claims about diversity's educational benefits. Their strategy was to virtually concede that such benefits existed while arguing that the point was irrelevant because those benefits do not offset the harm that race-conscious admissions policies do to the white and Asian American applicants rejected as a result of them. Because the Center for Individual Rights was not focused on challenging the educational diversity rationale for affirmative action, it obtained but never bothered to present to the courts the early 1990s study by the University of Michigan's own administrators showing that a large share of the university's students thought its policies promoted racial division, not racial understanding. Michigan's lawyers, understandably, did not bring up the study themselves. If the National Association of Scholars, an organization critical of affirmative action, had not submitted to the Supreme Court briefs seeking to debunk the research that the University of Michigan had entered into the record, the justices and their clerks might not have heard criticisms of the research at all.

On the other side of the issue, the Supreme Court was deluged with friend-of-the-court briefs insisting that an overwhelming body of research had proven the educational benefits of race-conscious admissions policies beyond the shadow of a doubt. Among those submitting amicus curiae briefs were public universities and a long list of higher education associations whose leaders had heard lawyers and education experts on their own side acknowledge that none of the studies convincingly proved their point.

As the Supreme Court was weighing the cases, the University of Michigan's general counsel, Marvin Krislov, told me in a *Chronicle* interview, "We have focused on the educational benefits and the learning environment because that is, quite frankly, why we do what we do." Given how many other justifications for racial preferences had earlier been rejected by the Supreme Court, it was also the case that persuading the court to accept the educational diversity rationale for race-conscious admissions represented the single best hope of keeping affirmative action alive.

Chapter 10

Supreme Reckoning
The Changing Legal Landscape

The U.S. Supreme Court does not wade into just any dispute. It grants only a small fraction of requests that it hear cases, and generally will not try to decide a question of Constitutional law that is not a source of significant disagreement or confusion among the lower courts. The members of the court are aware that, when it comes down to it, their power rests in the willingness of other branches of government to abide by their wishes, and accordingly they historically have been reluctant to put themselves in the position of issuing orders that might be defied by elected officials or provoke rioting in the streets. It is telling that the high court often hands down its most divisive and controversial opinions at the very end of its term, just before the July Fourth holiday, when Americans are most likely to be on vacation, oblivious to evening newscasts, and in a patriotic mood.

The Supreme Court has good reason to regard the topic of race as especially treacherous. Its 1857 decision to deny Dred Scott citizenship and freedom from slavery was a key development precipitating the Civil War. Its 1944 ruling allowing the wartime internment of Japanese Americans has been ranked with its *Dred Scott* decision as one of the most shameful in its history. Its 1950s rulings requiring the desegregation of public colleges and public schools went largely ignored for a decade, and their eventual enforcement triggered tremendous strife and social upheaval as lawmakers vowed resistance and whites fought and fled race-based busing.

As the 1990s drew to a close, however, it was becoming clear that the debate over race-conscious college admissions policies had reached a point where the Supreme Court could not put off revisiting the issue much longer. Lower courts were all over the map as to their views on such policies' legality, and some judges had begun rejecting the diversity rationale articulated by Justice Lewis Powell in the Supreme Court's last major ruling on the matter, the 1978 *Bakke* decision.

To understand why there was so much disagreement and confusion among the lower courts, it is important to realize that the legal challenges to race-conscious admissions did not just involve conflicting views of how to apply the Fourteenth Amendment, the equal protection clause. They also involved the question of how to balance the need to safeguard civil rights against the principle of academic freedom, which colleges were asserting as a defense against judicial intrusion into their affairs. The principle of academic freedom was hardly something colleges' lawyers were pulling out of thin air. It was one of the primary reasons for academe's sacred tradition of tenure and had been embraced by the Supreme Court in earlier rulings. The court's definition of what academic freedom entails stems from a 1957 decision involving a University of New Hampshire lecturer accused of being a communist. In that ruling, Justice Felix Frankfurter had held that every university has "four essential freedoms," those being "to determine for itself on academic grounds who may teach, what may be taught, how it shall be taught, and who may be admitted to study."[1] A decade later, in a ruling involving a New York state law intended to purge academe of communists, the Supreme Court regarded academic freedom as a form of free speech covered by the First Amendment.

The Supreme Court has not held the principle of academic freedom to be so sacred that it justifies Jim Crow–era admissions policies excluding blacks, and it similarly has not let claims of the benefits of single-sex education deter it from ordering all-male colleges open to women. But in the *Bakke* ruling, Justice Powell held that colleges' freedom to set their own admissions policies included the freedom to take applicants' race into consideration if doing so had educational benefits.

The *Bakke* decision was exceptionally messy and difficult to interpret. The nine members of the court issued a total of six different opinions, with four strongly opposing race-conscious admissions policies, four strongly favoring them, and Powell agreeing with one faction that some consideration of race was permissible and with the other faction that the use of racial quotas crossed the line. The four justices who thought colleges should be allowed to consider race in admissions did not sign on to Powell's diversity rationale, instead maintaining that colleges need such policies to offset and remedy the effects of societal discrimination. But Powell's view would take on increasing importance over time as the Supreme Court placed new limits on affirmative action in a series of rulings involving minority preferences in employment and contracting.

In its 1986 decision in *Wygant v. Jackson Board of Education,* a lawsuit brought by white teachers who were laid off before minority teachers with less seniority, the court explicitly rejected the idea that societal discrimination justified the use of racial preferences by a government agency. Writing for the majority, Justice Powell said the only way the school system could have avoided running afoul of the equal protection clause was by showing its policy was needed to remedy racial discrimination that it had committed. In the court's 1989 ruling in *City of Richmond v. J.A. Croson,* involving a requirement that construction companies doing city-financed work subcontract with minority-owned firms, Justice Sandra Day O'Connor challenged the city's assertion that racial discrimination was the only possible explanation for the low number of minorities in the construction industry. She also practically ridiculed Richmond's claim that the need to remedy its own past discrimination justified the policy at hand, which included Native Alaskans and people from India among the list of those favored. "It may well be that Richmond has never had an Aleut or Eskimo citizen," much less discriminated against one, she said. The majority opinion asserted that the consideration of race in such a nonremedial context "may in fact promote notions of racial inferiority and lead to a politics of racial hostility."

In its 1995 ruling in *Adarand Constructors v. Pena,* involving a federal minority contracting requirement, the court held that any consideration of race by state or federal agencies was unconstitutional unless it could pass a standard of judicial review known as "strict scrutiny." As spelled out in earlier court decisions, strict scrutiny has three prongs. First, the policy at hand must seek to fulfill a compelling government interest. Second, the policy must be "narrowly tailored" to consider race no more than necessary for such purposes. And, third, no "less drastic means" of fulfilling the compelling government interest at issue other than considering race must exist. The Justice Department responded to the ruling by warning colleges that merely citing the *Bakke* decision may not be enough to justify race-conscious admissions programs, and "a court might demand some proof of a nexus between the diversification of the student body and the diversity of viewpoints expressed on campus."

By the early 1990s, some critics of race-conscious college admissions policies were arguing that even if Justice Powell's diversity rationale still applied, colleges were giving far too much weight to race for their policies to pass the narrow-tailoring test. As Roger Clegg, the chief lawyer for the Center for Equal Opportunity, later remarked in a *Chronicle of Higher Education* interview: "Justice Powell intended to leave the door slightly ajar for careful and limited use of racial considerations, and universities, under pressure to be politically correct, have driven a truck right through that door."

Lawyers for the Center for Individual Rights, which helped represent the plaintiffs in four key lawsuits challenging race-conscious admissions policies, went beyond these assertions to argue that Justice Powell's diversity rationale was irrelevant because it was his view alone, not that of the *Bakke* majority.

The federal courts ended up issuing a patchwork of conflicting decisions on the question of whether Powell's diversity rationale applied. In its 1996 *Hopwood v. Texas* decision, the U.S. Court of Appeals for the Fifth Circuit held that Powell spoke only for himself, and therefore there was no high court precedent holding diversity to be a compelling interest. But in a 2000 decision in *Smith v. University of Washington Law School,* the U.S. Court of Appeals for the Ninth Circuit, which covers nine Pacific and Rocky Mountain states, held that Powell spoke for the *Bakke* majority and his diversity rationale remains binding until the Supreme Court revisits the issue and declares otherwise. In a 2001 ruling striking down the race-conscious admissions policy at the University of Georgia, the U.S. Court of Appeals for the Eleventh Circuit side-stepped the whole diversity rationale dispute by focusing on the question of whether the university's policy was narrowly tailored. The answer was no, the court held, because the university used a numerical index that automatically gave minority applicants a point boost that put them ahead of white applicants, including some who came from disadvantaged backgrounds or otherwise had "greater potential to contribute to a diverse student body" than some minority students who got in.

Meanwhile, the University of Michigan cases—*Grutter v. Bollinger* involving Michigan's law school and *Gratz v. Bollinger* involving Michigan's chief undergraduate admissions policy—each went before separate U.S. District Court judges, who ended up reaching markedly different conclusions.

In the undergraduate case, the briefs submitted to the court by the lawyers representing Jennifer Gratz and other rejected applicants did not bother challenging the assertion that racial diversity yields educational benefits. Instead, they argued that the concept of diversity was too amorphous and ill-defined for its promotion to be seen as a compelling government interest. Because the two sides were in agreement on the basic facts of the case, Judge Patrick Duggan did not bother holding a trial, and he issued his December 2000 ruling in the form of a summary judgment on the disputed points of law. He upheld the point-based admissions system Michigan used in evaluating undergraduate applicants because, he said, the university's briefs had presented him with "solid evidence" that diversity has educational benefits and, therefore, is something that universities have "a permanent and ongoing interest" in promoting.

In the law school case, U.S. District Judge Bernard Friedman held a trial. The university's lawyers presented a series of expert witnesses who testified about the benefits of educational diversity and said the law school needs race-conscious admissions policies to enroll sufficient numbers of minority students. The lawyers for Barbara Grutter sought to prove that the law school was operating an illegal quota system, by noting that its total enrollment from the various minority groups granted preference never dropped below 10 percent.

In his March 2001 decision, Judge Friedman ruled against the university and struck down the law school's admission policy. He accepted the arguments that Powell's diversity rationale was not the opinion of the *Bakke* majority and that the remedial rationale expressed by other justices in that case had been invalidated by subsequent Supreme Court decisions. Regardless of the applicability of the diversity rationale, Friedman held, the law school's policy violated the *Bakke* decision's prohibition against the use of racial quotas.

Friedman said the law school's admissions policies were "practically indistinguishable from a quota system" for several different reasons. In all the years for which he had been given admissions data, the total enrollment from favored minority groups never sank below 10 percent or rose above 17 percent. During the admission cycle, the law school's dean and admissions director received daily reports on the racial composition of the pool of applicants accepted, which suggested that they were fine-tuning admissions criteria to get desired results. Among applicants with certain grade point average and LSAT-score combinations, the university was admitting virtually every black applicant while white and Asian American applicants had a less than 1 in 40 chance of getting in. Michigan's lawyers had struggled to articulate a clear definition of the "critical mass" that the law school's admission policies were purportedly intended to achieve.

The U.S. Court of Appeals for the Sixth Circuit, which encompasses Kentucky, Michigan, Ohio, and Tennessee, agreed in October 2001 to take up appeals of the Duggan and Friedman rulings and decided to hear both cases at the same time. Usually, federal circuit courts assign a three-member panel of judges to hear cases, with the parties involved having the option of appealing the three-member panel's ruling to a full panel of judges if they wish. At the request of the lawyers for Grutter and Gratz, the Sixth Circuit agreed to take up the two cases *en banc*—before nine judges—at the outset, based on the cases' importance and the assumption that any ruling by a three-judge panel would be appealed anyway.

By that time, it was generally assumed that the Michigan cases were the most likely of any of the pending challenges to race-conscious admissions to wind up being settled by the highest court in the land. The Supreme Court had already refused twice to consider appeals of the *Hopwood v. Texas* decision, with Justice Ruth Bader Ginsburg issuing a statement that suggested the court viewed the matter as moot because the law school had already changed the policy that the Fifth Circuit struck down. Likewise, the Supreme Court had already declined to take up an appeal of the Ninth Circuit's decision to uphold race-conscious admissions in the University of Washington case after the university's lawyers argued that the dispute had been transformed into a mere academic exercise by Washington State's subsequent adoption of a preference ban. No one was about to even ask the Supreme Court to take up the Eleventh Circuit's ruling striking down a race-conscious admissions policy at the University of Georgia. Civil rights groups had convinced the university that its case was so weak—with a heavy-handed policy at issue and little evidence of the educational benefits of diversity entered into the record—that appealing it to the Supreme Court would just invite a high court decision banning such policies everywhere.

It would later be alleged that supporters of affirmative action—recognizing that the Sixth Circuit's eventual rulings in the Michigan cases would frame how the dispute was presented to the Supreme Court—did everything they could behind the scenes to make sure the nine-member panel would be dominated by judges sympathetic to their side.

In his dissenting opinion in the law school case, Judge Danny Boggs accused Chief Judge Boyce Martin Jr. of manipulating the court's calendar and procedures to ensure that the case would not be heard until two judges critical of affirmative action had gone into semiretirement, precluding their involvement. The court would remain bitterly divided on the procedural matter for years to come, with some judges supporting Boggs's allegations, and others disputing them and calling them unjustified and unwarranted.

A congressional staff memo leaked in 2003 suggests that efforts were also mounted in Washington, D.C., to make sure the panel hearing the cases was stacked in Michigan's favor. The author of the April 17, 2002, memo was Olatunde C. A. (Olati) Johnson, an aide to Senator Edward Kennedy, a Democratic member of the Senate Judiciary Committee. In it, she urged that steps be taken to delay the committee's confirmation of Julia Scott Gibbons, a Sixth Circuit nominee with an uncontroversial but fairly conservative record, until after the Sixth Circuit has decided the Michigan cases: "The thinking is that the current 6th Circuit will sustain the affirmative action program, but if a new judge with conservative views is confirmed before the case is decided, that new judge will be able, under 6th Circuit rules, to review the case and vote on it." Johnson wrote that she was making her recommendation that the committee delay action at the request of Elaine Jones, the president of the NAACP Legal Defense and Educational Fund. Johnson acknowledged being "a little concerned about the propriety of scheduling hearings based on the resolution of a particular case." But, she said, "the Michigan case is important."[2] Gibbons was not confirmed until after the Sixth Circuit ruled.

The Sixth Circuit issued its decision in the *Grutter* case in May 2002, ruling 5 to 4 in the law school's favor. The majority opinion, written by Chief Judge Martin, endorsed Powell's diversity rationale as "the law until the Supreme Court instructs otherwise." It also rejected U.S. District Court Judge Friedman's conclusion that the law school had been operating a quota system. It held that the "critical mass" that the law school seeks to enroll is not a "fixed goal or target," and that the law school's consideration of race and ethnicity does not insulate minority applicants from competition or knock nonminority applicants out of the running.

Perhaps because of the deep rift among its members caused by the law school case, the court never got around to issuing a decision on the *Gratz* challenge to Michigan's undergraduate policies. In fact, it was still debating the *Gratz* lawsuit when the Supreme Court announced in December 2002 that it was taking up both the *Grutter* and *Gratz* cases.

For the Supreme Court to hear a case before a circuit court has decided it, as the justices did with the *Gratz* lawsuit, was unusual but not unprecedented. The court's rules say that the justices can take such a step when a case is of "imperative public importance." Given the widespread confusion caused by conflicting circuit court opinions on the legality of race-conscious admissions, both of the Michigan cases clearly fit that bill.

Chapter 11

The Worried White House

Bush Faces an American Dilemma

In helping to give rise to the widespread use of racial preferences through-out American society, President Richard Nixon hoped to create an issue that would wreak havoc within the Democratic Party. He calculated, correctly, that the ensuing debate over preferences would drive a wedge between blacks and working-class whites, straining the coalition of civil rights groups and labor unions that had played a key role in putting Presidents Kennedy and Johnson in the White House.

What Nixon failed to foresee was how the affirmative action issue would bedevil his own party for decades to come. Among those in the Republican fold, social conservatives who strongly opposed affirmative action prefer-ences as an affront to individual rights would find themselves at odds with business leaders—who increasingly saw these preferences as a way to stave off lawsuits and help their companies' bottom lines—and with political pragmatists who hated to see the GOP stake out positions that might alien-ate women or Hispanic voters.

Such were the political crosscurrents that swirled around George W. Bush when the debate over race-conscious college admissions reached the

U.S. Supreme Court in late 2002. Under pressure to take a position on the University of Michigan cases, Bush would end up performing a contortionist act in which he seemed to bend in every direction to try to please everyone. He would say that selective colleges need to be concerned about enrolling a diverse student body, while he simultaneously would insist that these institutions should judge applicants based solely on merit. He would promote—as "race-neutral" alternatives to Michigan's practices—"percent plans" and other policies that had been adopted by California, Florida, and Texas specifically with the intent of propping up black and Hispanic enrollments. He declined to stand on principle against all race-conscious admissions policies, but he nonetheless urged the Supreme Court to strike down the University of Michigan's, which were fairly representative of those in use elsewhere.

The general public seemed appreciative. A nationwide *Los Angeles Times* poll conducted in early 2003 found that 55 percent of Americans approved, and just 27 percent disapproved, of the Bush administration's decision to oppose Michigan's policies. Among those endorsing the administration's actions were 44 percent of liberals and 46 percent of respondents belonging to racial or ethnic minority groups.[1] But the Supreme Court's justices would join lawyers on both sides of the dispute in seeing the administration's position on the cases as too convoluted to offer much useful guidance. Many prominent members of the administration would feel badly betrayed by Bush's refusal to give White House lawyers the go-ahead to try to deal a death blow to affirmative action when they had the chance.

To be fair to Bush, he was hardly the first president to waffle when confronted with the affirmative action issue. The first president to use the term "affirmative action," John F. Kennedy, avoided even discussing the possibility of having the federal government endorse racial preferences. Richard Nixon, the president who first crossed that line in calling for the use of preferences to integrate Philadelphia's trade unions, reversed himself and became an outspoken opponent of racial quotas within the space of a year. When the Supreme Court decided in 1973 to take up a lawsuit challenging race-conscious admissions at the University of Washington's law school, the Nixon administration then pursued a third course—staying out of the fray entirely.[2]

Nixon's immediate successor, Gerald Ford, was too preoccupied with a deteriorating economy and too politically conservative to concern himself much with the enforcement of those federal affirmative action requirements that had survived Nixon's change of heart.[3] Jimmy Carter, who won the 1976 election with 94 percent of the black vote, initially antagonized liberals by saying he opposed the use of racial quotas, but soon changed his tack and began calling on employers and colleges to set numerical goals to ensure they were providing enough access to minorities and women.[4] When the Supreme Court took up a challenge to admissions quotas in the *Bakke* case in 1977, the Carter administration filed a brief in which it sided with the University of California and argued that race-conscious admissions policies are acceptable as remedies for societal discrimination.

Ronald Reagan was voted into office in 1980 on a Republican platform that opposed any federal use of racial quotas, goals, or timetables. He was a harsh critic of affirmative action during his two terms in office, and some of his key appointees, such as William Bradford Reynolds, the head of the Justice Department's civil rights division, favored doing away with racial preferences entirely. But despite his tough talk, Reagan failed to issue a single executive order ending or even restricting affirmative action.[5]

Many historians believe a controversy that erupted a year after Reagan took office left his administration gun-shy in dealing with matters of race. The flap was triggered by a decision by the Justice and Treasury departments to reverse a 12-year-old Internal Revenue Service policy denying tax exemptions to racially discriminatory private institutions such as South Carolina's Bob Jones University, which admitted a few black students but prohibited interracial dating. The administration came under such intense criticism over the move that it took Reagan just four days to declare that he was "unalterably opposed to racial discrimination in any form" and was reinstituting the old policy denying Bob Jones U. its tax-exempt status.[6] When Attorney General Edwin Meese later considered rewriting federal affirmative action requirements to make compliance with hiring goals and timetables voluntary, he met with resistance even from within the administration's own ranks. Adam Meyerson, who worked closely with the White House as an official of the Heritage Foundation, would later observe that conservatives had made "a strategic decision" not to oppose racial quotas. "We felt we just couldn't win," he said. "Swing voters in the suburbs were too sensitive to the 'racist' label."[7]

Also discouraging any firm stand against racial preferences was strong and growing support for affirmative action from one of the Reagan administration's key constituencies: corporate America. Although a few companies still resented federal rules favoring minority-owned firms in the awarding of government contracts, most had been sold on affirmative action as good public relations, as a way for them to avoid discrimination lawsuits, and as a way to hire and promote employees who could help them tap into new markets. A poll of Fortune 500 and Service 500 chief executive officers conducted in February 1989, just months after Reagan left office, found that nearly three-fourths of their companies were using hiring goals or quotas. Most were happy with the results of their affirmative action efforts and did not have any plans to change course any time soon.[8]

When it came to higher education, the only people that the Reagan administration felt comfortable trying to protect from exclusion were Asian Americans. In May 1988, as the University of California at Berkeley was being investigated by state officials over complaints of anti-Asian bias, Reagan gave a speech denouncing any such discrimination as "a repudiation of everything America stands for." That August, the Education Department's Office for Civil Rights began investigating allegations of anti-Asian bias on the part of Harvard and the University of California at Los Angeles. The Justice Department's civil rights chief, William Bradford Reynolds, subsequently called discrimination against Asian American applicants the "inevitable result" of colleges' preferences for other racial groups.[9]

Reagan's successor, George H. W. Bush, had signaled a confrontational approach to racial politics during his campaign. He appealed to voters by running now-famous advertisements that sought to hold his Democratic opponent, Massachusetts governor Michael Dukakis, responsible for that state's decision to furlough a black prison inmate, William Horton, who proceeded to commit murder and rape. Once in office, however, Bush took an approach to affirmative action that would later be characterized by some historians as moderate, others, as muddled. Bush vetoed the Civil Rights Act of 1990, which sought to make it easier for people to sue for workplace discrimination. But then he signed the Civil Rights Act of 1991, which contained very similar provisions such as a requirement that employers have a sound, business-related justification for any job criteria that seem to have a disparate impact on minority applicants.[10] And in dealing with race in higher education, Bush, like Reagan, tended to rein in his appointees when they seemed to attack affirmative action too aggressively.

The Bush administration's desire to avoid racial controversy became evident in late 1990, when Michael Williams, the Education Department's assistant secretary for civil rights, stirred up a tempest by suggesting that he viewed most minority scholarship programs as violating the Civil Rights Act of 1964. Williams offered his opinion in the context of a letter to organizers of the Fiesta Bowl, who were planning to make $100,000 contributions for minority scholarships to each of the two colleges playing.[11] Colleges and civil rights groups expressed outrage, and the Education Department not only disavowed Williams's statement but kept a tight leash on him during his remaining two years in the job.[12]

In contrast to Bush and Reagan, Bill Clinton was elected with the support of civil rights groups and a large share of black voters. But like his immediate predecessors, he too was unwilling to take such a strong stand on affirmative action that he risked politically hurting himself or his party. The Democratic Leadership Council, the centrist national organization that Clinton had helped establish in 1985 as governor of Arkansas, operated on the assumption that many white voters had abandoned the Democratic Party over issues related to race. In the 1990 Congressional elections—when several Republican candidates appeared to be scoring points by tarring their Democratic opponents as "pro-quota"—the council, with Clinton as its chair, issued a statement declaring itself in favor of "equal opportunity, not equal results." In their successful bid for the White House in 1992, Clinton and Al Gore issued a campaign book in which they made no statements in favor of affirmative action and sought to assure voters that they opposed quotas, even though the broader Democratic Party had made support for affirmative action a plank.[13]

Soon after taking office, Clinton won applause from minority advocates by naming Norma Cantu, a lawyer for the Mexican American Legal Defense and Educational Fund, to the same civil rights post in the Education Department that Michael Williams had held. And Clinton's pick as secretary of education, Richard Riley, quickly signaled that his office had no objections to minority scholarships, the legality of which had remained a topic of debate within that agency under Bush.

Yet, despite such developments, Clinton continued for the next several years to keep a low profile on matters of race. When the U.S. Court of Appeals for the Fourth Circuit ruled in 1994 that the University of Maryland at College Park had engaged in illegal discrimination by operating a minority scholarship program, Clinton said little in defense of such scholarship programs, even as his administration's lawyers joined civil rights and higher education groups in (unsuccessfully) urging the Supreme Court to take up and reverse the decision. Advocacy groups such as the Citizens Commission on Civil Rights complained that the administration was slow to enforce desegregation agreements affecting public schools and public colleges. Key civil rights officials such as Cantu acknowledged that they were proceeding cautiously and focusing their efforts on enforcing well-established laws.[14]

Clinton's cautious approach seemed justified by the results of the November 1994 midterm elections, in which the GOP took over Congress largely as a result of what political analysts described as an "angry white male" backlash against affirmative action and other liberal social policies. With his advisors expressing fear that Southern and working-class whites would similarly rally behind the GOP's presidential candidate in 1996, Clinton told journalists in February 1995 that he was authorizing a review of the federal government's affirmative action policies, partly to determine whether there might be need-based alternatives that would be more effective and would generate more public support. Christopher Edley Jr., who directed the review as a White House special counsel, says there was a sense within the administration that "the Republican majority was going to put these programs in the legislative cross hairs," and top Clinton advisor George Stephanopoulos "wisely concluded that the president needed to get out in front of the issue and start developing a strategy before we found ourselves in the middle of a full-scale battle."

Civil rights groups and feminist organizations reacted angrily to the announcement of the review and sought assurances from Clinton that he had no plans to eliminate race- and gender-based programs. Jesse Jackson made it known that he would challenge Clinton in the Democratic presidential primaries leading up to that year's elections if he abandoned affirmative action.[15] But Clinton's aides argued that there was reason to believe a fine-tuning of affirmative action might be justified. A March 1995 *Forbes* magazine exposé on abuses of affirmative action in federal contracting noted that 80 percent of firms certified as "minority owned" had no employees and simply contracted out their work, and that the share of federal "minority" contracts going to black-owned firms had declined from two-thirds to one-third over the past 15 years.

In July 1995, Clinton gave a speech discussing the results of his administration's affirmative action review and his response to the Supreme Court's decision the month before, in *Adarand v. Pena*, to limit the use of affirmative action in federal contracting. He said he was directing federal agencies to hold their affirmative action programs to the following four standards: no quotas; no illegal discrimination (including reverse discrimination); no preferences for people who are unqualified; and "as soon as a program has succeeded, it must be retired." But, to the applause of civil rights groups, Clinton also said he thought affirmative action "always has been good for America" and that "the evidence suggests, indeed screams," that the work of ending discrimination in America is not done. Therefore, he said, "We should reaffirm the principle of affirmative action and fix the practices. We should have the simple slogan: Mend it, but don't end it."[16]

Clinton's commitment to affirmative action would be tested in the following year's elections. When voters in the crucial state of California went to the polls in 1996, they were voting not only on a president but on Proposition 209, banning the use of racial, ethnic, and gender preferences by public colleges and other state agencies. With Proposition 209 expected to pass easily, both Clinton's advisors and leaders of the Democratic Party made the calculation not to waste campaign dollars and political capital by taking a stand on the losing side of the issue. The party spent little money opposing the measure, and Clinton said little to denounce it.[17] On the national level, Clinton's approach to affirmative action was to show enough support to hang on to his political base, enough skepticism to avoid alienating white men. The Democratic Party's platform going into the 1996 elections said Clinton "is leading the way to reform affirmative action so that it works, it is improved, and promotes opportunity, but does not accidentally hold others back in the process."

On the other side of the partisan divide, Republicans were having a hard time deciding what stand to take on Proposition 209 and affirmative action in general. California governor Pete Wilson had thought that championing Proposition 209 would help position him to become the Republican nominee for president in 1996. But Wilson's presidential campaign never got off the ground and became a cautionary tale for other politicians who had thought they might get mileage out of opposing affirmative action preferences. At its 1996 national convention, the Republican Party adopted a platform that stated, "We scorn Bill Clinton's notion that any person should be denied a job, promotion, contract or chance at higher education because of race or gender." But Colin Powell gave a convention speech strongly defending affirmative action, and several prominent governors either expressed support for it or warned their fellow Republicans that attacking it would do more harm than good.[18] The Republican presidential nominee, Bob Dole, who as Senate majority leader had proposed legislation to abolish racial and gender preferences in federal contracting, softened his opposition to affirmative action throughout much of the summer and fall of 1996, turning the volume back up only when it became clear in October that he was badly behind in the polls.[19]

Clinton won easily in 1996, but so did California's Proposition 209. An analysis of exit poll data found that the preference ban was supported by 59 percent of whites, 42 percent of Asians, 37 percent of Hispanics, and 18 percent of blacks.[20]

Throughout both of Clinton's terms in office, his top appointees made token efforts to try to counter each new setback for affirmative action in higher education. Inevitably, however, they found themselves legally and politically constrained from putting up much of a fight. When the Fourth Circuit struck down race-exclusive scholarships as discriminatory in 1994, the Clinton administration held that minority scholarships remained legal elsewhere around the nation, but colleges in the five states covered by the court's decision had no choice but to open such programs to members of any race. The administration initially responded to the University of California regents' 1995 decision to stop using racial and gender preferences by threatening to withhold federal money from the system, but then it backed down. It rejected pleas by civil rights leaders to block implementation of Proposition 209 and, after launching an investigation of whether the admissions policies that remained in place at the UC system's law schools were biased in favor of white males, took no action. When the U.S. Court of Appeals for the Fifth Circuit issued its 1996 *Hopwood* ruling striking down race-conscious admissions at the law school at the University of Texas at Austin, the Education Department's Norma Cantu told other colleges in the Fifth Circuit that the decision applied only to the specific law school named in the suit. Both Texas's attorney general and Clinton's solicitor general disagreed, and Cantu changed her stand and said the ruling covered other colleges in the Fifth Circuit.

About the only place defenders of affirmative action seemed to be holding their own was on the legislative front. Throughout the 1990s, Congress failed to pass several bills intended to end the use of racial or gender preferences by federally financed programs or to prohibit these preferences in hiring decisions. In 1998, the House of Representatives voted 249 to 171 against a proposal to prohibit federal dollars from going to colleges that granted admissions preferences based on ethnicity, race, or gender. Fifty-five Republicans were among those who came out against the measure.

Outside Washington, state legislation seeking to ban preferences similarly ran into walls; even in relatively conservative states such as Arizona, Georgia, and South Carolina, such bills were voted down. The Michigan state legislators who helped recruit Jennifer Gratz and Barbara Grutter as plaintiffs for lawsuits challenging racial preferences at their state's flagship university did so after failing to win widespread support for a preference ban in the halls of the state capitol in Lansing.

In campaigning for the Oval Office in 2000, Vice President Al Gore expressed strong support for affirmative action and, during a campaign stop in Florida, criticized Governor Jeb Bush's plan to end race-conscious university admissions as ignoring "the reality of our situation in our country." George W. Bush, having signed the Texas Ten Percent plan into law in the aftermath of the Fifth Circuit's *Hopwood* decision, advocated a policy he called "affirmative access," although he was never entirely clear about what he meant.

Once in office, Bush named several veterans of the fight against racial preferences to key leadership posts. His picks as head of the Education Department's Office for Civil Rights, Gerald Reynolds, and as the department's general counsel, Brian Jones, were conservative African Americans who had previously been presidents of the antipreference Center for New Black Leadership. (Mr. Reynolds also had worked at Center for Equal Opportunity, a group in the very thick of the battle against race-conscious college admissions.) Bush named Theodore Olson as U.S. solicitor general; as a lawyer in private practice Olson had aided the Center for Individual Rights in representing the plaintiffs in the *Hopwood* case.

Ward Connerly, the prominent affirmative action critic, would later remark in a *Chronicle of Higher Education* interview that just as the Clinton administration "had an incestuous relationship" with minority-advocacy groups such as the NAACP, "there is an incestuous relationship now—it is just that there are different families involved."

The Bush administration was willing to take a strong stand against one type of affirmative action program—those that were completely off limits to members of certain races, usually whites and Asians. It was common, when Bush took office, for colleges to offer minority scholarships or fellowships or

to operate summer camps, orientations, internships, or academic enrich-
ment programs solely for members of certain racial or ethnic groups deemed
underrepresented on campus or in certain fields. When the Center for Equal
Opportunity began to file discrimination complaints challenging the legality of such programs in 2002, the Education Department's Office for Civil
Rights undertook investigations, pressured the colleges to offer the programs
to members of any race or ethnicity, and issued a statement that said, "Generally, programs that use race or national origin as sole eligibility criteria are
extremely difficult to defend."

When the Supreme Court agreed on December 2, 2002, to hear the
University of Michigan cases, opponents of race-conscious admissions expressed hope that the Bush administration would take a strong stand against
such policies and persuade the potential swing votes on the court, such as
Justice Sandra Day O'Connor, to ban preferences once and for all.

On December 5, 2002, at a party celebrating Senator Strom Thurmond's one hundredth birthday, the biggest gift exchanged may have been
the one that Senator Trent Lott inadvertently ended up giving to affirmative
action supporters. Referring to Thurmond's failed 1948 bid for the presidency—in which the South Carolina senator ran on a platform staunchly
defending racial segregation—Lott said that if Thurmond had won "we
wouldn't of had all of these problems over all of these years." Jaws dropped,
demands for Lott's resignation filled the air, and the Republican Party ended
up scrambling to do damage control to avoid going into the 2004 presidential election with an image as the party of unrepentant bigotry. The Bush administration's prospects of easily staking out a position on the Michigan
cases were wiped away like the birthday-cake frosting on old Strom's lips.

The administration spent a month debating what position to take before the court. On one side, social conservatives in the Justice Department,
such as Solicitor General Olson and Attorney General John Ashcroft, were
urging Bush to strongly oppose race-conscious admissions, both to uphold
their values and appeal to his conservative base. On the other side, some of
Bush's closest advisors, including White House counsel Alberto Gonzales,
expressed concern that by taking such a stand, Bush, who had barely
squeaked into office in 2000, would be sabotaging his own chances of appealing to minority voters in 2004. National security adviser Condoleezza
Rice, who had been Stanford University's first black provost, held the view
that it would be preferable if colleges could find race-neutral means of

achieving diversity, but they should have the option of considering applicants' race if they deemed necessary.[21]

Among the outside forces putting pressure on the administration were some conservative organizations that had played a key role in getting Bush elected, retained close ties with many of the administration's top lawyers, and were not going to be satisfied with anything but Bush's rejection of all race-conscious admissions policies as discriminatory. On the opposite side of the issue, the leaders of 12 prominent Hispanic organizations issued an open letter to Bush warning that "the percentage of Latino youth graduating from higher education would drop substantially" if the Supreme Court rejected Michigan's policies. Bush also was urged to back Michigan in an open letter signed by the leaders of major higher education associations, including several representing private or religious colleges. Somewhat predictably, Bush heard calls to support Michigan coming from Democratic members of Congress, but four moderate Republican senators—Lincoln Chafee of Rhode Island, Susan Collins and Olympia Snowe of Maine, and Arlen Specter of Pennsylvania—sent him a letter urging him to support racial diversity as "a compelling government interest." A long list of major U.S. corporations had already filed friend-of-the-court briefs supporting Michigan's defense of affirmative action in the lower federal courts, so Bush was well aware of where much of the business sector stood.

In January 2003, in remarks delivered to the White House press corps, Bush said his lawyers would be urging the U.S. Supreme Court to strike down the University of Michigan's race-conscious admissions policies as "impossible to square with the Constitution" because they "amount to a quota system that unfairly rewards or penalizes prospective students, based solely on their race." At the time, however, Bush said he remained a strong supporter of diversity on campus, and administration officials made it clear that the Justice Department's brief to the Supreme Court would stop short of asking the justices to declare that colleges should never consider race in admissions. In a briefing after Mr. Bush's announcement, a senior administration official who spoke on condition of anonymity said the Justice Department would file "a narrowly tailored brief" that would focus on Michigan's policies, not on "the outer limits of what the Constitution does or does not permit."[22]

The briefs that Solicitor General Olson ended up submitting to the Supreme Court sought to indirectly bring about the preference ban that conservatives wanted. The briefs stopped short of arguing that *all* race-conscious admissions policies are unconstitutional, but their criticisms of Michigan's policies were so broad that lawyers on both sides of the debate found it difficult to envision any college's race-conscious admissions policies meeting their standards. The briefs' definition of an illegal admissions quota encompassed Michigan's efforts to enroll a "critical mass" of minority students.[23] They suggested that colleges must exhaust all race-neutral means for diversifying their student bodies before they can legally use race as a factor in admitting students, and faulted Michigan for failing to do enough to explore options other than considering race.

Ted Shaw, then the associate director of the NAACP Legal Defense and Educational Fund, said, "I think the intent of the briefs is to make race-conscious affirmative action in higher education always unconstitutional because there are always, in their view, race-neutral alternatives."

Fortunately for the University of Michigan, plenty of other powerful entities weighed in on the *Grutter* and *Gratz* cases, and their voices would largely drown out the arguments of President Bush's lawyers.

Chapter 12

Voices from on High
The Establishment Speaks

It's amazing how some things change.

Flash back to the 1960s, when colleges were adopting race-conscious admissions policies in response to black unrest on their campuses and in the nation's major cities. If you were to ask the militant black protesters of that era "Who are you fighting?" they almost certainly would have ranked high on their list "the establishment," big business, the leaders of America's military, and those college officials whom they suspected of doing the bidding of any of the above.

Now focus on the winter and spring of 2003, when race-conscious college admissions policies were being challenged before the U.S. Supreme Court. If you were to make a list of the key forces that came to the defense of such policies—and probably deserve most of the credit for saving them—at the top would have to be the establishment, big business, military leaders, and college officials doing the bidding of the above.

In the space of four decades, affirmative action had become an integral part of American society, deeply valued by many members of the nation's elite. It transformed colleges and workplaces, spawned an entire movement and an entire industry focused on promoting diversity, and helped many blacks and Hispanics embark on lucrative careers and break into—or, more recently, stay within—the upper middle class. The world was filled with people who either benefited from affirmative action, made a living promoting affirmative action, or saw the advocacy of affirmative action as a prerequisite for rising to positions of power in business, politics, or academe. Many in the top echelons of society had come to see the allotment of racial and ethnic preferences as a way to offer minority groups enough hope to buy into the system. Both those with an interest in maintaining the status quo and those who saw affirmative action as a means of moving up in the world were not about to sit on their hands if they believed affirmative action was at risk.

As 2003 rolled around, the risk to affirmative action was very, very real. At least half of the Supreme Court had displayed ideological conservatism, and its members had already curtailed the use of racial preferences in employment and contracting. Among legal analysts trying to predict how the court would rule in the two University of Michigan cases, it seemed evident that placing *Gratz v. Bollinger* and *Grutter v. Bollinger* in the hands of the justices not only jeopardized race-conscious college admissions policies but also posed a grave threat to affirmative action as a whole. The Equal Employment Advisory Council, an organization of 340 large private-sector companies committed to promoting affirmative action in the workplace, was one of many groups worried that the Supreme Court would use one or both of the Michigan cases as a vehicle for issuing a sweeping rebuke of affirmative action wherever it was practiced. Accordingly, the council submitted a brief to the justices urging that, should the court rule against Michigan, "to craft its opinion carefully so as not to invalidate existing legitimate activities by employers," some of which "do not even arguably involve any race-based preference." The National School Boards Association joined 10 other education groups in signing a brief urging the court not to render any decision that would curtail the power of public and private schools to make race-based decisions to promote integration and diversity at the K–12 level.

Many affirmative action advocates were especially worried about how the Supreme Court would rule in the *Gratz* case, involving the admissions policies at Michigan's chief undergraduate program. If any justices were looking for an opportunity to knock affirmative action out of the ballpark, the *Gratz* case offered them the equivalent of a slow, easy pitch. The admissions system at its center did not treat applicants as individuals or consider race as a mere "plus," as Justice Lewis Powell had urged in the 1978 *Bakke* decision. Instead, it automatically awarded black, Hispanic, and American Indian applicants an advantage equal to the difference between a 3.0 and a 4.0 GPA, making it seem so far outside Powell's *Bakke* guidelines that it raised doubts whether colleges could be trusted to consider race in a restrained manner, or inevitably would take miles if allowed inches. In adopting the point-based system, the University of Michigan had been warned even by its own lawyers that what it was doing would not pass legal muster. A careful reading of the briefs that various colleges and higher education associations submitted in the *Gratz* case shows that they were reluctant to even bring up, much less get behind, Michigan's use of a point-based system, no matter how strongly they defended the broader principles espoused by the university.

All told, the Supreme Court received more than 60 briefs supporting the University of Michigan's consideration of race in admissions. Seldom in the court's history had so many briefs been filed on behalf of one side of a dispute.[1] Among the more than 300 organizations that signed on to briefs backing Michigan were 88 colleges, 50 higher education associations, dozens of minority-advocacy and student groups, labor unions, nearly 70 Fortune 500 companies, 29 former top-ranking officers and civilian leaders of the military, 22 states' attorneys general, and more than 110 members of Congress. Many had been urged to step forward by lawyers for the University of Michigan and its allies in higher education and the minority-advocacy community. Each brief seemed to come at the case from a somewhat different perspective, but nearly all put forward the idea that race-conscious admissions policies serve a compelling government interest, and many described how campus diversity benefits particular institutions, or career fields, or society as a whole.[2]

In a speech delivered as the briefs were pouring in, the University of Michigan's president, Mary Sue Coleman, described the many submissions as "an unprecedented flood that speaks volumes about the importance and far-reaching impact of this upcoming decision."

On the other side of the cases, 20 briefs were submitted on behalf of the plaintiffs suing Michigan. Among those weighing in were the groups that had already been in the thick of the fight against race-conscious admissions, such as the American Civil Rights Institute, the Center for Equal Opportunity, and the Pacific Legal Foundation. Most of the other briefs came from think tanks with a conservative or libertarian bent, such as the Cato Institute, the Center for New Black Leadership, and the Reason Foundation. Nearly all mainly echoed the arguments put forward by the lawyers representing Barbara Grutter and Jennifer Gratz. Among the few exceptions were briefs submitted by the National Association of Scholars, which sought at this late stage in the game to try to debunk the assertion—put forward by the University of Michigan and in many of the briefs filed on its behalf—that research has clearly shown that race-conscious admissions policies produce educational benefits.

As the Supreme Court deliberated, critics of affirmative action expressed confidence that the overwhelming show of support for the other side would not have much impact on how the cases were decided. Experts on the Supreme Court observed that, as a practical matter, few of the *amicus* briefs submitted to it are ever read by the justices themselves—most are passed off to clerks. Ronald Rotunda, a professor of law at George Mason University, noted that "Congress is supposed to be impressed when there is a deluge of letters, but the court is supposed to react to arguments and reasoning."

In hindsight, however, the impact of the briefs filed on Michigan's behalf was huge. In a speech delivered to the Chicago Bar Association in September 2003, three months after the court's rulings in the *Grutter* and *Gratz* cases, Justice John Paul Stevens said he had argued during the court's deliberations that the task at hand was not determining as a technical point whether Justice Powell had spoken for the *Bakke* majority, but determining as a practical matter how much American society had come to rely on Powell's reasoning. His argument to the other justices boiled down to the basic question of whether the fate of affirmative action should be decided by "the nine of us sitting in the chambers of the Supreme Court" or by "the accumulated wisdom of the country's leaders." If the court left affirmative action intact, the leaders of society could always choose to reduce or end it on their own, he had reasoned. But a Supreme Court decision striking down affirmative action would produce a "sea change" that could not easily be undone.[3]

Among the many groups urging the justices to leave well enough alone was the American Council on Education, which represents 1,800 colleges. It enlisted dozens of other higher education associations to sign on to briefs telling the court it would be wise to leave admissions decisions to colleges. "American higher education is considered the best in the world because of our longstanding tradition of government deference to an institution's judg-ment on academic questions, such as what combination of students yields the best educational outcomes," said the council's president.

Several briefs sought to dissuade the court from thinking there may be effective race-neutral alternatives to the policies currently in place. Amherst College joined 27 other selective private colleges in arguing that none of the race-neutral alternatives (such as "percent plans") being proposed to the court would work at small private institutions. Several public universities, led by the University of Pittsburgh, argued that percent plans would not work in states with little diversity in their populations. Of the 959 minority students who enrolled at the University of Minnesota at Twin Cities in 2002, for example, just 178 had graduated in the top tenth of their class and 360 in the top fourth at one of the state's high schools. The authors of the Texas Ten Percent Plan submitted a brief arguing that minority enrollments at that state's public colleges had yet to return to where they had been be-fore a federal court struck down race-conscious admissions there in 1996.

On the other side of the debate over race-neutral alternatives, Governor Jeb Bush of Florida submitted a brief on behalf of the plaintiffs arguing that the minority enrollments in his state's public universities have "remained steady and perhaps even increased" through the use of alternatives to race-conscious admissions. At the federal level, George W. Bush's appointees ex-tolled the virtues of percent plans and other alternatives to race-conscious admissions in the solicitor general's brief before the Supreme Court and in a report that the Education Department issued in March 2003, just as the Supreme Court was about to hear oral arguments. Secretary of Education Roderick Paige acknowledged "it will take time, creativity and constant at-tention" to achieve diversity through race-neutral means. But, he said, "as Americans we owe it to our heritage and to our children to meet those chal-lenges head on, rather than looking for shortcuts that divide us by race and betray the nation's fundamental principles." The Civil Rights Project at Har-vard University responded by issuing a statement saying the Education De-partment report "offers little more than a series of unsubstantiated hopeful expressions."

With the exception of the Bush brothers and their appointees, politi-cians willing to take a stand against race-conscious admissions policies were hard to find. The Republican governors of Ohio and Virginia effec-tively blocked public colleges in their states from submitting briefs on the

University of Michigan's behalf, and Michigan's Republican attorney general told the Democratic governor she was on her own if she wanted to file a brief in support of her state's flagship university (which she did). But other than that, Republicans in the states and in Congress stayed out of the fray.

On the other side of the partisan divide, Democrats seemed to come out of the woodwork to declare their support for the University of Michigan. The Democratic attorneys general of 21 states signed a brief arguing that the Supreme Court should defer to colleges' judgments and that any oversight of public colleges should be left to the states. New Jersey's attorney general submitted a separate brief arguing that educational diversity is a compelling state interest. Four separate briefs in support of the University of Michigan were signed by multiple members of Congress. Twelve senators, including John Edwards, John Kerry, Edward Kennedy, and Hillary Rodham Clinton, noted in theirs that Congress has consistently endorsed and abided by the *Bakke* decision. Another brief bore the signatures of more than 100 Democratic members of the U.S. House of Representatives, including the minority leader at the time, Nancy Pelosi of California, as well as leading members of the Congressional Black Caucus, the Congressional Hispanic Caucus, and the Congressional Asian-Pacific American Caucus. It argued that a Supreme Court decision to strike down race-conscious college admissions could adversely affect a host of federal programs in education and other areas that consider race in seeking to help the nation overcome past discrimination.

The many large corporations that rallied behind Michigan argued that colleges need diverse enrollments to produce graduates who can work effectively in the global economy. General Motors asserted that "a stratified workforce, in which whites dominate the highest levels of the managerial corps and minorities dominate the labor corps, may foment racial divisiveness." Many briefs bore the signatures of companies that themselves had recently been the targets of lawsuits alleging racial discrimination. They included Boeing, Eastman Kodak, and Texaco, which had been sued by large groups of their black employees, and Nationwide Mutual Insurance, which had been accused of bias against black customers. Some critics of affirmative action suggested that companies saw their signing on to briefs endorsing Michigan's policies as a low-cost way to try to repair their relationships with minority groups.

Among the many groups from the professions that submitted briefs were the American Bar Association, the Association of American Law Schools, and the Association of American Medical Colleges (which listed 30 health care associations as cosigners). The Massachusetts Institute of Technology was joined by the International Business Machines Corporation, the National Academy of Sciences, and the National Academy of Engineering in submitting a brief arguing that racial diversity leads to increased productivity and success in the science and engineering fields. "Diverse work teams create better and more innovative products and ideas than homogenous teams," the brief said.

Of all of the briefs submitted on Michigan's behalf, one of the least expected—and, in the long run, most influential—was one signed by 29 former leaders of the U.S. military, including three former chairmen of the Joint Chiefs of Staff, former NATO military chief General Wesley Clark, and Persian Gulf war chief General H. Norman Schwarzkopf. It essentially suggested that ruling in Michigan's favor was a matter of national security. Recalling the Vietnam War era, when the overwhelmingly white officer corps "faced racial tension and unrest" among the largely integrated enlisted ranks and the military dealt with "hundreds of race-related incidents," it warned that similar problems could recur if the military is unable to maintain racial and ethnic diversity among those in positions of command. It argued that the armed forces' officer corps is unlikely to remain racially and ethnically diverse without the continued use of race-conscious admissions policies by the nation's military service academies and by the various selective colleges that have Reserve Officer Training Corps units. Left out of the brief were any qualms about the basic fact of military life that it sought to address: the substantial overrepresentation of African Americans among those on the front lines in our nation's wars.[4]

Mainly for strategic reasons, minority-advocacy organizations submitted *amicus* briefs to the Supreme Court on behalf of the University of Michigan, rather than on behalf of the minority students who had intervened in both the *Grutter* and *Gratz* cases. Instead of contending that race-conscious admissions policies were needed to remedy societal discrimination—an argument that had been rejected by the *Bakke* majority in 1978 and seemed doubly unlikely to fly in 2003—they generally echoed Michigan's argument that its race-conscious admissions policies were justified given their educational benefits.

Perhaps no minority population had more at stake in the cases than African Americans, who received the biggest boost from race-conscious admissions policies. A brief submitted on behalf of "veterans of the civil rights movement and family members of murdered civil rights activists" of the 1950s and 1960s warned that the attack on affirmative action posed a "great threat" to the progress made by blacks since that time. The National Urban League joined Jesse Jackson's Rainbow/PUSH Coalition in arguing that percent plans are not an acceptable alternative to race-conscious admissions because they have the effect of condoning and perpetuating the segregation that still exists in the nation's elementary and secondary schools.

Among other minority groups, Hispanic-advocacy organizations weighed in on the cases with the knowledge that nearly six out of ten of the people they represent live in one of three states—California, Florida, and Texas—where public colleges already had been precluded from considering race or ethnicity in admissions. Texas, as the only one of the three in which race-conscious admissions had been eliminated through a federal court order, was the only one in which the Supreme Court's rulings could change anything. The National Council of La Raza and 27 other Latino organizations argued that race-conscious admissions policies can draw more Hispanics into college, helping to remedy the Hispanic population's high unemployment and incarceration rates.[5] A dozen Native American tribes and organizations submitted briefs, with several from Michigan arguing that, without race-conscious admissions, the University of Michigan would be unable to provide them with the educational services promised them under an 1817 federal treaty. Because American Indians account for less than 1 percent of the nation's population, and most American high schools educate only a handful or none at all, several of the briefs submitted on their behalf emphatically argued that percent plans would do nothing to prop up their numbers.[6]

For Asian American and Pacific Islander groups, the question of how to approach the Michigan cases was complicated. Because most undergraduate programs hold Asian American applicants to standards equal to, or greater than, those applied to most white students, some studies have suggested that the abolition of race-conscious admissions policies would cause Asian American enrollments to climb. In 1997, the year after a federal appeals court precluded the University of Texas at Austin from using race-conscious admissions, the university accepted 81 percent of its Asian applicants, up from 68 percent the year before. But, because Asian Americans still benefit from affirmative action in many workplaces, it seemed entirely possible that court rulings in favor of Grutter or Gratz would harm Asian Americans in the job market while helping them in higher education.

The only Asian American group that ended up supporting Grutter and Gratz was the Asian American Legal Foundation, which in the 1990s had waged a successful legal fight against a San Francisco Unified School District policy of limiting Chinese enrollment in certain schools to promote integration. Its brief in the Michigan cases argued that "diversity-based admissions schemes are almost always used to exclude Asian-Americans from educational institutions."

Twenty-eight other organizations, including the Japanese American Citizens League, the Organization of Chinese Americans, and other groups representing people from Cambodia, Korea, Laos, Vietnam, and the Philippines, signed on to a brief supporting Michigan. They argued that Americans from Asia and the Pacific Islands still face serious discrimination and should be the beneficiaries of affirmative action in some cases.

Jewish organizations found themselves deeply divided on what stand to take on the *Grutter* and *Gratz* cases—a reflection, partly, of how much their status in higher education had improved in the past few decades. Mindful of their bitter past experiences with college admission quotas, Jews had been some of the harshest critics of affirmative action in its early days. The records of the Nixon White House contain a memo from six Jewish organizations protesting the preferential treatment that universities were giving blacks and citing, as one of 33 examples, the complaint of reverse discrimination that Marco DeFunis Jr., a Sephardic Jew, had leveled in his lawsuit against the University of Washington.[7] When the Supreme Court took up the *Bakke* case in 1977, the Anti-Defamation League of B'Nai Brith joined the Jewish Labor Committee, the National Jewish Commission on Law and Public Affairs, and various labor groups in submitting a brief arguing that racial quotas are always wrong and that affirmative action should address true disadvantage, which cannot always be equated with race. The American Jewish Committee and the American Jewish Congress joined groups representing Poles, Greeks, Italians, and Ukrainians in making similar arguments and alleging that race-conscious admissions policies assume people of the same race all think alike.

But in the decades leading up to the Supreme Court's consideration of the *Grutter* and *Gratz* cases, the odds of Jewish students being accepted into top colleges had increased substantially.[8] In fact, figures compiled by the national Jewish campus organization Hillel show that Jewish enrollments at most top colleges are robust under the current admissions regimen. While Jews account for about 2 percent of America's population, they account for more than 10 percent of the enrollment at about half of the colleges that *Barron's* ranks as "highly competitive" or "most competitive," with the chief exceptions being Christian colleges, military service academies, and small liberal arts colleges out in the hinterlands. They account for about 30 percent of undergraduates at Harvard and the University of Pennsylvania, and only two members of the Ivy League—Dartmouth and Princeton—have undergraduate enrollments that are less than 20 percent Jewish.

The American Jewish Congress was so internally torn over what position to take in the Michigan cases it ended up never filing a brief at all. The Anti-Defamation League filed a brief billed as taking neither side in the case and argued that, although some consideration of race may be appropriate, the University of Michigan's policies were too heavy-handed to be seen as narrowly tailored to achieving its educational goals.

The American Jewish Committee joined nine other Jewish groups in filing a brief in support of Michigan. They argued that the historical Jewish opposition to racial quotas does not preclude them from supporting colleges' use of flexible goals aimed at increasing minority enrollments. Their brief said, "Only if diversity is permitted to continue and flourish in our universities will our children receive the rich and rewarding education that they deserve."

Fortunately for those who sided with the University of Michigan, the Supreme Court was heavily stocked with justices who not only cared strongly about what the establishment thought, but had a deep personal interest in and appreciation of the prestigious higher education institutions that serve the elite's children.

Chapter 13

Affirmative Action Affirmed

The Supreme Court Grants a Reprieve

The Supreme Court heard oral arguments in the University of Michigan cases in 2003 on a cold April Fools' Day.

Outside the courthouse were tens of thousands of protesters, many of whom had ridden buses to Washington, D.C., overnight. The overwhelming majority were affirmative action supporters, many holding placards with slogans such as "Save Brown v. Board of Education" and "Defend Affirmative Action and Integration." A large share had been summoned here by the Coalition to Defend Affirmative Action and Integration and Fight for Equality By Any Means Necessary, the group that had intervened on behalf of minority students in the law school case. BAMN's lawyers had been denied a chance to speak to the Supreme Court directly this morning, but the group was determined to be heard somehow, even if all that reached the ears of the justices were muffled chants outside thick marble walls.[1]

The nine justices seated at the bench were as firmly entrenched in America's establishment as the mottos etched over the building's doorways, and all had close ties to the higher education institutions that produce an overwhelmingly disproportionate share of the nation's elite. Stephen Breyer and

Anthony Kennedy each had followed a parent's footsteps into Stanford University and kept the new family tradition alive by sending their own children there. Sandra Day O'Connor earned both her undergraduate and law degrees at Stanford, served on Stanford's board of trustees, and then enrolled two of her three sons in her alma mater. Justice Ruth Bader Ginsburg and her daughter both attended Harvard law. John Paul Stevens took after his father in earning his undergraduate degree at the University of Chicago and his law degree at Northwestern. Of the others, Antonin Scalia and David Souter graduated from Harvard law, while Chief Justice William Rehnquist earned his Stanford law degree alongside Justice O'Connor. Clarence Thomas, the only one of the bunch to grow up in poverty, had found his way from rural Georgia into Yale's law school.[2]

Although Thomas had endured discrimination as a black man, and O'Connor and Ginsburg experienced it as women, all three had made it to the very pinnacle of their profession, with the top law schools serving as their key stepping stones. It would take at least a small leap of the imagination—as well as a bit of humility—for them to feel empathy toward those who, having failed to make it into prestigious colleges and professional schools despite solid grades and test scores, regard such institutions as arbitrary deniers of opportunity rather than as training grounds for the truly deserving. In a commencement address delivered at Stanford in 1982, while her son Jay was still an undergraduate there, O'Connor had declared, "There is no greater, more foresighted office in this land of ours than the admissions office of Stanford University." If she had possessed any skepticism at all toward the admissions process of her alma mater and its capacity to identify the best and brightest, she had kept such thoughts well hidden.[3]

Of the nine justices on the court, O'Connor was the one being watched most carefully as the oral arguments in the Michigan cases began. Most court analysts pegged four justices—Breyer, Ginsburg, Souter, and Stevens—as clearly supportive of affirmative action. Four others—Rehnquist, Scalia, Thomas, and Kennedy—had been highly critical of any use of racial preferences. O'Connor had gone both ways on affirmative action cases, functioning as a key swing vote in several 5–4 decisions. Her preference had seemed to be to base her judgments on the specifics of whatever program was under review, rather than making sweeping declarations for or against affirmative action preferences.

Guessing a Supreme Court's decision based on what is said during oral arguments is tricky business. Justices can hammer away at lawyers espousing views similar to their own just to get them to state positions more persuasively, or they can lob affirming statements toward those advancing ideas they find abhorrent in hopes of setting rhetorical traps for them. But nearly every veteran Supreme Court observer who heard the Michigan cases argued before the Supreme Court walked away believing, beyond a shadow of a doubt, that affirmative action was going to be preserved. Several justices had made comments showing that they had heeded briefs submitted on the university's behalf warning that the interests of businesses and the military were at stake. Justice O'Connor betrayed her reluctance to issue a broad-brush decision by admonishing a lawyer for Barbara Grutter that he was "speaking in absolutes" when reality "isn't quite like that."

The court handed down its rulings on June 23, 2003, shortly before adjourning for the summer. Just as many had predicted at the outset, it struck down the undergraduate admissions policy at the center of the *Gratz v. Bollinger* case as too heavy-handed in its automatic awarding of large point bonuses to black, Hispanic, and Native American applicants.[4] In keeping with the expectations of those who witnessed the oral arguments, the court ruled in *Grutter v. Bollinger,* involving Michigan's law school, that race-conscious admissions policies are constitutionally justified—at least in principle—because they serve a compelling government interest.

On balance, the court's rulings were a victory for the University of Michigan and the colleges and higher education associations that had backed it. Although Michigan's undergraduate College of Literature, Science and the Arts would need to go back to the drawing board and come up with a new admissions policy, the key thing all of them were fighting for—the power of higher education institutions to take applicants' race or ethnicity into account—had been preserved.

The court's primary vehicle for sorting through the big questions posed by the cases was its 5–4 *Grutter* decision, in which O'Connor wrote a majority opinion signed by the pro–affirmative action stalwarts Breyer, Ginsburg, Souter, and Stevens.

On the central point of whether the law school's admissions policies served a compelling government interest, the majority deferred to the law school's judgment that racial and ethnic diversity is essential to its educational mission. In explaining their reluctance to wade into the matter,

O'Connor cited past Supreme Court decisions interpreting the First Amendment as covering various academic freedoms, including the freedom of colleges to decide which students to admit. She added, however, that the majority had decided regardless that the law school almost certainly was on solid ground, having been swayed by the many assertions of diversity's educational benefits made in the case.

"These benefits are not theoretical but real, as major American businesses have made clear that the skills needed in today's increasingly global marketplace can only be developed through exposure to widely diverse people, cultures, ideas, and viewpoints," O'Connor wrote. Noting that "universities, and in particular, law schools, represent the training ground for a large number of our nation's leaders," O'Connor said that society as a whole benefits when colleges enroll diverse student bodies.

On the question of whether the Michigan law school's race-conscious admissions policy was an appropriate means of promoting diversity, the majority said yes because the policy "bears the hallmarks of a narrowly tailored plan." Applicants undergo a "holistic review" and are judged as individuals, "not in a way that makes race or ethnicity the defining feature."

The *Grutter* majority rejected the allegation that the law school's efforts to maintain a "critical mass" of minority students amount to an illegal quota system, saying its black, Hispanic, and Native American enrollments fluctuated too much for a quota to be at work. Their opinion likewise rejected the Bush administration's argument that the law school's policies were not narrowly tailored because the school had not adequately explored other options. "Narrow tailoring does not require exhaustion of every conceivable race-neutral alternative," O'Connor wrote. Colleges should give "serious, good-faith consideration" to such alternatives, but Michigan's law school appeared to have done so. She dismissed the percentage plans touted by the Bush administration as unworkable for graduate and professional schools, and said two alternatives suggested by the district court judge who had ruled against Michigan—using a lottery system or placing less weight on Law School Admissions Test scores and undergraduate grades—were unacceptable because they "would require a dramatic sacrifice of diversity, the academic quality of all admitted students, or both." The majority said it was taking the law school at its word that it would like nothing better than to find a race-neutral admissions formula and will cease considering race as soon as practicable.

The five justices side-stepped the long-running debate over whether Justice Lewis Powell had spoken for a majority of the badly divided Supreme Court in his 1978 *Bakke* opinion espousing the educational benefits of diversity. O'Connor wrote that, even if Powell had then lacked a majority in support of his belief in such a justification for race-conscious admissions, she now had a majority in support of hers. Even if Powell's opinion wasn't binding precedent, her opinion would be.

Each of the four dissenting justices in the *Grutter* case wrote his own opinion, with some signing on to the words of others.

All four dissenters signed on to Chief Justice Rehnquist's opinion, in which he argued that the law school had operated a quota system, and he dismissed as hokum the law school's claims of trying to achieve only a "critical mass" of each underrepresented minority group. Rehnquist noted that from 1995 through 2000, the number of Native Americans enrolled by the law school ranged from 13 to 19, the number of Hispanics from 47 to 56, and the number of blacks from 91 to 108, and yet the law school had never offered any explanation as to why it defined the size of a "critical mass" differently for each group. He argued that there was too strong a correlation between the racial breakdown of each year's applicant pool and the racial breakdown of the student body enrolled in any given year to be explained as anything other than an attempt at racial balancing.

Justice Kennedy argued in his own dissent that the majority had accepted the law school's assertions so readily, it had failed to fulfill the requirement that it subject the admissions policy to strict scrutiny.

Ironically, it was the two most ideologically conservative members of the court, Scalia and Thomas, who seemed most bent on calling for a complete rethinking of selective colleges' admissions policies to provide more opportunity to society's downtrodden. In tag-team fashion, they attacked the basic assumptions underlying the defense of the law school's policies, and rejected many of the choices posed to them—such as presumed choice between a quality education and a lack of diversity—as false dilemmas. Scalia's dissent, which Thomas signed, questioned whether the State of Michigan even had a compelling interest in maintaining a prestigious public law school with such high admissions standards that many minority applicants could not get in without affirmative action. "If that is a compelling state interest, everything is," Scalia wrote. He ridiculed the law school's assertion that the educational benefits provided by its race-conscious admissions policies include "cross-racial understanding" and better preparation for "an increasingly diverse workforce and society." He noted that neither law professors nor bar exams grade law students on such knowledge, and he asserted that such lessons are learned by "people three feet shorter and twenty years younger than the full-grown adults at the University of Michigan Law School, in institutions ranging from Boy Scout troops to public school kindergartens."

Thomas came out swinging even harder. His opinion, signed by Scalia, argued that the law school is seeking to engage in racial discrimination to remedy "self-inflicted wounds" stemming from its insistence on "an exclusionary admissions system that it knows produces racially disproportionate results." He contended that the law school could achieve more diversity through race-neutral means, were it not too worried about any decline in its reputation for academic selectivity to consider such a step. The interest that the law school and the Supreme Court's majority finds compelling, Thomas alleged, is the law school's desire "to improve marginally the education it offers without sacrificing too much of its exclusivity and elite status." Thomas echoed Scalia's assertion that the State of Michigan does not have a compelling interest in maintaining an elite public law school. He noted that five states—Alaska, Delaware, Massachusetts, New Hampshire, and Rhode Island—get by without operating any accredited public law schools at all, and cited statistics from the University of Michigan law school revealing that only about 27 percent of its students come from within the Great Lakes State, and fewer than 16 percent stick around Michigan to practice law after graduating.

Pointing to several studies suggesting that African American students actually achieve at higher levels at historically black colleges than at predominantly white institutions, Thomas questioned whether even the black students at Michigan's law school are benefiting from its race-conscious admissions policies. He scolded the law school for failing to present any evidence at all that the minority students admitted in such a manner are performing at or near the level of other students, and he called the school's silence on the matter "deafening to those of us who view higher education's purpose as imparting knowledge and skills to students, rather than a communal, rubber-stamp, credentialing process." Thomas accused the law school of caring more about its reputation for diversity than the real educational problems facing minority students, many of whom enroll there "only to find they cannot succeed in the cauldron of competition." One consequence of racial preferences, he said, is that "when blacks take positions in the highest places of government, industry, or academia, it is an open question today whether their skin color played a part in their advancement."

Alleging that the admissions processes of colleges are "poisoned" by various exceptions to merit, such as preferences for legacy applicants, Thomas suggested that affirmative action preferences are being defended partly for the sake of keeping the rest of the admissions system intact. "Were this Court to have the courage to forbid the use of racial discrimination in admissions," he wrote, "legacy preferences (and similar practices) might quickly become less popular—a possibility not lost, I am certain, on the elites (both individual and institutional) supporting the Law School in this case."

In the companion *Gratz* case, both O'Connor and Breyer (usually an affirmative action supporter) joined Kennedy, Rehnquist, Scalia, and Thomas in rejecting Michigan's chief undergraduate admissions policy as violating both the Constitution's equal protection clause and Title VI of the Civil Rights Act of 1964. Writing for the majority in the 6–3 decision, Chief Justice Rehnquist said the policy was not narrowly tailored enough to the goal of promoting educational diversity. The university's practice of automatically awarding black, Hispanic, and Native American applicants a 20-point bonus on a 150-point scale had the effect of making race the decisive factor "for virtually every minimally qualified underrepresented minority applicant," regardless of what they could contribute to the educational climate.

Higher education researchers who analyzed the academic credentials of those being admitted to the University of Michigan would later note that, ironically, the law school policy upheld by the court gave much more weight to race and ethnicity than the undergraduate policy that the court shot down. What made the bigger edge awarded by the law school's admissions officers acceptable was that it was thrown into the mix subjectively, inside the admissions officers' own heads, rather than precisely quantified on paper.

In dissenting from the *Gratz* majority and endorsing the undergraduate admissions policy, Justice Souter said "it seems especially unfair to treat the candor of the admissions plan as an Achilles heel." He wrote: "Equal protection cannot become an exercise in which the winners are the ones who hide the ball."

The Supreme Court's companion decisions were cheered by many of the colleges and organizations that had submitted briefs on the University of Michigan's behalf. Thirty-three of the nation's leading higher education associations jointly issued a statement that said, "These decisions enable our institutions to maintain their strong commitment to be welcoming places to students of all races and walks of life and to continue to pursue a wide range of legally permissible means of attaining a diverse student body."

The intervenors in the cases were pleased as well. The NAACP Legal Defense and Educational Fund applauded the *Grutter* ruling as a major victory and an acknowledgment that colleges and universities should continue to assist in remedying the effects of racial discrimination. "The message in the Court's ruling is that race still matters, not necessarily because it should, but because it does," the group said.

Despite the Supreme Court's rejection of nearly every argument that his administration's lawyers put forward, President George W. Bush said, "I applaud the Supreme Court for recognizing the value of diversity on our nation's campuses."

The chief groups that had been attacking race-conscious admissions policies conceded a major loss. But, they said, the battle was hardly over. They planned to vigorously monitor colleges to make sure their admissions policies stayed within the Supreme Court's guidelines, and there was nothing in the *Grutter* and *Gratz* decisions that precluded them from seeking to abolish race-conscious admissions policies through state ballot initiatives, state legislation, or acts of Congress. Roger Clegg, general counsel at the Center for Equal Opportunity, said, "The Supreme Court's decisions mean that these issues will have to be fought out school by school and state by state, and we are prepared to do that."

Jennifer Gratz, frustrated that her lawyers had failed to persuade the Supreme Court to abolish all race-conscious admissions policies, picked up the phone and called Ward Connerly. Her hope was that he could help her mount a campaign for a Michigan ballot measure banning affirmative action preferences, just as he had helped lead campaigns for such measures in California and Washington. The University of Michigan's practice of considering applicants' race had survived scrutiny by the Supreme Court, with a majority of justices citing the purported educational benefits of racial diversity as reason to maintain the status quo. But Gratz was confident that racial and ethnic preferences would not fare quite as well in the hands of Michigan's voters.

Chapter 14

The Struggle Continues
Democracy Rears Its Head

A few weeks after the Supreme Court handed down its decisions in the University of Michigan affirmative action cases, the leaders of 48 colleges held a private meeting at Harvard University to discuss what the rulings meant. According to several attendees who spoke to me on the condition of anonymity, the mood was one of relief for having dodged a bullet. Although a Supreme Court majority had said colleges should give "serious, good-faith consideration" to race-neutral alternatives to affirmative action preferences, such alternatives received little mention at the Harvard gathering. The college leaders focused instead on finding ways to shield their existing policies from legal challenges down the road.[1]

The movement against legacy preferences in admissions lost much of its steam as a result of the high court's decision. Civil rights organizations, for one, had much less interest in going after legacy preferences now that they had been reassured colleges would continue to give an edge to certain minority groups to offset their favoritism toward white applicants from privileged backgrounds.

Senator Edward Kennedy kept the legacy issue alive through the summer of 2004, when he proposed an amendment to the Higher Education Act—the federal law governing most student aid programs—that would have forced colleges to annually report how many of their entering students were legacies or had benefited from early decision programs. College lobbyists staunchly opposed the measure; the president of the American Council on Education, higher education's umbrella organization, told Kennedy in a letter that the proposal represented "the camel's nose under the tent" of federal intrusion into college admissions and would set "a very desirable precedent" for those seeking to rid colleges of affirmative action. Kennedy eventually abandoned the amendment for the sake of marshalling support for other priorities.

In an act of political jujitsu, George W. Bush thwarted Democratic efforts to make his own legacy status an issue in the 2004 presidential election by declaring that he, too, opposed preferences for the children of alumni. His reelection suggested that his handling of the Michigan cases and other affirmative action controversies might have helped his popularity and certainly did him no real harm.[2]

The Michigan decisions did not end the broader discussion of income-based disparities in selective college access brought to the fore by the affirmative action debate. In fact, having been reassured that affirmative action was no longer on the line, some higher education leaders became emboldened to talk about class more candidly than before. In a 2005 forum at the Brookings Institution, the Mellon Foundation's William Bowen acknowledged that he and other education researchers had avoided discussing class in the years leading up to the Michigan rulings because they did not want the federal courts' consideration of affirmative action "confused by claims that if you only paid attention to class, you wouldn't have to pay attention to race." He said, "we thought it was better" to let the dispute over the constitutionality of race-conscious admissions "be settled before we turn to the question of socioeconomic status."[3]

The Supreme Court having ruled, the parameters of discussions of class and college access changed. Reassured that the Supreme Court would defer to colleges' judgments, higher education leaders were now in a position to decide which ideas would be on the table and which ones would be off limits. Now that they no longer faced the prospect of needing to find a replacement for race-conscious admissions, they could put aside any talk of overhauling their admissions policies or adopting drastic measures such as "percent plans."

Partly because selective colleges saw admitting more low-income students as a way to increase their black and Hispanic enrollments, they began giving serious thought to finding ways of increasing their enrollments from the very bottom of the socioeconomic pile. But they clearly were in no hurry to curtail access for those at the top, and their strategies for improving low-income access almost invariably called for the squeeze to be put on those in the middle. Bowen offered an example of such thinking in an April 2004 speech at the University of Virginia in which he argued that "allegiance to this country's ideals" required selective colleges to do more to enroll the economically disadvantaged. Rather than propose curtailing legacy preferences and other admissions policies that benefit the privileged, he suggested that selective colleges simply create another preference category for low-income applicants, giving them the same degree of preference that legacies continue to enjoy.

Bowen's preference proposal did not catch on, but several prestigious colleges have decided in recent years to step up their efforts to help students from low-income families. In most cases, they have been offering to fully cover these students' college costs and offering such aid in the form of grants rather than loans. The University of North Carolina at Chapel Hill, for example, adopted a policy of fully meeting the financial needs of students from families with incomes below about $40,000. Similar policies were put in place at other public flagships, such as the University of Virginia and the University of Maryland at College Park, and at elite private institutions such as Harvard, Princeton, Stanford, and the Massachusetts Institute of Technology.

Such policies are a boon to those low-income students who qualify for admission and have somewhat increased their numbers on campus. After Harvard offered to pay the full costs of students from families earning less than $40,000, their share of enrollment rose from 6.6 percent to 7.9 percent in the space of a year, due almost entirely to a big increase in the number applying.

The problem, however, is that only a small share of people from low-income backgrounds are ever considered selective-college material. An analysis of the impact of Harvard's policy determined that the relative paucity of low-income students on its campus is not due so much to their financial constraints as to the small number who make it into the pool of applicants meeting Harvard's standards.[4]

Guarantees of financial assistance also are expensive; the University of Virginia's efforts to cover the cost of low-income students have set it back about $20 million annually. As a result, the only colleges that generally can afford such policies are those with exceptionally large endowments and public colleges in states willing to cough up enough tax dollars. The efforts of public colleges especially are vulnerable to economic downturns, because state governments often respond to recession-induced budget shortfalls by making deep cuts in higher education spending.[5]

Financial considerations are seen as also likely to limit colleges' interest in another change that a few elite colleges have adopted to bolster low-income enrollments—eliminating early admission and early decision policies. Both policies have long been seen as most benefiting wealthy students with the savvy to take advantage of them, and early decision policies are mainly an option for those who can afford to commit to a college before they know how its financial aid offerings will stack up against other institutions'. Most of the colleges that have abandoned such policies entirely have deep pockets; Princeton, Harvard, and the University of Virginia are in the forefront here as well. In moments of candor in private conversations, some college leaders argue that their institutions simply cannot afford to take in fewer wealthy students and more poor ones—if their enrollments truly represented the class make-up of society, the resulting drop-off in donations and escalation of financial aid costs would force them to rewrite their budgets and profoundly change how they do business.

One of the great ironies of the Supreme Court battle over Michigan's policies was that even as the nation was caught up in a bitter debate involving a small share of seats at selective colleges and professional schools, state governments met little resistance as they slashed spending on public colleges and student aid programs to close budget gaps, and the White House and Congress similarly felt free to adopt a series of budgets that froze or reduced federal spending on student financial aid. Lawmakers described such austerity measures as necessary to cope with declines in tax revenue resulting from the economic downturn that followed the September 11, 2001 attacks. But the federal and state treasuries also were feeling the effects of past tax reductions—many of which had been pushed by the same business interests that rallied behind the University of Michigan's policies. Colleges responded to reductions in their public support by eliminating course offerings, turning away students, or raising tuition to levels that made them unaffordable to a growing share of the population, including many blacks, Hispanics, and Native Americans. Among the education programs that ended up under the budget knife were some adopted as alternatives to admissions preferences. In California, for example, lawmakers reduced financial support for the University of California's efforts to reach out to high schools to try to increase the share of minority students going on to college.

Given the financial constraints that most selective colleges operate under, it may be the case that some believe their only affordable means of promoting educational opportunity is by focusing on the ends of the class spectrum—combining tuition assistance for the most disadvantaged with admissions policies favoring those wealthy enough to help bankroll such altruism. But at least one prominent Ivy League college president, Amy Gutmann of the University of Pennsylvania, has called such an approach "politically stupid" because it squeezes the middle class and eventually will provoke "the same kind of resentment that now exists against race-based preference." She also has said it's "the wrong thing to do" because working-class and middle-class students "have an awful lot to contribute to our country and to our campuses."[6]

For their part, the financially well-off seem capable of looking out for themselves. That much has been made apparent in Texas, where the parents of children in private schools and public schools in prosperous suburbs have been pressuring state lawmakers to repeal the "Ten Percent Plan" guaranteeing students in the top tenth of their high school class admission to any public university. As the share of students admitted to the University of Texas at Austin under the plan has risen from about half to more than two-thirds, the institution has become less dominated by students from privileged backgrounds, prompting complaints that the law is unfair to those who fail to make it into the top tenth of students in competitive high schools. Supporters of the plan—whose ranks include many black, Hispanic, and rural lawmakers who believe it is the only thing getting many of their constituents' children into UT-Austin—were in a much better position to fend off attacks as long as the state remained bound by the Fifth Circuit court's *Hopwood* decision. The Texas legislature, which meets every two years, came close to rewriting or abandoning the law in 2005. The measure was saved in that session by some skillful parliamentary maneuvering by a few well-positioned black and Hispanic legislators, but supporters of the plan were uncertain they would be able to stave off similar attacks down the road.

For the most part, race-conscious admissions policies remain the chief mechanism by which colleges seek to enroll black, Hispanic, and Native

American students in numbers they regard as sufficient. But, despite the higher education establishment's initial jubilation over the Supreme Court's 2003 decisions, it turns out that such policies may be on even shakier ground now than they were before the Michigan cases were decided.

Advocates of affirmative action in higher education had known straight off that the Supreme Court's Michigan rulings contained at least some bad news for them. The *Gratz v. Bollinger* decision, striking down the point-based policy of Michigan's chief undergraduate program, made absolutely clear that a solid majority of the justices believed admissions formulas that automatically award a bonus to minority applicants are too heavy-handed to be deemed acceptable. In the ensuing months, Ohio State University and the University of Massachusetts at Amherst joined the University of Michigan in replacing point-based undergraduate admissions systems with new policies that relied partly on applicants' answers to essay questions intended to gauge how they will contribute to diversity.

What was not immediately apparent when the Supreme Court issued its rulings, but would become clear once lawyers for colleges had taken the time to thoroughly analyze the opinions and compare notes, was how much the decisions had placed new limits on colleges' consideration of ethnicity and race.

Over the course of the next few months, some lawyers would warn colleges not to even use the term "affirmative action" because it historically had referred to efforts to remedy societal discrimination—a rationale for race-conscious admissions policies that clearly was off-limits now, if it had not been off-limits before. Colleges were likewise advised by their lawyers to avoid using the term "underrepresented minority," which could be interpreted as suggesting that they were pursing the forbidden goal of having a student body that reflected the general population, rather than engaging in the court-approved pursuit of a "critical mass" of minority students that would offer educational benefits. Colleges also were instructed to document the educational benefits of diversity wherever possible—an acknowledgment that they previously had used affirmative action preferences without having any tangible educational benefits in mind. Many college administrators and lawyers called for much more research on the concept of "critical mass" and on the educational benefits of diversity, neither of which, they now conceded, were very well defined.

In holding that colleges must treat students as individuals rather than as members of particular racial and ethnic groups, the Supreme Court was

seen by most colleges' lawyers as removing any doubt that they were breaking the law in operating programs solely for members of certain minority
populations. Since 2003, often in response to pressure from the advocacy
groups the Center for Equal Opportunity and the American Civil Rights
Institute, many colleges have scrapped race- and ethnicity-based eligibility
requirements that had restricted who could qualify for certain fellowships
or scholarships or who could take part in recruitment, orientation, aca-
demic-enrichment, internship, and job-fair programs. In some cases, colleges have opened the doors of these programs to white or Asian American
students who could demonstrate that they came from disadvantaged backgrounds. In others, students now have to show some sort of commitment
to diversity to qualify. Federal agencies such as the National Institutes of
Health have made similar revisions in the eligibility criteria of diversity-
oriented grant programs.

In cases where colleges have refused to open programs to members of
any race or ethnicity, the Center for Equal Opportunity generally has filed
complaints with the Education Department's Office for Civil Rights. The
office has then launched investigations that almost inevitably result in the
colleges backing down. By late 2005 the Justice Department also had gotten
into the act, pressuring the Southern Illinois University system into agreeing
to open fellowship programs to members of any race to avoid being formally
accused of violating Title VII of the Civil Rights Act, which prohibits employment discrimination. Roger Clegg, the Center for Equal Opportunity's
general counsel, said in a *Chronicle of Higher Education* interview that his
group had no intention of forcing colleges to abandon such programs, because that outcome would only hurt his side in the court of public opinion.
"Bureaucratically it is easier to persuade a school to change a program than
to end it," he said. But some colleges discontinued programs that they no
longer viewed as worth operating if the beneficiaries were not solely minority students. The National Association for College Admission Counseling
conducted a survey finding that the share of all colleges that reported providing outreach to minority students dropped from 63 percent in 2003 to
47 percent in 2004.[7]

Among the colleges that have kept programs intact but opened them to
members of other races, some have expanded the programs to take in more
participants and thus guard against a decline in the number of minority students benefiting. Others, however, have kept the programs the same size,

which means the inclusion of new populations has come at the expense of those served before.

In contrast to college programs that previously served only minority students, most colleges' admissions offices have been advised not to make any major changes, and to continue to operate much as they did before. Colleges may have needed to tweak what they had in writing to make sure their policy documents gave concepts such as "educational diversity" and "critical mass" their due, but they felt they were on fairly safe ground as long as they gave applications an individualized review and avoided using formulas or points. As was the case before the Supreme Court's Michigan rulings, higher education institutions continue to resist discussing the nuts and bolts of their admissions practices. But some researchers who have looked into the matter say that many colleges and professional schools maintain diversity in their enrollments by engaging in a casual form of "race norming"—informally comparing blacks against blacks, whites against whites, and choosing the most desirable from each group—or by simply making sure they admit enough minority applicants from among the qualified to ensure their enrollments roughly mirror the racial and ethnic breakdown of the overall applicant pool.[8]

Among the groups opposed to racial preferences, the National Association of Scholars has sought to monitor whether colleges are operating within the Supreme Court's limits by using state open-records laws to try to determine how much weight such institutions are giving applicants' race. The Center for Equal Opportunity, based on its analyses of admissions data, has asked the Education Department's civil rights office to investigate a few colleges and law and medical schools that it suspects of going too far in their diversification efforts. As of late 2006, however, there had been no significant new lawsuits challenging colleges' race-conscious admissions policies.

For its part, the Bush administration, although willing to go after colleges for operating minority-only programs, has been hesitant to wade into the discussion of how colleges should consider race and ethnicity in admissions. More than three years after the Supreme Court's *Grutter* and *Gratz* rulings, the Education Department's Office for Civil Rights had yet to issue any sort of guidance as to how it interpreted and planned to enforce the court's opinions. Usually, the civil rights office responds to such rulings by promptly issuing guidelines for colleges on how to proceed.

In the long term, President Bush's chief impact on the affirmative action debate may have come through his selection of two jurists with con-

servative reputations, John Roberts Jr. and Samuel Alito Jr., to replace
Chief Justice William Rehnquist after his death and Justice Sandra Day
O'Connor upon her retirement. In its 2006–2007 session, the court took
up two lawsuits involving challenges to the use of race in determining
public school assignments in Seattle and Jefferson County, Kentucky. Although the cases did not deal with higher education, some observers believed that the court's opinions in them could contain language that
might further guide or limit college affirmative action efforts or might at
least signal how the Supreme Court will rule on such policies down the
road. In the December 2006 oral arguments in the cases, it was clear that
Justices Roberts and Alito took a dim view of affirmative action and that
Justice Anthony Kennedy's opposition to it had intensified, indicating
that the court had acquired a solid five-member majority likely to reject
the use of racial preferences by colleges if the issue were to come up any
time soon.

Among the colleges that had been precluded from considering applicants' ethnicity or race under earlier federal court rulings, neither Texas
A&M University nor the University of Georgia seemed to be in any hurry
to go back to using affirmative action preferences, despite getting the green
light from the Supreme Court to do so. Texas A&M simply decided such
preferences were not the best approach for it, while Georgia was bent on
proceeding cautiously given the conservative political climate that it operated under and the strong likelihood that any new race-conscious policy it
adopted would promptly face legal challenge.

In both states where voters had banned such preferences, California and
Washington, efforts to reverse the bans have had trouble getting off the
ground. Even supporters of affirmative action acknowledge that the bans remain too popular to challenge at the polls.

Ward Connerly, the former University of California system regent who
was key to both states' preference-ban campaigns, helped bankroll the 2006
campaign for a ban on affirmative action preferences in Michigan. Known
as the Michigan Civil Rights Initiative and appearing on the ballot as Proposal 2, the measure amended the constitution of the Great Lakes State to
prohibit all state agencies, including public colleges, from operating affirmative action programs that grant preferences based on race, color, ethnicity, national origin, or gender. Jennifer Gratz, the plaintiff at the center of
Gratz v. Bollinger, led the initiative campaign.

The biggest obstacle that Proposal 2's sponsors faced may have been getting past legal challenges intended to keep the measure from ever going before voters. Lawyers for the Coalition to Defend Affirmative Action and Integration and Fight for Equality by Any Means Necessary, the militant group that had assumed a prominent role in the defense of the University of Michigan's admissions policies, argued in state and federal courts and before state elections officials that Proposal 2 should be kept off the ballot because many people had been deceived about its intent and thought it would actually expand the state's affirmative action efforts. With its provisions calling for an end to state-sponsored discrimination, the measure looked like something civil rights groups might be behind when in fact they were bitterly opposed to it.

Once the measure got on the ballot, the campaign against it was led by One United Michigan, an umbrella organization representing more than 200 groups that, taken together, accounted for a huge share of Michigan's political and economic establishment. Its members included the American Federation of Teachers, the American Jewish Committee, the Detroit Urban League, the Michigan Catholic Conference, the Michigan Democratic Party, and the United Auto Workers. The Michigan Republican Party declared itself neutral on the measure, while the Republican candidate for governor joined the Democratic candidate in voicing opposition to it. One United Michigan outspent the campaign on behalf of Proposal 2 by a ratio of more than three to one.

I traveled to Michigan to cover the Proposal 2 referendum for *The Chronicle* and found the strategies of the two sides fairly transparent.

Opponents of the measure sought to depict affirmative action as vital to Michigan's struggling economy. Realizing that Proposal 2 would almost certainly pass if voting fell along racial lines in their badly segregated state, they focused much of their energy on trying to appeal to white women, partly by making strongly disputed assertions that passage of the amendment would lead to the closure of breast and cervical cancer clinics.

The campaign on behalf of Proposal 2 stuck close to the message that the measure was all about equal treatment and fairness. "Let the doors be open and let the chips fall where they may," Gratz declared at one debate forum. Her campaign organization had clearly reached the conclusion that, in this day and age, Michigan's white voters would respond to black militancy by rebelling against affirmative action. Its Web site sought to associate

One United with BAMN and featured video clips showing black teenagers and children mobilized by the latter group overturning a table at a meeting of state elections officials, harassing Proposal 2 supporters, and shouting obscenities at the camera.

Proposal 2 passed with an overwhelming 58 percent of the vote, despite a strong turnout at the polls among Democrats, who tend to be much more supportive of affirmative action than Republicans. The only parts of the state where a majority of voters rejected the measure were predominantly black Detroit and the areas surrounding Michigan State University and the University of Michigan at Ann Arbor. An exit poll of 3,000 voters conducted for the *Detroit News* found that when voting patterns were broken down by education level, the strongest opponents of the measure were people at the extremes of the spectrum, who either had never earned a high school diploma or had graduated from college and gone on to graduate or professional school. Those in the middle—who had graduated from high school but not gone beyond earning a bachelor's degree—generally supported Proposal 2.

BAMN immediately filed a lawsuit challenging the election's results. The University of Michigan's president, Mary Sue Coleman, initially said she would direct her university's lawyers to look for ways to fight to preserve its policies. She later backed down and pledged to comply with Proposal 2 after coming under intense criticism and learning that some key university donors who opposed racial preferences were threatening to withhold planned contributions if her institution put up a fight. Having overcome similar efforts to resist California's preference ban, Ward Connerly was confident that the Michigan amendment would go into effect and change how public colleges there did business.

Calling Michigan "a very tough state," Connerly said Proposal 2's passage had inspired him to undertake similar campaigns elsewhere. He soon announced plans to set up exploratory campaign committees in nine states, with the intent of trying to get such measures on the ballot in at least two, and maybe five or more, in the November 2008 elections. He predicted that the era of affirmative action was coming to an end. "If we can win in Michigan," he said, "I think we can win anywhere."

Epilogue

Thurgood Marshall, the first black member of the U.S. Supreme Court, knew firsthand his nation's troubled racial history. The grandson of a slave, he was rejected by the University of Maryland School of Law in 1930 because of his skin color. Later, as chief counsel for the NAACP, he helped persuade the Supreme Court to hand down two 1950 rulings ending the segregation of public colleges and its 1954 *Brown v. Board of Education* decision striking down laws calling for "separate but equal" public schools.

It has been reported that as the Supreme Court engaged in deliberations leading to its first major ruling upholding college affirmative action, the 1978 *Bakke* decision, Justice John Paul Stevens wondered aloud how long black Americans would need the help of such racial preferences. Justice Marshall gave his answer: One hundred more years.[1]

In writing for the majority in the Supreme Court's 2003 decision upholding race-conscious admissions at the University of Michigan law school, Justice Sandra Day O'Connor offered a much more optimistic prediction, in essence reducing by half the timetable that Justice Marshall had envisioned. Noting that it had been 25 years since the *Bakke* decision, and that since then "the number of minority applicants with high grades and test scores has indeed increased," Justice O'Connor said, "We expect that 25 years from now, the use of racial preferences will no longer be necessary to further the interest approved today."

Personally, if I had to bet on who guessed closest the year that black America will be on an equal footing—Justice Marshall with 2078 or Justice O'Connor with 2028—I would not hesitate to go with Marshall. I have yet to encounter an expert on education or social policy who thinks the playing field is being leveled as quickly as O'Connor predicted.

The problem is not just ongoing racism, but one of the chief legacies of racism in the past: black, Hispanic, and Native Americans are disproportionately represented among those earning low incomes and stuck on the wrong side of a growing class divide.

In a 2005 study, three well-known economists—Alan Krueger and Jesse Rothstein of Princeton and Sarah Turner of the University of Virginia—used economic and education data to subject Justice O'Connor's 25-year deadline to a reality check. They looked at how much progress there has been over the past 25 years in closing the income and standardized-test score gaps between blacks and whites, and projected what things will look like 25 years down the road if the same amount of progress is made. The researchers admitted that the assumptions underlying their work were almost certainly way too optimistic. Given that black America's educational gains largely stalled in the mid-1980s, they (as well as Justice O'Connor) were likely making the same error of logic as someone who looks at a 5-foot-tall 25-year-old and predicts that person will be 10 feet tall at the age of 50. Nevertheless, despite assuming the best, the researchers concluded that black students still will need admissions preferences to remain at least as represented on selective college campuses in 2028 as they are today.[2]

Although racial disparities are likely to persist well into the future, it is an open question whether the nation's courts, lawmakers, and voters will allow colleges to continue using race-conscious college admissions policies much longer.

Even if the Supreme Court's Michigan decisions hold up, it is important to keep in mind that they embraced a justification for race-conscious admissions policies that has little to do with ensuring minority members equal access to higher education. Michigan's stated goal was not enrolling minority students in numbers that reflected their share of the population; its goal was to maintain a "critical mass" so that everyone on its Ann Arbor campus could reap the purported educational benefits of diversity. Its law school believed it had reached this critical mass when black, Hispanic, and Native American students accounted for 10 to 17 percent of its enrollment. In much of the country, it is already possible for colleges using the same logic to declare they have achieved a critical mass for educational purposes when their enrollments are not nearly as diverse as the populations of the states they serve.

Many thinkers who have looked critically at today's college admissions policies—Lani Guinier, Nicholas Lemann, and Jerome Karabel among them—have expressed concern that our delusions of meritocracy have left us with an elite whose members, believing they have earned their privileges and owe nothing to society, are either blind to the need for change or unwilling to make any effort to bring it about.

Back in 1840, Alexis de Tocqueville predicted: "If ever America undergoes great revolutions, they will be brought about by the presence of the black race on the soil of the United States—that is to say, they will owe their origin, not to the equality, but to the inequality, of conditions."[3] Black demands for equal opportunity have already brought about two revolutions in higher education, the first carried out through desegregation, the second, through affirmative action. What remains to be seen is whether the shortcomings of those policies will lead to another revolution down the road.

If such a revolution occurs, will it be triggered by some edict from above such as a Supreme Court decision? Or will the catalyst be a new explosion of social unrest among those at the bottom of the heap? Will the future be determined by factions of our society loudly demanding sacrifices from others, or by individuals quietly demanding sacrifice of themselves?

Which will we find ourselves longing for more, peace or justice?

Can we have both?

Notes

Introduction

1. U.S. Supreme Court, *Grutter v. Bollinger,* 539 U.S. 306 (2003).
2. A caveat and apology is in order at the outset. There will be many times in this book when I seem to ignore certain minority populations, particularly Native Americans and Asian Americans, in presenting historical or statistical analyses. In some discussions of history, their absence in this book reflects that they simply were not a focus when a given event transpired. In many of my discussions of statistics and research, the absence of Native Americans and Asian Americans reflects their omission from the research cited, often because they were not present in sample populations in sufficient numbers for researchers to draw meaningful or reliable conclusions regarding them.
3. Anthony P. Carnevale and Stephen J. Rose, "Socioeconomic Status, Race/Ethnicity, and Selective College Admissions," in *America's Untapped Resource: Low-Income Students in Higher Education,* ed. Richard D. Kahlenberg (New York: Century Foundation, 2003).
4. Daniel Golden, "For Supreme Court, Affirmative Action Isn't Just Academic," *Wall Street Journal,* May 14, 2003.
5. The chief exceptions, where Asian American enrollments declined without race-conscious admissions, are those higher education institutions that had granted members of certain Asian ethnic groups the same preferences they gave other minority applicants.
6. See, for example, Douglas S. Massey, Camille Z. Charles, and Margarita Mooney, "Black Immigrants and Black Natives Attending Selective Colleges and Universities in the United States," *American Journal of Education* 113 (February 2007).
7. Michael Chandler, "Secrets of the SAT," *Frontline,* aired on PBS Oct. 4, 1999 (WGBH Educational Foundation transcript); Lani Guinier, "Colleges Should Take 'Conformative Action' in Admissions," *The Chronicle of Higher Education,* December 14, 2001; Lani Guinier, "Saving Affirmative Action," *Village Voice,* July 2–8, 2003.
8. See, for example, Peter Sacks, "Class Rules: the Fiction of Egalitarian Higher Education," *The Chronicle of Higher Education,* July 25, 2003.
9. See Michael Lind, *The Next American Nation: The New Nationalism and the Fourth American Revolution* (New York: Free Press, 1995). For a discussion of the theory that the upper class selectively offers upward mobility to co-opt the leadership of working class and create the illusion of equal opportunity, see also Robert Perrucci and Earl Wysong, *The New Class Society: Goodbye American Dream?* (Lanham, MD: Rowman & Littlefield, 2003).

10. Cornel West, *Race Matters* (New York: Vintage Books, 1994), 156–58.

11. David Karen and Kevin J. Dougherty, "Necessary but Not Sufficient: Higher Education as a Strategy of Social Mobility," in *Higher Education and the Color Line: College Access, Racial Equity, and Social Change,* ed. Gary Orfield, Patricia Marin, and Catherine L. Horn (Cambridge, MA: Harvard Education Press, 2005), 36.

12. William G. Bowen, Martin A. Kurzweil, and Eugene M. Tobin, *Equity and Excellence in American Higher Education* (Charlottesville: University of Virginia Press, 2005), 132. See also Alexander W. Astin and Leticia Osequera, "The Declining 'Equity' of American Higher Education," *Review of Higher Education* (East Lansing, MI: Association for the Study of Higher Education), Spring 2004, 321–41.

13. Tom Hertz, *Understanding Mobility in America* (Washington, D.C.: Center for American Progress, 2006).

14. Jerome Karabel, *The Chosen: The Hidden History of Admission and Exclusion at Harvard, Yale, and Princeton* (New York: Houghton Mifflin, 2005).

15. For the most widely cited study on this point, see Stacy Berg Dale and Alan B. Krueger, "Estimating the Payoff of Attending a More Selective College: An Application of Selection on Observables and Unobservables," *Quarterly Journal of Economics* 107 (November 2002), 1491–1527.

16. Carnevale and Rose, "Socioeconomic Status," 12–13.

17. Ibid., 14. See also Paul W. Kingston and John C. Smart, "The Economic Pay-Off of Prestigious Colleges," in *The High Status Track: Studies of Elite Schools and Stratification,* ed. Paul W. Kingston and Lionel S. Lewis (Albany: State University of New York Press, 1990), 147–74.

18. Astin and Osequera, "The Declining Equity," 323.

19. William G. Bowen and Derek Bok, *The Shape of the River: Long-term Consequences of Considering Race in College and University Admissions* (Princeton, NJ: Princeton University Press, 1998), 136–40. See also Bowen, Kurzweil, and Tobin, *Equity and Excellence,* 123–25.

20. Bowen, Kurzweil, and Tobin, *Equity and Excellence,* 125.

21. Michael Useem and Jerome Karabel, "Pathways to Top Corporate Management," 175–207; Charles L. Cappell and Ronald M. Pipkin, "The Inside Tracks: Status Distinctions in Allocations to Elite Law Schools," 211–30; both in *High Status Track.*

22. Christopher Lasch, *The Revolt of the Elites and the Betrayal of Democracy* (New York: W. W. Norton, 1995).

Chapter 1

1. Anthony P. Carnevale and Stephen J. Rose, "Socioeconomic Status, Race/Ethnicity, and Selective College Admissions," in *America's Untapped Resource: Low-Income Students in Higher Education,* ed. Richard D. Kahlenberg (New York: Century Foundation, 2003), 11.

2. Most of the colleges in *Barron's* top two tiers that were excluded from the study were either military service academies or highly specialized institutions. A few institutions were excluded because they declined or were unable to provide researchers with the necessary data.

3. Carnevale and Rose, "Socioeconomic Status," 11.

4. Ibid.

5. Dave Newbart, "Wealthy Squeeze Out Low-Income Students at Many Top Colleges," *Chicago Sun-Times,* June 13, 2004.

6. Michael S. McPherson and Morton O. Schapiro, *Reinforcing Stratification in American Higher Education: Some Disturbing Trends* (Stanford, CA: Stanford University, National Center for Postsecondary Improvement, 1999), 22–27.

7. Alexander W. Astin and Leticia Osequera, "The Declining Equity of American Higher Education," *Review of Higher Education* (East Lansing, MI: Association for the Study of Higher Education), Spring 2004, 329–32.

8. James C. Hearn, "Pathways to Attendance at the Elite Colleges," in *The High Status Track: Studies of Elite Schools and Stratification,* ed. Paul W. Kingston and Lionel S. Lewis (Albany: State University of New York Press, 1990), 121–45.

9. Karin Fischer, "Elite Colleges Lag in Serving the Needy," *Chronicle of Higher Education,* May 12, 2006.

10. Danette Gerald and Kati Haycock, *Engines of Inequality: Diminishing Equity in the Nation's Premier Public Universities* (Washington, D.C.: Education Trust, 2006).

11. Kenneth Oldfield and Richard F. Conant, "Professors, Social Class, and Affirmative Action: A Pilot Study," *Journal of Public Affairs Education* 7, no. 3 (2001): 171–85.

12. Jake Ryan and Charles Sackrey, *Strangers in Paradise: Academics from the Working Class* (Boston: South End Press, 1984). My observation here is also based on numerous conversations with professors and on e-mails exchanged with members of the group Working Class and Poverty Class Academics.

13. Scott Smallwood, "Inflation Beats Faculty Salaries Again," *Chronicle of Higher Education,* April 28, 2006.

14. "The Million-Dollar President, Soon to Be Commonplace?" *Chronicle of Higher Education,* Nov. 24, 2006.

15. Jeffrey Selingo, "Leaders' Views About Higher Education, Their Jobs, and Their Lives," *Chronicle of Higher Education,* Nov. 4, 2005.

16. William G. Bowen and Derek Bok, *The Shape of the River: Long-term Consequences of Considering Race in College and University Admissions* (Princeton, NJ: Princeton University Press, 1998), 23–24.

17. Jerome Karabel, *The Chosen: The Hidden History of Admission and Exclusion at Harvard, Yale, and Princeton* (New York: Houghton Mifflin, 2005), 2–6.

18. Harold S. Wechsler, *The Qualified Student: A History of Selective College Admission in America* (New York: John Wiley, 1977), 3–15.

19. Karabel, *The Chosen,* 13–38.

20. William G. Bowen, Martin A. Kurzweil, and Eugene M. Tobin, *Equity and Excellence in American Higher Education* (Charlottesville: University of Virginia Press, 2005), 3–15.

21. Wechsler, *Qualified Student,* 16–35.

22. Karabel, *The Chosen,* 23, 39–76.

23. Richard Farnum, "Prestige in the Ivy League: Democratization and Discrimination at Penn and Columbia, 1890–1970" in *High Status Track,* 53–73.

24. Karabel, *The Chosen,* 2, 87, 120.

25. Nicholas Lemann, *The Big Test: The Secret History of the American Meritocracy* (New York: Farrar, Straus & Giroux, 1999); David Owen and Marilyn Doerr, *None of the Above: The Truth Behind the SATs* (Lanham, MD: Rowman & Littlefield, 1999).

26. Lemann, *The Big Test.*

27. Karabel, *The Chosen,* and Lemann, *The Big Test.*

28. Merrill D. Peterson, *The Portable Thomas Jefferson* (New York: Penguin, 1975), 533–39.

29. Karabel, *The Chosen,* 159, 174.

30. Lemann, *The Big Test.*

31. Lemann, *The Big Test,* Owen and Doerr, *None of the Above.*

32. Karabel, *The Chosen,* 4, 262–93. William G. Bowen and Sarah A. Levin, *Reclaiming the Game: College Sports and Educational Values* (Princeton, NJ: Princeton University Press, 2003), 59–60.

33. Richard Farnum, "Patterns of Upper-Class Education in Four American Cities: 1875–1975," in *High Status Track,* 53–73.

34. Karabel, *The Chosen,* 539–40.

35. James M. Summer, "Faked Figures Make Fools of Us," in *College Unranked: Ending the College Admissions Frenzy,* ed. Lloyd Thacker (Cambridge, MA: Harvard University Press, 2005), 68–71.

36. Lloyd Thacker, "Introduction," in *College Unranked,* 1–6. Figures derived from a survey by the National Association for College Admission Counseling.

37. Rachel Toor, *Admissions Confidential: An Insider's Account of the Elite College Selection Process* (New York: St. Martin's Griffin, 2002), 27.

38. Christopher Avery, Mark Glickman, Caroline Hoxby, and Andrew Metrick, "A Revealed Preference Ranking of U.S. Colleges and Universities" (NBER Working Paper 10803, National Bureau of Economic Research, Cambridge, MA, 2004).

39. Christopher Avery, Andrew Fairbanks, and Richard Zeckhauser, "What Worms for the Early Bird: Early Admissions at Elite Colleges" (unpublished paper presented to the National Association for College Admission Counseling, 2000).

40. In 2003, *U.S. News* editors announced that they would no longer consider yield, in an attempt to extricate their magazine from the whole debate. See Jeffrey R. Young, "In Response to Critics, 'U.S. News' Changes Its Formula for Ranking Colleges," *Chronicle of Higher Education,* July 18, 2003.

41. Caroline Hodges Persell and Peter W. Cookson Jr., "Chartering and Bartering: Elite Education and Social Reproduction," in *High Status Track,* 25–49. The prestigious prep schools commonly known as the "Select 16" are Choate Rosemary Hall, Hotchkiss School, Kent School, and Taft School in Connecticut; Deerfield Academy, Groton School, Middlesex School, Phillips (Andover) Academy, and St. Mark's School in Massachusetts; Phillips Exeter Academy and St. Paul's School in New Hampshire; Lawrenceville School in New Jersey; Hill School in Pennsylvania; St. George's School in Rhode Island; Episcopal High School and Woodbury Forest School in Virginia.

42. Avery, Fairbanks, and Zeckhauser, "What Worms for the Early Bird." See also Christopher Avery, Andrew Fairbanks, and Richard Zeckhauser, *The Early Admissions Game: Joining the Elite* (Cambridge, MA: Harvard University Press, 2003).

43. Bowen, Kurzweil, and Tobin, *Equity and Excellence,* 173, 174. The research conducted for *Equity and Excellence,* cited repeatedly throughout this book, was based on admissions data on more than 180,000 young people who applied for admission as freshmen in the fall of 1995 to at least one of 19 selective colleges. The 19 institutions examined included 5 Ivy League universities (Columbia University, Harvard University, Princeton University, the University of Pennsylvania, and Yale University), 7 academically selective, coeducational liberal arts colleges (Bowdoin, Macalester, Middlebury, Oberlin, Pomona,

Swarthmore, and Williams), 3 academically selective liberal arts colleges for women (Barnard, Smith, and Wellesley), and 4 leading state universities (Pennsylvania State University, the University of California at Los Angeles, the University of Illinois at Urbana-Champaign, and University of Virginia).

44. Karabel, *The Chosen,* 449–82.

45. Ibid., 485.

46. Selingo, "Leaders' Views."

47. Bowen, Kurzweil, and Tobin, *Equity and Excellence,* 167, 168.

48. Bowen and Levin, *Reclaiming the Game.* See also Douglas S. Massey and Margarita Mooney, "The Effects of America's Three Affirmative Action Programs on Academic Performance," *Social Problems,* February 2007.

49. Massey and Mooney, "The Effects."

50. Ibid. The 28 selective colleges referenced here are those that agreed to contribute data to what would be called the National Longitudinal Survey of Freshmen. The book *The Source of the River* and a host of other studies by Massey and other researchers are based on the information they provided. There is a large overlap between this subset of colleges and the 28 colleges in the College and Beyond database that was relied upon by the authors of *The Shape of the River.* Both databases include the following 9 liberal arts colleges: Barnard, Bryn Mawr, Denison, Kenyon, Oberlin, Smith, Swarthmore, Wesleyan, and Williams. Both include the following 15 research universities: Columbia, Emory, Northwestern, Pennsylvania State, Princeton, Rice, Stanford, Tufts, Tulane, Yale, Miami University of Ohio, the University of Michigan at Ann Arbor, the University of North Carolina at Chapel Hill, the University of Pennsylvania, and Washington University in St. Louis. Where the College and Beyond database had included Duke and Vanderbilt universities and Hamilton and Wellesley colleges, the National Longitudinal Survey has substituted Georgetown and Howard universities, Notre Dame, and the University of California at Berkeley.

51. Thomas J. Espenshade and Chang Y. Chung, "The Opportunity Cost of Admissions Preferences at Elite Universities," *Social Science Quarterly,* June 2005.

52. At the private colleges studied for *Equity and Excellence,* legacies were 21 percentage points more likely than nonlegacies with equal academic qualifications to be admitted—if a college admitted 30 percent of nonlegacy applicants with a particular academic profile, it admitted 51 percent of legacy applicants with the same qualifications. At the public colleges studied, legacies were 5.5 percentage points more likely than nonlegacies to gain admission at each skill level. Bowen, Kurzweil, and Tobin, *Equity and Excellence,* 108.

53. Bowen, Kurzweil, and Tobin, *Equity and Excellence,* 167–68.

54. Cameron Howell and Sarah E. Turner, "Legacies in Black and White: The Racial Composition of the Legacy Pool" (NBER Working Paper 9448, National Bureau of Economic Research, Cambridge, MA, 2004).

55. Espenshade and Chung, "Opportunity Cost of Admissions Preferences."

56. Jacques Steinberg, "Of Sheepskin and Greenbacks," *New York Times,* Feb. 13, 2003.

57. Daniel Golden, "'Buying' Your Way Into College," *Wall Street Journal,* March 12, 2003.

58. Toor, *Admissions Confidential,* 209–21.

59. Ben Gose, "Old 'Quota' Under Attack," *The Chronicle of Higher Education,* June 29, 1994.

60. John J. Siegfried and Malcolm Getz, "Where Do the Children of Professors Attend College?" (working paper, Vanderbilt University, Nashville, TN, 2003).

61. In research conducted for *Reclaiming the Game,* Bowen and Levin and their colleagues found that male and female recruited athletes were at least 50 percentage points more likely than nonathletes with the same academic qualifications to gain admission to one of the Ivy League universities they examined. At most of the prestigious small colleges they examined, including women's colleges, athletes had at least a 20-percentage-point edge and generally fared much better than that. The aforementioned study of three large private universities conducted by Espenshade and Chung found that being a recruited athlete gave an applicant an advantage equal to 200 out of 1600 SAT points. At the 28 selective colleges studied by Massey and Mooney, recruited athletes were advantaged to the tune of about 108 extra SAT points. See Espenshade and Chung, "Opportunity Cost of Admissions Preferences"; Massey and Mooney, "The Effects"; Bowen and Levin, *Reclaiming the Game.*

62. Bowen and Levin, *Reclaiming the Game,* 116.

63. Massey and Mooney, "The Effects."

64. Bowen, Kurzweil, and Tobin, *Equity and Excellence,* 106.

65. Ibid., 102–105, 181.

66. Gordon C. Winston and Catherine B. Hill, *Access to the Most Selective Private Colleges By High-Ability, Low-Income Students: Are They Out There?* Discussion paper no. 69, Williams Project on the Economics of Higher Education, Williams College, Oct. 2005.

67. Paul Marthers, "Admissions Messages vs. Admissions Realities," in *College Unranked: Ending the College Admissions Frenzy,* ed. Lloyd Thacker (Cambridge, MA: Harvard University Press, 2005), 73–77.

68. James Fallows, "The New College Chaos," *Atlantic Monthly,* Nov. 2003.

69. Jay Mathews and Susan Kinzie, "Colleges, Awash in Applications, Turning Away Even Top Students," *Washington Post,* April 27, 2006.

Chapter 2

1. Peter Schmidt, "Pursuing a Vision of Equality in Connecticut Court," *Education Week,* May 6, 1992.

2. Gunnar Myrdal, *An American Dilemma: The Negro Problem and Modern Democracy* (New York: Harper & Brothers, 1944), xliii.

3. After 1995, pollsters no longer bothered asking the question. See Howard Schuman, Charlotte Steeh, Lawrence Bobo, and Maria Krysan, *Racial Attitudes in America: Trends and Interpretations* (Cambridge, MA: Harvard University Press, 1997), 38, 39.

4. Richard D. Kahlenberg, *All Together Now: Creating Middle-Class Schools through Public School Choice* (Washington, D.C.: Brookings Institution Press, 2001), 47. U.S. General Accounting Office, *Per-Pupil Spending Differences between Selected Inner City and Suburban Schools Varied by Metropolitan Area* (Washington, D.C.: U.S. General Accounting Office, 2002).

5. Ellen Brantlinger, *Dividing Classes: How the Middle Class Negotiates and Rationalizes School Advantage* (New York: Routledge Falmer, 2003).

6. Thomas J. Sugrue, *The Origins of the Urban Crisis: Race and Inequality in Postwar Detroit* (Princeton, NJ: Princeton University Press, 1996), 181–207.

7. Stephen Richard Higley, *Privilege, Power and Place: The Geography of the American Upper Class* (Lanham, MD: Rowman & Littlefield, 1995), 1–30.

8. Sheryll Cashin, *The Failures of Integration: How Race and Class Are Undermining the American Dream* (New York: Public Affairs, 2004), 83–124. Higley, *Privilege, Power and Place*, 31–47.

9. Cashin, *Failures of Integration*, 83–124.

10. Jerry Johnson and Marty Strange, *Why Rural Matters 2005: The Facts about Rural Education in the 50 States* (Arlington, VA: Rural School and Community Trust, 2005).

11. Douglas S. Massey and Mary J. Fischer, *The Geography of Inequality in the United States* (Washington, D.C.: Brookings-Wharton Papers on Urban Affairs, 2003).

12. Jason C. Booza, Jackie Cutsinger, and George Galster, *Where Did They Go? The Decline of Middle-Income Neighborhoods in Metropolitan America* (Washington, D.C.: Brookings Institution, 2006).

13. John R. Logan, *The New Ethnic Enclaves in America's Suburbs* (Albany, NY: Lewis Mumford Center for Comparative Urban and Regional Research, 2001).

14. Patrick Bayer, Hamming Fang, Robert McMillan, "Separate When Unequal? Racial Inequality and Residential Segregation" (Working Paper 11507, National Bureau of Economic Research, Cambridge, MA, 2005).

15. Camille Zubrinsky Charles, "Can We Live Together? Racial Preferences and Neighborhood Outcomes," *The Geography of Opportunity: Race and Housing Choice in Metropolitan America*, ed. Xavier de Souza Briggs (Washington, D.C.: Brookings Institution Press, 2005), 45–80.

16. John R. Logan, *How Race Counts for Hispanic Americans* (Albany, NY: Lewis Mumford Center for Comparative Urban and Regional Research, 2003).

17. Margery Austin Turner, Stephen L. Ross, George C. Galster, and John Yinger, *Discrimination in Metropolitan Housing Markets: National Results from Phase I HDS 2000* (Washington, D.C.: Urban Institute Metropolitan Housing and Communities Policy Center, 2002).

18. National Fair Housing Alliance, *Unequal Opportunity—Perpetuating Housing Segregation in America: 2006 Fair Housing Trends Report* (Washington, D.C.: National Fair Housing Alliance, 2006).

19. John R. Logan, *Separate and Unequal: The Neighborhood Gaps for Blacks and Hispanics in Metropolitan America* (Albany, NY: Lewis Mumford Center for Comparative Urban and Regional Research, 2002).

20. Cashin, *Failures of Integration*, 83–124.

21. John R. Logan, Dierdre Oakley, Polly Smith, Jacob Stowell, and Brian Stults, *Separating the Children* (Albany, NY: Lewis Mumford Center for Comparative Urban and Regional Research, 2001).

22. John R. Logan, Jacob Stowell, and Dierdre Oakley, *Choosing Segregation: Racial Imbalance in American Public Schools, 1999–2000* (Albany, NY: Lewis Mumford Center for Comparative Urban and Regional Research, 2002).

23. "Almost No Blacks at Many of the Nation's Highest-Rated Public High Schools," *Journal of Blacks in Higher Education*, Autumn 2003.

24. See David N. Figlio and Maurice E. Lucas, "What's in a Grade? School Report Cards and House Prices" (NBER Working Paper 8019, National Bureau of Economic Research, Cambridge, MA, 2000); David L. Weimer and Michael J. Wolkoff, "School Performance and Housing Values," *National Tax Journal*, June 1, 2001; Theodore M. Crone, "Housing Prices and the Quality of Public Schools: What Are We Buying?" *Business Review,*

Sept.-Oct. 1998; Sandra E. Black, "Do Better Schools Matter? Parental Valuation of Elementary Education"(Research Paper 9729, Federal Reserve Bank of New York, 1997).

25. Lynn Olson, "Financial Evolution," *Education Week,* Jan. 6, 2005.

26. The Education Trust, *Funding Gap 2005: Most States Shortchange Poor and Minority Students* (Washington, D.C.: Education Trust, 2005).

27. James S. Coleman, E. Q. Campbell, C. J. Hoson, James McPartland, A. M. Mood, F. D. Weinfeld, and R. L. York, *Equality of Educational Opportunity* (Cambridge, MA: Harvard University Press, 1966).

28. David Glenn, "Study Links High-School Quality with Likelihood of Earning a Degree," *The Chronicle of Higher Education,* April 10, 2006.

29. Bruce J. Biddle and David C. Berliner, *What Research Says about Unequal Funding for Schools in America* (San Francisco, CA: WestEd, 2003).

30. Kahlenberg, *All Together Now,* xvi.

31. Caroline Hodges Persell and Peter W. Cookson Jr., "Chartering and Bartering," in *The High Status Track: Studies of Elite Schools and Stratification,* ed. Paul W. Kingston and Lionel S. Lewis (Albany: State University of New York Press, 1990), 25–49.

32. Peter Schmidt, "La Crosse to Push Ahead With Income-Based Busing Plan," *Education Week,* Aug. 5, 1992; "Bold Busing Plan Leads to Deep Divides in Wausau," *Education Week,* Dec. 15, 1993; "Five on Wausau Board Voted Out over Busing Stands," *Education Week,* Jan. 12, 1993; "New Board Members in Wausau Ditch Controversial Busing Scheme," *Education Week,* May 18, 1994. See also Robert C. Johnston, "N.C. District to Integrate by Income," *Education Week,* April 26, 2000.

33. Alan Richard, "Broad Effort to Mix Students by Wealth under Fire in N.C.," *Education Week,* May 22, 2002; Karla Scoon Reid, "Integration by Income Proving Unpopular," *Education Week,* Nov. 12, 2003.

34. Jennifer L. Hoschild, "Social Class in Public Schools," *Journal of Social Issues* 59, no. 4 (Dec. 2003).

35. As of the 1999–2000 academic year, about 77 percent of students at private schools were white, compared to 63 percent of those at public schools. See the National Center for Education Statistics report, *Private Schools: A Brief Portrait* (Washington, D.C.: U.S. Department of Education, 2002).

36. Julian R. Betts and Robert W. Fairlie, "Does Immigration Induce 'Native Flight' from Public Schools into Private Schools?" *Journal of Public Economics* 87 (2003): 987–1012.

37. Charles T. Clotfelter, *After Brown: The Rise and Retreat of School Desegregation* (Princeton, NJ: Princeton University Press, 2004), 100–25.

38. National Center for Education Statistics, *Private Schools.*

39. Mary Ann Zehr, "Tuition at Independent Schools Continues to Rise," *Education Week,* Sept. 15, 2004. See also the Education Week Research Center, "Private Schooling" (http://www.edweek.org/rc/issues/private-schooling).

40. Phil Oreopoulos, Mark Stabile, Randy Wald, and Leslie Roos, "Short, Medium, and Long Term Consequences of Poor Infant Health: An Analysis Using Siblings and Twins" (NBER Working Paper 11998: National Bureau of Economic Research, Cambridge, MA: 2006).

41. Harold L. Hodgkinson, *Leaving Too Many Children Behind: A Demographer's View on the Neglect of America's Youngest Children* (Washington, D.C.: Institute for Educational Leadership, 2003).

42. Kahlenberg, *All Together Now,* 49.

43. Richard J. Coley, *An Uneven Start: Indicators of Inequality in School Readiness* (Princeton, NJ: Educational Testing Service, 2002).

44. Susan E. Mayer, *What Money Can't Buy: Family Income and Children's Life Chances* (Cambridge, MA: Harvard University Press, 1997), 1–15, 39–54.

45. Annette Lareau, *Unequal Childhoods: Class, Race, and Family Life* (Berkeley, CA: University of California Press, 2003).

46. David N. Figlio, "Names, Expectations and the Black-White Test Score Gap" (NBER Working Paper, National Bureau of Economic Research, Cambridge, MA, 2005).

47. John Hartigan Jr., *Odd Tribes: Toward a Cultural Analysis of White People* (Durham, NC: Duke University Press, 2005), 158–59, 205–29.

48. Edward Morris, *An Unexpected Minority: White Kids in an Urban School* (New Brunswick, NJ: Rutgers University Press, 2006).

49. Asian American Legal Center of Southern California, *A Community of Contrasts: Asian Americans and Pacific Islanders in the United States* (Washington, D.C.: Asian American Justice Center, 2006).

50. See Rachel Toor, *Admissions Confidential: An Insider's Account of the Elite College Selection Process* (New York: St. Martin's Griffin, 2002), 100, 207.

51. Peter Schmidt, "Academe's Hispanic Future," *The Chronicle of Higher Education,* Nov. 28, 2003.

52. Douglas S. Massey, Camille Z. Charles, Garvey F. Lundy, and Mary J. Fischer, *The Source of the River: The Social Origins of Freshmen at America's Selective Colleges and Universities* (Princeton, NJ: Princeton University Press, 2003), 70–86, 95.

53. Harold L. Hodgkinson, *Leaving Too Many Children Behind.*

54. Roland G. Fryer Jr. and Steven D. Levitt, "The Black-White Test Score Gap through Third Grade" (NBER Working Paper 11049, National Bureau of Economic Research, Cambridge, MA, 2005).

55. "Why Suburban Blacks from Affluent Families Fail to Close the Racial Gap in SAT Scores," *Journal of Blacks in Higher Education,* Summer 2004.

56. Brent Bridgeman and Cathy Wendler, *Characteristics of Minority Students Who Excel on the SAT and in the Classroom* (Princeton, NJ: Educational Testing Service, 2004).

57. Massey, Charles, Lundy, and Fischer, *Source of the River,* 104–5.

58. William G. Bowen, Martin A. Kurzweil, and Eugene M. Tobin, *Equity and Excellence in American Higher Education* (Charlottesville: University of Virginia Press, 2005), 76–77.

59. Bridgman and Wendler, *Characteristics of Minority Students Who Excel.*

60. Gordon C. Winston and Catherine B. Hill, *Access to the Most Selective Private Colleges By High-Ability, Low-Income Students: Are They Out There?* Discussion paper no. 69, Williams Project on the Economics of Higher Education, Williams College, Oct. 2005.

61. Bowen, Kurzweil and Tobin, *Equity and Excellence,* 76–77, 80–81.

62. Kenneth R. Weiss, "New Test-Taking Skill: Working the System," *Los Angeles Times,* Jan. 9, 2000.

63. David Owen and Marilyn Doerr, *None of the Above: The Truth Behind the SATs* (Lanham, MD: Rowman & Littlefield, 1999), 91–136; Michael Chandler, "Secrets of the SAT," *Frontline* aired on PBS Oct. 4, 1999 (WGBH Educational Foundation transcript).

64. Emily Nelson and Laurie P. Cohen, "Why Jack Grubman Was So Keen to Get His Twins into the Y," *Wall Street Journal,* Nov. 15, 2002.

65. Robert Worth, "For $300 an Hour, Advice on Courting Elite Schools," *New York Times,* Oct. 25, 2000. Lloyd Thacker, "College Admission: Profession or Industry?" *The Journal of College Admission Ethics Series,* 29–46.

66. Tamar Lewin, "How I Spent Summer Vacation: Going to Get-into-College Camp," *New York Times,* April 18, 2004.

67. June Kronholtz, "For High Schoolers, Summer Is Time to Polish Resumes," *Wall Street Journal,* April 21, 2005.

68. William M. Shain, "Let Them Be Students," in *College Unranked: Ending the College Admissions Frenzy,* ed. Lloyd Thacker (Cambridge, MA: Harvard University Press, 2005), 14.

69. See Persell and Cookson, "Chartering and Bartering," in *High Status Track,* 25–49.

70. Paul E. Barton, One-Third of a Nation: Rising Dropout Rates and Declining Opportunities (Princeton, NJ: Educational Testing Service, 2005).

71. Andrea Venezia, Michael W. Kirst, and Anthony L. Antonio, *Betraying the College Dream: How Disconnected K–12 and Postsecondary Education Systems Undermine Student Aspirations* (Stanford, CA: Stanford Institute for Higher Education Research, 2003).

72. Christopher Avery, Andrew Fairbanks, and Richard Zeckhauser, "What Worms for the Early Bird: Early Admissions at Elite Colleges" (unpublished paper presented to National Association for College Admission Counseling, 2000).

73. "When Aptitude Goes Unnurtured," *Johns Hopkins Magazine,* Sept. 1999.

74. Kristin Klopfenstein and M. Kathleen Thomas, "The Advanced Placement Performance Advantage: Fact or Fiction" (working paper presented at the 2005 annual conference of American Economic Association 2005).

75. Charles T. Clotfelter, "Interracial Contact in High School Extracurricular Activities" (NBER Working Paper 7999, National Bureau of Economic Research, Cambridge, MA, 2000).

76. Advisory Committee on Student Financial Assistance, *Empty Promises: The Myth of College Access in America* (Washington, D.C.: U.S. Department of Education, 2002).

77. Donald E. Heller, "Can Minority Students Afford College in an Era of Skyrocketing Tuition?" in *Higher Education and the Color Line: College Access, Racial Equity, and Social Change,* ed. Gary Orfield, Patricia Marin, and Catherine L. Horn (Cambridge, MA: Harvard Education Press, 2005), 83–106.

78. Jeffrey Selingo, "Leaders' Views About Higher Education, Their Jobs, and Their Lives," *The Chronicle of Higher Education,* Nov. 4, 2005.

79. Danette Gerald and Kati Haycock, *Engines of Inequality: Diminishing Equity in the Nation's Premier Public Universities* (Washington, D.C.: Education Trust, 2006).

80. Sandy Baum and Lucie Lapovsky, *Tuition Discounting, Not Just a Private College Practice* (New York: The College Board, 2006).

81. Bowen, Kurzweil, and Tobin, *Equity and Excellence,* 187,188.

82. Alexander W. Astin and Leticia Osequera, "The Declining 'Equity' of American Higher Education," *Review of Higher Education* (East Lansing, MI: Association for the Study of Higher Education), Spring 2004, 323.

83. Matthew Quirk, "The Best Class Money Can Buy," *Atlantic Monthly,* Nov. 2005.

84. Karin Fischer, "State Spending on Student Financial Aid Picked Up in 2004–5, Survey Finds," *The Chronicle of Higher Education,* June 2, 2006.

85. Heller, "Can Minority Students Afford College?"

86. Elizabeth F. Farrell, "Richer Students Receive Much More Merit-Based Aid Than Do Poorer Ones," *The Chronicle of Higher Education,* Jan, 17, 2007.

87. Lawrence Gladieux and Laura Perna, *Borrowers Who Drop Out* (San Jose, CA: National Center for Public Policy and Higher Education, 2005).

88. Stephen Burd, "Working-Class Students Feel the Pinch," *The Chronicle of Higher Education,* June 9, 2006.

89. Michelle Higgins, "'Buying' Your Way Into College—More Families Hide Assets to Qualify for Financial Aid," *Wall Street Journal,* March 12, 2003.

90. David Karen and Kevin J. Dougherty, "Necessary but Not Sufficient: Higher Education as a Strategy of Social Mobility," in *Higher Education and the Color Line,* 33–34. See also Jerome Karabel, *The Chosen: The Hidden History of Admission and Exclusion at Harvard, Yale, and Princeton* (New York: Houghton Mifflin, 2005), 5.

Chapter 3

1. Peter Schmidt, "Protesters Stage Sit-In at University of Michigan," Associated Press, March 20, 1987; Peter Schmidt, "Jackson Praises University's Response to Racial Tensions," Associated Press, March 24, 1987; Jim Mitzelfeld, "600 Jam Hearing to Protest Racism on Campus," Associated Press, March 6, 1987; Larry R. Kosteke, "Virtual Racism at the University of Michigan in the Winter of 1987," downloaded Jan. 30, 2006 (http:\\m3peeps.org); Isabel Wilkerson, "Campus Race Incidents Disquiet U. of Michigan," *New York Times,* March 9, 1987.

2. Mark Fritz, "Activist's Suicide Leap Unfathomable to Friends, Family," Associated Press, March 28, 1987.

3. James W. Brann, "Colleges' Negro-Aid Activities Spurred by Dr. King's Death," *Chronicle of Higher Education,* April 22, 1968.

4. U.S. Commission on Civil Rights, *Statement on Affirmative Action* (Washington, D.C.: U.S. Government Printing Office, 1977).

5. David Karen and Kevin J. Dougherty, "Necessary but Not Sufficient: Higher Education as a Strategy of Social Mobility," in *Higher Education and the Color Line: College Access, Racial Equity, and Social Change,* ed. Gary Orfield, Patricia Marin, and Catherine L. Horn (Cambridge, MA: Harvard Education Press, 2005), 41; John D. Skrentny, *The Minority Rights Revolution* (Cambridge, MA: Belknap Press of Harvard University Press, 2002); David Karen, "The Politics of Class, Race, and Gender: Access to Higher Education in the United States, 1960–1986," *American Journal of Education* 99, Feb. 1991.

6. Dana Y. Takagi, *The Retreat from Race: Asian-American Admissions and Racial Politics* (New Brunswick, NJ: Rutgers University Press, 1992); John Aubrey Douglass, "Anatomy of Conflict: The Making and Unmaking of Affirmative Action at the University of California," in *Color Lines: Affirmative Action, Immigration, and Civil Rights Options for America,* ed. John D. Skrentny (Chicago: University of Chicago Press, 2001), 128.

7. Skrentny, *The Minority Rights Revolution.*

8. U.S. Commission on Civil Rights, *Toward Equal Educational Opportunity: Affirmative Admissions Programs at Law and Medical Schools* (Washington, D.C.: U.S. Government Printing Office, 1978).

9. William G. Bowen, Martin A. Kurzweil, and Eugene M. Tobin, *Equity and Excellence in American Higher Education* (Charlottesville: University of Virginia Press, 2005), 20–23.

10. U.S. Commission on Civil Rights, *Toward Equal Educational Opportunity.*

11. Jerome Karabel, *The Chosen: The Hidden History of Admission and Exclusion at Harvard, Yale, and Princeton* (New York: Houghton Mifflin, 2005), 397–409.

12. Charles T. Clotfelter, *After Brown: The Rise and Retreat of School Desegregation* (Princeton, NJ: Princeton University Press, 2004), 7.

13. Ibid., 22; U.S. Commission on Civil Rights, *Toward Equal Educational Opportunity.*

14. Ibid.

15. Clotfelter, *After Brown,* 16–17.

16. John D. Skrentny, *The Ironies of Affirmative Action: Politics, Culture, and Justice in America* (Chicago: University of Chicago Press, 1996), 67–110.

17. Karabel, *The Chosen,* 380–409.

18. "Vigorous Berkeley Program Doubles Minority Groups," *The Chronicle of Higher Education,* Nov. 8, 1967.

19. Thomas J. Sugrue, *The Origins of the Urban Crisis: Race and Inequality in Postwar Detroit* (Princeton, NJ: Princeton University Press, 1996), 259. See also the *Report of the National Advisory Commission on Civil Disorders* (New York: Bantam Books, 1968).

20. *Report of the National Advisory Commission on Civil Disorders.*

21. Karabel, *The Chosen,* 407–409.

22. Ibid., 397–409.

23. Robert L. Jacobson, "Admissions Help Urged," *The Chronicle of Higher Education,* Nov. 8, 1967.

24. James W. Brann, "Colleges' Negro-Aid Activities Spurred by Dr. King's Death," *The Chronicle of Higher Education,* April 22, 1968.

25. Karabel, *The Chosen,* 402–9.

26. James W. Brann, "Negro Students Are Organizing National Group," *The Chronicle of Higher Education,* May 6, 1968.

27. Lucia Mouat, "Sit-In at Northwestern: A University and Its Negro Students Reach an Understanding," *The Chronicle,* May 20, 1968.

28. Philip W. Semas, "San Francisco State: 'Mirror of the Turmoil Dividing America,'" June 1969; James W. Brann, "Response to Armed Negroes Divides Cornell Community," May 5, 1969; Ian E. McNett, "Jackson State Shootings Stir New Wave of Unrest," May 25, 1970; all in *The Chronicle of Higher Education.*

29. Philip W. Semas, "Shortages of Money, Faculty, Time Plague Black Studies Programs," *The Chronicle of Higher Education,* May 4, 1970.

30. Malcolm G. Scully, "Raids of Negro College Staffs Are Condemned as 'Immoral,'" *The Chronicle of Higher Education,* Jan. 13, 1969.

31. Philip W. Semas, "Admissions Officers Say Nonwhite Students Should Be 10 Pct. Of Colleges' Enrollment," *The Chronicle of Higher Education,* Oct. 20, 1969.

32. Ian E. McNett, "Change—and Fear of It—Dominates ACE Discussions," *The Chronicle of Higher Education,* Oct. 20, 1969.

33. Robert L. Jacobson, "Black Enrollment Rising Sharply, U.S. Data Show," Oct. 4, 1971; Peter A. Janssen, "Higher Education and the Black American: Phase 2," May 30, 1972; both in *The Chronicle of Higher Education.*

34. Janssen, "Higher Education and the Black American."

35. Skrentny, *The Minority Rights Revolution.*

36. U.S. Commission on Civil Rights, *Statement on Affirmative Action* (Washington, D.C.: U.S. Government Printing Office, 1977); John D. Skrentny, "Introduction," in *Color*

Lines: Affirmative Action, Immigration, and Civil Rights Options for America, ed. John D. Skrentny (Chicago: University of Chicago Press, 2001) 4–5; Skrentny, *The Ironies of Affirmative Action;* Richard D. Kahlenberg, *The Remedy: Class, Race, and Affirmative Action* (New York: Basic Books, 1996), 8–10.

37. Thomas J. Sugrue, "Breaking Through: The Troubled Origins of Affirmative Action in the Workplace," in *Color Lines,* 40–52.

38. Skrentny, *The Ironies of Affirmative Action,* 177–211.

39. Hugh Davis Graham, *The Civil Rights Era: Origins and Development of National Policy 1960–1972* (New York: Oxford University Press, 1990), 340.

40. John Ehrlichman, *Witness to Power: The Nixon Years* (New York: Simon & Schuster, 1982), 228–29.

41. Skrentny, *The Ironies of Affirmative Action,* 177–211; Kahlenberg, *The Remedy,* 21–24.

42. Skrentny, *The Minority Rights Revolution.*

43. "How Universities Differ in Their Competition for Black Students," *Journal of Blacks in Higher Education,* Summer 2002.

44. National Association for College Admission Counseling, *Diversity and College Admission in 2003: A Survey Report,* September 2003.

45. Karabel, *The Chosen,* 397–409, 483–84.

46. See, for example, John Aubrey Douglass, "Anatomy of Conflict: The Making and Unmaking of Affirmative Action at the University of California," in *Color Lines,* 118–44.

47. Clotfelter, *After Brown,* 75, 81.

48. Ibid., 37, 100–25.

49. Peter Schmidt, "Desegregation Study Spurs Debate over Equity Remedies," *Education Week,* Jan. 12, 1993.

50. John R. Logan, Jacob Stowell, and Dierdre Oakley, *Choosing Segregation: Racial Imbalance in American Public Schools, 1999–2000* (Albany, NY: Lewis Mumford Center for Comparative Urban and Regional Research, 2002); John R. Logan, *Resegregation in American Public Schools? Not in the 1990s* (Albany, NY: Lewis Mumford Center for Comparative Urban and Regional Research, 2004).

51. Peter Schmidt, "Reforms, Not Court, Seen as Key in Equity Fight," *Education Week,* April 27, 1994.

52. Peter Schmidt, "Urban Officials' Views on Desegregation Surveyed," *Education Week,* July 12, 1995.

53. Jaekyung Lee, "Racial and Ethnic Achievement Gap Trends: Reversing the Progress Toward Equity," *Educational Researcher* 31, no. 1 (Jan.-Feb. 2002); Derek Neal, "Why Has the Black-White Skill Convergence Stopped?" (NBER Working Paper 11090, National Bureau of Economic Research, Cambridge, MA, 2005).

54. U.S. Commission on Civil Rights, *Toward Equal Educational Opportunity.*

55. Karen, "The Politics of Class, Race, and Gender."

56. Ibid.

57. Ibid.

58. Karabel, *The Chosen,* 448.

59. Julian R. Betts and Robert W. Fairlie, "Does Immigration Induce 'Native Flight' from Public Schools into Private Schools?" *Journal of Public Economics* 87 (2003), 987–1012.

60. Peter Schmidt, "Cursed by Success," *Education Week,* April 5, 1995.

61. Sigal Alon, "Racial, Ethnic and Socioeconomic Disparities in College Destination, 1982 and 1992" (Working Paper No. 2001–02, Princeton University Office of Population Research, Princeton, NJ, 2001).

62. Takagi, *The Retreat from Race,* 27–28.

63. Karabel, *The Chosen,* 501.

64. Takagi, *The Retreat from Race,* 9.

65. Ibid., 9. In 1993, under Clinton, the Office for Civil Rights reversed its finding of discrimination at UCLA.

66. John R. Logan and Glenn Deane, *Black Diversity in Metropolitan America* (Albany, NY: Lewis Mumford Center for Comparative Urban and Regional Research, 2003).

67. Massey, Charles, Mooney, *Black Immigrants and Black Natives.* The 28 colleges referenced here are those that were part of the National Longitudinal Survey of Freshmen. See Chapter 1, endnote 50.

68. *Trends in College Admission 2000: A Report of the National Survey of Undergraduate Admission Policies, Practices, and Procedures,* ACT, Inc., Association for Institutional Research, College Board, Educational Testing Service, National Association for College Admission Counseling, 2002.

69. Hugh Davis Graham, "Affirmative Action for Immigrants? The Unintended Consequences of Reform," in *Color Lines,* 53–70.

70. Peter Wood, *Diversity: The Invention of a Concept* (San Francisco: Encounter Books, 2003), 25–26.

71. Douglas S. Massey, Camille Z. Charles, Garvey F. Lundy, and Mary J. Fischer. *The Source of the River: The Social Origins of Freshmen at America's Selective Colleges and Universities* (Princeton, NJ: Princeton University Press, 2003), 40.

72. K. Edward Renner, "Racial Equity in Higher Education," *Academe* 89, no. 1 (Jan.-Feb. 2003).

Chapter 4

1. Megan Twohey, "U-Wisconsin Feels Effects of Poor Diversity," *Milwaukee Journal Sentinel,* April 8, 2006. In my own reporting from Madison on the university system and Wisconsin's state legislature, I found the Madison campus to be caught between black students and employees who complained of a hostile climate and conservative state lawmakers who accused it of being engaged in liberal indoctrination, coddling black administrators, and giving far too much weight to race in admissions.

2. Erin Kelly and Frank Dobbin, "How Affirmative Action Became Diversity Management: Employer Response to Antidiscrimination Law, 1961–1996," in *Color Lines: Affirmative Action, Immigration, and Civil Rights Options for America,* ed. John D.Skrentny (Chicago: University of Chicago Press, 2001), 87–117; Frederick R. Lynch, *The Diversity Machine: The Drive to Change the "White Male Workplace"* (New York: Free Press, 1997), 11–12; Terry H. Anderson, *The Pursuit of Fairness: A History of Affirmative Action* (New York: Oxford University Press, 2004), 220.

3. Lisa Cooper-Patrick, Joseph D. Gallo, Junius J. Gonzales, Hong Thi Vu, Neil R. Powe, Christine Nelson, and Daniel E. Ford, "Race, Gender, and Partnership in the Patient-Physician Relationship," *JAMA* 282, no. 6 (Aug. 11, 1999).

4. Timothy Ready, "The Impact of Affirmative Action on Medical Education and the Nation's Health," in *Diversity Challenged: Evidence on the Impact of Affirmative Action,* Gary

Orfield and Michael Kurlaender, eds. (Cambridge, MA: Harvard Education Publishing Group, 2001) 213. A separate 1990 study of California physicians found that the average black doctor served in a community that had five times as many black residents as the community where the average nonblack physician worked, and cared for a fourth again as many black patients as nonblack doctors in communities with comparable demographics. See Miriam Komaromy, Kevin Grumbach, Michael Drake, Karen Vranizan, Nicole Lurie, Dennis Keane, and Andrew Bindman, "The Role of Black and Hispanic Physicians in Providing Health Care for Underserved Populations," *New England Journal of Medicine* 34, no. 20 (May 16, 1996).

5. Richard H. Sander, "A Systemic Analysis of Affirmative Action in American Law Schools," *Stanford Law Review* 57, no. 2 (Nov. 2004).

6. Ibid. See also Linda F. Wightman, "The Threat to Diversity in Legal Education: An Empirical Analysis of the Consequences of Abandoning Race as a Factor in Law School Admission Decisions," *New York University Law Review* 72, no. 1 (April 1997).

7. Derek Bok, "The Uncertain Future of Race Sensitive Admissions" (unpublished paper circulated in 2003), 12–13, 20.

8. Typical of the research on this point is an American Council on Education study of 12,000 students who entered college in 1995. It found that just 62.5 percent of black and Hispanic students seeking majors in science, technology, engineering, or mathematics had earned bachelor's degrees within six years, compared to 94.8 percent of Asian American and 86.7 percent of white students.

9. Scott L. Miller, Mehmet D. Ozturk, and Lisa Chavez, *Increasing African American, Latino, and Native American Representation among High Achieving Undergraduates at Selective Colleges and Universities* (Berkeley, CA: Institute for the Study of Social Change, 2005).

10. Among the studies cited by those who argue that it is degrees, not grades, that matter is one that looked at medical school students at the University of California at Davis and found that those granted special consideration in admissions—while being less likely than others there to receive top grades or pass the national physicians' certification test on their first try—went on to have very similar careers and be as successful. See Robert G. Davidson and Ernest L. Lewis, "Affirmative Action and Other Special Consideration Admissions at the University of California, Davis, School of Medicine," *JAMA* 278, no. 14 9 (Oct. 8, 1997).

11. William G. Bowen and Derek Bok, *The Shape of the River: Long-term Consequences of Considering Race in College and University Admissions* (Princeton, NJ: Princeton University Press, 1998), 61, 63.

12. Wightman, "The Threat to Diversity in Legal Education."

13. Sander, "A Systemic Analysis of Affirmative Action in American Law Schools."

14. David L. Chambers, Timothy T. Clydesdale, William C. Kidder, and Richard O. Lempert, "The Real Impact of Eliminating Affirmative Action in American Law Schools: An Empirical Critique of Richard Sander's Stanford Law Review Study"; David B. Wilkins, "A Systemic Response to Systemic Disadvantage"; Michele Dauber, "The Big Muddy"; Ian Ayres and Richard Brooks, "Does Affirmative Action Reduce the Number of Black Lawyers?"; all in *Stanford Law Review* 57 no. 6 (Feb. 2005). Daniel E. Ho, "Why Affirmative Action Does Not Cause Black Students to Fail the Bar," *Yale Law Journal,* June 2005. See also Katherine S. Mangan, "Does Affirmative Action Hurt Black Law Students?" *The Chronicle of Higher Education,* Nov. 12, 2004.

15. Stephen Cole and Elinor Barbar, *Increasing Faculty Diversity: The Occupational Choices of High Achieving Minority Students* (Cambridge, MA: Harvard University Press, 2003). Robin Wilson, "The Unintended Consequences of Affirmative Action," *The Chronicle of Higher Education,* Jan. 31, 2003.

16. Richard H. Sander, "The Racial Paradox of the Corporate Law Firm," *North Carolina Law Review,* June 2006.

17. James E. Coleman Jr. and Mitu Gulati, "A Response to Professor Sander: Is It Really All About the Grades?" *North Carolina Law Review,* June 2006.

18. U.S. Glass Ceiling Commission, *Good for Business: Making Full Use of the Nation's Human Capital* (Washington, D.C.: U.S. Government Printing Office, 1995), 12; Richard L. Zweigenhaft and G. William Domhoff, *Diversity in the Power Elite: Have Women and Minorities Reached the Top?* (New Haven, CT: Yale University Press, 1998).

19. U.S. Glass Ceiling Commission, *A Solid Investment: Making Full Use of the Nation's Human Capital* (Washington, D.C.: U.S. Government Printing Office, 1995).

20. Sharon M. Collins, "The Marginalization of Black Executives," *Social Problems* 36, no. 4 (Oct. 1989). See also Deborah C. Malamud, "Affirmative Action and Ethnic Niches," in *Color Lines,* 327–28.

21. Zweigenhaft and Domhoff, *Diversity in the Power Elite.*

Chapter 5

1. Harry Jaffe, "Our Sons Have Something to Say," *Washingtonian,* Oct. 2003.

2. "The Progress of Black Student Enrollments at the Nation's Highest-Ranked Colleges and Universities," *Journal of Blacks in Higher Education,* Autumn 2004.

3. Julianne Basinger, "How Nan Keohane Is Changing Duke," Nov. 3, 2000; Denise K. Magner, "Duke U. Struggles to Make Good on Pledge to Hire Black Professors," March 24, 1993; both in *The Chronicle of Higher Education.*

4. "At Duke University, Racial Diversity Is Not Just a Slogan," *Journal of Blacks in Higher Education,* Summer 2000.

5. Basinger, "How Nan Keohane Is Changing Duke."

6. All of these developments have been extensively reported in the media in a story that continued to evolved last spring. One of the best resources for readers who wish to learn more is the Web site of the *News and Observer* of Raleigh (http://www.newsobserver. com). The description of the Duke lacrosse team's behavior is based on an internal report prepared by an ad hoc committee established by Duke University officials and from Sarah Lipka, "Duke Incident Raises Issues About Culture of the Campus," *The Chronicle of Higher Education,* April 21, 2006.

7. Jennifer Yachnin, "Black and White (and Red All Over)," *The Chronicle of Higher Education,* Sept. 29, 2000.

8. Jennifer Jacobson, "In Brochures, What You See Isn't Necessarily What You Get," *The Chronicle of Higher Education,* March 16, 2001.

9. Daryl G. Smith, Jose Moreno, Alma R. Clayton-Pedersen, Sharon Parker, and Daniel Hiroyuki Teraguchi, *"Unknown" Students on College Campuses: An Exploratory Analysis"* (San Francisco: James Irvine Foundation, 2005).

10. Gary Orfield and Dean Whitla, "Diversity and Legal Education: Student Experiences in Leading Law Schools," in *Diversity Challenged: Evidence on the Impact of Affirmative Action,* ed. Gary Orfield and Michael Kurlaender (Cambridge, MA: Harvard Education Publishing Group, 2001), 143–74.

11. Cranbrook is not just 86 percent white; it has sought to remain fairly homogenous in the old-school white-Anglo-Saxon-Protestant sense. In the late 1980s, admissions officers there were caught drawing little circle-within-circle bagel symbols on applications to signal that those seeking admission were Jewish.

12. In 1989, a year in which 50 percent of the nation's college-age blacks and 22 percent of its college-age whites came from families that the researchers of *The Shape of the River* defined as having low socioeconomic status—with incomes less than $22,000 and no parent who had graduated from college—14 percent of black and 2 percent of white students at the 28 selective institutions in the College and Beyond database met this profile. But while just 3 percent of blacks and 11 percent of whites of college age came from families defined as having high socioeconomic status—with incomes over $70,000 and at least one parent who was a college graduate—15 percent of blacks and 44 percent of whites at those colleges had this profile. See William G. Bowen and Derek Bok, *The Shape of the River: Long-term Consequences of Considering Race in College and University Admissions* (Princeton, NJ: Princeton University Press, 1998), 48.

13. Douglas S. Massey, Camille Z. Charles, Garvey F. Lundy, and Mary J. Fischer, *The Source of the River: The Social Origins of Freshmen at America's Selective Colleges and Universities* (Princeton, NJ: Princeton University Press, 2003).

14. Douglas S. Massey, Camille Z. Charles, and Margarita Mooney, "Black Immigrants and Black Natives Attending Selective Colleges and Universities in the United States," *American Journal of Education,* 113 (February, 2007).

15. Sara Rimer and Karen W. Arenson, "Top Colleges Take More Blacks, But Which Ones?" *New York Times,* June 24, 2004; Nathan Heller, "People Who Look Like You," *Harvard Magazine,* January 2004.

16. Massey, Charles, Lundy, and Fischer, *Source of the River,* 44–45, 201.

17. Ben Gose, "Interracial Dating Angers Many Black Women at Brown U.," *The Chronicle of Higher Education,* May 10, 1996.

18. Massey, Charles, Lundy, and Fischer, *Source of the River,* 205; Bowen and Bok, *Shape of the River,* 233.

19. Institute for the Study of Social Change, *The Diversity Project: Final Report* (Berkeley: University of California at Berkeley, 1991), 15, 27.

20. Karen Kurotsuchi Inkelas, "Diversity's Missing Minority: Asian Pacific American Undergraduates' Attitudes toward Affirmative Action," *Journal of Higher Education,* Nov. 1, 2003.

21. Bowen and Bok, *Shape of the River,* 233.

22. Institute for the Study of Social Change, *The Diversity Project,* 11–15.

23. Ibid., iii-iv.

24. Beverly Daniel Tatum, *"Why Are All the Black Kids Sitting Together in the Cafeteria?"* (New York: Basic Books, 1997).

25. Eric Wills and Jeffrey Brainard, "Black Student Sent Hate Mail at Trinity College, Police Say," *The Chronicle of Higher Education,* May 6, 2005.

26. Scott Smallwood, "California Jury Convicts Former Professor of Lying About Hate Crime She Is Said to Have Staged," *The Chronicle of Higher Education,* Aug. 20, 2004.

27. Mary Geraghty, "Student Told Not to Reveal Black Classmates' Scores and Grades," *The Chronicle of Higher Education,* Feb. 28, 1997.

28. Douglas S. Massey and Margarita Mooney, "The Effects of America's Three Affirmative Action Programs on Academic Performance," *Social Problems,* February 2007.

29. Ibid.

30. Paul M. Sniderman and Thomas Piazza, *The Scar of Race* (Cambridge, MA: Harvard University Press, 1993).

31. Roland G. Fryer Jr. and Glenn C. Loury, "Affirmative Action and Its Mythology" (NBER Working Paper 11464: National Bureau of Economic Research, Cambridge, MA, 2005).

Chapter 6

1. Hamacher soon faded into the background of the Center for Individual Rights' publicity efforts, even though he remained a named plaintiff.

2. Thomas J. Sugrue, "Breaking Through: The Troubled Origins of Affirmative Action in the Workplace," in *Color Lines: Affirmative Action, Immigration, and Civil Rights Options for America,* ed. John D. Skrentny (Chicago: University of Chicago Press, 2001), 45–52.

3. Robert J. Hoy, "Lid on a Boiling Pot," *The New Right Papers,* ed. Robert W. Whitaker (New York: St. Martin's Press, 1982), 84–103.

4. John D. Skrentny, *The Minority Rights Revolution* (Cambridge, MA: Belknap Press of Harvard University Press, 2002), 278; John D. Skrentny, *The Ironies of Affirmative Action: Politics, Culture, and Justice in America* (Chicago: University of Chicago Press, 1996), 182.

5. Carol A. Horton, *Race and the Making of American Liberalism* (New York: Oxford University Press, 2005), 219.

6. Terry H. Anderson, *The Pursuit of Fairness: A History of Affirmative Action* (New York: Oxford University Press, 2004).

7. Horton, *Race and the Making of American Liberalism,* 191–229.

8. Nathan Glazer, *Affirmative Discrimination: Ethnic Inequality and Public Policy* (New York: Basic Books, 1975), 220–21.

9. Carnegie Council on Policy Studies in Higher Education, *The Relevance of Race in Admissions* (Berkeley, CA: Carnegie Council on Policy Studies in Higher Education, 1977).

10. Richard H. Sander, "A Systemic Analysis of Affirmative Action in American Law Schools," *Stanford Law Review* 57, no. 2 (Nov. 2004).

11. "Affirmative Action Supporters at U. of Texas Are Offered Dare by Conservative Group," *The Chronicle of Higher Education,* Oct. 3, 1997.

12. Under the point-based admissions system used by Michigan's undergraduate College of Literature, Science, and the Arts as of 1999, applicants could earn up to 110 points based on academic profiles and up to 40 points based on other considerations. Those with scores of at least 100 on its 150-point scale were automatically admitted, while those with 90 to 99 points were put on a waiting list. Those with 89 or fewer points generally were rejected, although the university reserved the option of granting a reprieve to some applicants with scores as low as 75 by delaying consideration of their application or placing them in remedial programs. Among the purely academic factors considered, students could receive up to 80 points based on their grade point average, up to 10 points based on the quality of their high school, up to 8 points based on the courses they took, and up to 12 points based on their SAT scores. Among nonacademic factors considered, they could receive up to 10 points based on geography, up to 4 based on legacy status, up to 3 for their application essay, up to 5 for their personal achievement, and up to 5 for their demonstrated leadership ability and commitment to public service. They automatically got a 20-point bonus if they were from a disadvantaged background, a recruited athlete,

or black, Hispanic, or American Indian. If they were men going into nursing, they automatically got 5 extra points. The provost had the discretion to award 20 points to any applicant he or she chose.

13. John Aubrey Douglass, "Anatomy of Conflict: The Making and Unmaking of Affirmative Action at the University of California," in *Color Lines,* 118–144.

14. Institute for the Study of Social Change, *The Diversity Project: Final Report* (Berkeley: University of California at Berkeley, 1991), 2–4.

15. Heather M. Dalmage, "Introduction," *The Politics of Multiracialism: Challenging Racial Thinking,* ed. Heather M. Dalmage (Albany: State University of New York Press, 2004), 1–16.

16. Ward Connerly, "My Fight Against Race Preferences: a Quest Toward 'Creating Equal,'" *The Chronicle of Higher Education,* March 10, 2000, adapted from Connerly's book, *Creating Equal: My Fight Against Race Preferences* (San Francisco: Encounter Books, 2000).

17. Nicholas Lemann, *The Big Test: The Secret History of the American Meritocracy* (New York: Farrar, Straus & Giroux, 1999), 278–292; Anderson, *The Pursuit of Fairness,* 233.

18. Ibid.

19. Kit Lively, "University of California Ends Race-Based Hiring, Admissions," *The Chronicle of Higher Education,* July 28, 1995.

20. Lee Cokorinos, *The Assault on Diversity: An Organized Challenge to Racial and Gender Justice* (Lanham, MD: Rowman & Littlefield, 2002).

Chapter 7

1. U.S. Commission on Civil Rights, *Statement on Affirmative Action* (Washington, D.C.: U.S. Government Printing Office, 1977).

2. Jerome Karabel, *The Chosen: The Hidden History of Admission and Exclusion at Harvard, Yale, and Princeton* (New York: Houghton Mifflin, 2005), 493.

3. Theodore M. Shaw, "The Debate Over Race Needs Minority Students' Voices," *The Chronicle of Higher Education,* Feb. 25, 2000.

4. At a March 2001 BAMN-organized rally in Berkeley, high school students looted an athletic-shoe store, beating two bystanders; see Carrie Sturrock, "Affirmative Action Rally Becomes Tumultuous as Looting Shuts Down Streets," *Contra Costa Times,* March 9, 2001.

5. Maryanne George, "Students Can't Address Supreme Court in U-M Case," *Detroit Free Press,* March 11, 2003.

Chapter 8

1. Fischer, "Elite Colleges Lag in Serving the Needy," *The Chronicle of Higher Education,* May 12, 2006.

2. Richard D. Kahlenberg, *The Remedy: Class, Race, and Affirmative Action* (New York: Basic Books, 1996), ix-xvii; David Halberstam, *The Unfinished Odyssey of Robert Kennedy* (New York: Random House, 1968), 128–29.

3. Jeffery Selingo, "What Americans Think About Higher Education," *The Chronicle of Higher Education,* May 2, 2003.

4. There was a brief surge of public interest in the fairness of selective colleges' admissions standards in the late 1970s, as it became clear that the *University of California Board of Regents v. Bakke* case was headed to the Supreme Court. Little changed, however. Selective

colleges generally give less preference to the children of alumni now than they did a few decades ago, but most have adopted a host of new practices, such as tuition discounting and early decision admissions, that favor applicants with money.

5. An exception was made for the children of people employed by the university system at facilities outside California, such as the Los Alamos National Laboratory in New Mexico.

6. Some skeptics of system administrators' commitment to complying with Proposition 209 have alleged that the comprehensive review policy has become a backdoor way to grant racial preferences and seldom operates to the benefit of Asian Americans, whose numbers the university is most concerned with restricting. A 2004 internal review of the system did indeed find that fewer Asians were being admitted than might be expected, but it characterized the shortfall as small and said it could not conclusively pin the blame on considerations of ethnicity or race.

7. Richard H. Sander, "Experimenting with Class-based Affirmative Action," *Journal of Legal Education* 47, no. 4 (Dec. 1997).

8. David Montejano, "Access to the University of Texas at Austin and the Ten Percent Plan: A Three-year Assessment" (downloaded April 27, 2006 from www.utexas.edu/student/admissions/research/montejanopaper.html).

9. Gary M. Lavergne and Bruce Walker, *Implementation and Results of the Texas Automatic Admissions Law at the University of Texas at Austin* (Austin: University of Texas, 2002).

10. Julie Berry Cullen, Mark C. Long, and Randall Reback, "Jockeying for Position: High School Student Mobility and Texas' Top-Ten Percent Rule" (working paper). Information here is also based on interviews and e-mail exchanges with Cullen.

11. Florida State University had recently acted on its own to stop giving preference to minority applicants after its lawyers concluded that such policies were legally vulnerable.

12. Patricia Marin and Edgar K. Lee, *Appearance and Reality in the Sunshine State: The Talented 20 Program in Florida* (Cambridge, MA: Civil Rights Project at Harvard University, 2003).

13. Marin and Lee, *Appearance and Reality in the Sunshine State.*

14. Sara Hebel, "In Michigan and Many Other States, 'Percent Plans' Could Undermine Diversity," *The Chronicle of Higher Education,* March 21, 2003.

15. Sara Hebel, "'Percent Plans' Don't Add Up," *The Chronicle of Higher Education,* March 21, 2003.

16. Catherine L. Horn and Stella M. Flores, *Percent Plans in College Admissions: A Comparative Analysis of Three States' Experiences* (Cambridge, MA: Civil Rights Project at Harvard University, 2003).

17. Studies of how well the SAT predicts the college performance of Hispanic students have yielded mixed results, with some saying it overpredicts and others saying it underpredicts how well they will do. Those students, Hispanic and other, who grow up speaking a language other than English at home generally do better in college than might be predicted based on their SAT scores.

18. Sara Hebel, "Education Dept. Releases Final Version of Guide on Use of Standardized Tests," *The Chronicle of Higher Education,* Jan. 5, 2001.

19. Kahlenberg, *The Remedy,* x, 118–19.

20. Abigail Thernstrom, "The Perils of Class-Based Preferences," *The Chronicle of Higher Education,* July 14, 1995.

21. Ibid. See also Douglas Laycock, "The Broader Case for Affirmative Action: Desegrega-tion, Academic Excellence, and Future Leadership," *Tulane Law Review* 78, no. 6 (2004).

22. Nicholas Lemann, *The Big Test: The Secret History of the American Meritocracy* (New York: Farrar, Straus & Giroux, 1999), 268–77.

23. Rebecca Zwick, *Fair Game? The Use of Standardized Admissions Tests in Higher Education* (New York: RoutledgeFalmer, 2002), 138–40.

24. See Roger E. Studley, *Inequality, Student Achievement, and College Admissions: A Remedy for Underrepresentation* (Berkeley: Center for Studies in Higher Education at the University of California at Berkeley, 2003).

25. Debra Thomas and Terry Shepard, "Legacy Preferences Are Defensible, Because the Process Can't Be 'Fair,'" *The Chronicle of Higher Education,* March 14, 2003.

Chapter 9

1. Peter Wood, *Diversity: The Invention of a Concept* (San Francisco: Encounter Books, 2003), 99–145.

2. Alan M. Dershowitz and Laura Hanft, "Affirmative Action and the Harvard College Diversity-Discretion Model: Paradigm or Pretext?" *Cardozo Law Review,* 1979, 379–424.

3. Gary Orfield, "Introduction," *Diversity Challenged: Evidence on the Impact of Affirmative Action,* ed. Gary Orfield and Michael Kurlaender (Cambridge, MA: Harvard Education Publishing Group, 2001), 3–4.

4. John Friedl, "Making a Compelling Case for Diversity in College Admissions," *University of Pittsburgh Law Review* 61, no. 1 (Fall 1999): 1–44.

5. Ibid.

6. Months before my analysis, Harry J. Holzer, a professor of public policy at Georgetown University, and David Neumark, a professor of economics at Michigan State University, conducted a similar review of the research done so far and similarly concluded that "the jury is still very much out" on how much, if anything, is gained educationally from diverse campuses. They also found little evidence that the pursuit of such diversity by colleges causes educational harm to students. See Holzer and Neumark, "Assessing Affirmative Action," *Journal of Economic Literature* 38 (September 2000): 483–568.

7. William G. Bowen and Derek Bok, *The Shape of the River: Long-term Consequences of Considering Race in College and University Admissions* (Princeton, NJ: Princeton University Press, 1998).

8. Terrance Sandalow, "Minority Preferences Reconsidered," *Michigan Law Review* 97, no. 6 (May 1999).

9. Stanley Rothman, Seymour Martin Lipset, and Neil Nevitte, "Racial Diversity Reconsidered," *Public Interest,* Spring 2003.

Chapter 10

1. Frankfurter derived his summary of the four basic freedoms of universities from a statement that South African scholars had issued in response to that nation's law banning the instruction of whites and members of other races at the same university.

2. After Johnson's memo came to light, the Center for Individual Freedom, an advocacy group, filed an ethics complaint against her with the state bar in New York, where she is licensed. A bar official dismissed the complaint, saying the memo amounted to permissible political advice. In early 2006, Johnson was appointed to the faculty of Columbia

University's law school, where Lee Bollinger, the named defendant in the *Grutter v. Bollinger* and *Gratz v. Bollinger* cases, had assumed the presidency after leaving the University of Michigan's top post in 2002. Curt Levey, a former director of legal and public affairs for the Center for Individual Rights, alleged in an op-ed published on March 24, 2006, in the *New York Sun* that the appointment "raises questions about a conflict of interest and a possible payoff for services rendered." Columbia University officials denied any wrongdoing, described Johnson as qualified for the job, and said Bollinger, who also holds a position on the law school's faculty, was not personally involved in the decision to hire her.

Chapter 11

1. Jill Darling Richardson, "Poll Analysis: U.S. Nowhere Near Eliminating Racism, But Race-Based Affirmative Action Not the Answer," *Los Angeles Times,* Feb. 6, 2003.
2. John D. Skrentny, *The Minority Rights Revolution* (Cambridge, MA: Belknap Press of Harvard University Press, 2002). John D. Skrentny, *The Ironies of Affirmative Action: Politics, Culture, and Justice in America* (Chicago: University of Chicago Press, 1996). Richard D. Kahlenberg, *The Remedy: Class, Race, and Affirmative Action* (New York: Basic Books, 1996).
3. Terry H. Anderson, *The Pursuit of Fairness: A History of Affirmative Action* (New York: Oxford University Press, 2004), 145–60.
4. Ibid.
5. Ibid., 161–216.
6. Ibid.
7. Frederick R. Lynch, *The Diversity Machine: The Drive to Change the "White Male Workplace"* (New York: Free Press, 1997), 30–31.
8. Alan Farnham, "Holding Firm on Affirmative Action," *Fortune,* March 13, 1989.
9. Dana Y. Takagi, *The Retreat from Race: Asian-American Admissions and Racial Politics* (New Brunswick, NJ: Rutgers University Press, 1992), 100–4. As discussed in chapter 3, both institutions were later cleared.
10. Ibid., 205–16.
11. At the time Fiesta Bowl organizers announced their plan to finance minority scholarships, civil rights groups had been calling on colleges to boycott the bowl game in response to Arizonans' rejection of a November 1990 ballot measure to make the birth of Martin Luther King a state holiday.
12. Williams's only other major foray into the affirmative action debate was a 1992 finding by his office's lawyers—based on an investigation of anti-Asian bias undertaken under Reagan—that the Boalt Hall School of Law at the University of California at Berkeley was illegally operating separate admissions tracks for different races and ethnicities. The office declined to take legal action, however, after the law school promised to ensure its admissions policies complied with the law. Other higher education institutions took the view that the admissions bias at the Berkeley law school was so blatant that it was an anomaly, and therefore they had no reason to worry that federal government's finding against Boalt Hall meant their own policies would be challenged.
13. Anderson, *The Pursuit of Fairness,* 217–73. Kahlenberg, *The Remedy,* 197, 314–16.
14. Peter Schmidt, "Clinton Civil Rights Agenda Cloudy, Advocates Say," *Education Week,* Jan. 25, 1995.

15. Nicholas Lemann, *The Big Test: The Secret History of the American Meritocracy* (New York: Farrar, Straus & Giroux, 1999), 307.

16. Christopher Edley Jr., *Not All Black and White: Affirmative Action, Race, and American Values* (New York: Hill and Wang, 1996).

17. Lemann, *The Big Test,* pp. 293–336; confirmed in an October 2006 interview with Edley.

18. Anderson, *The Pursuit of Fairness,* 252. Among the GOP governors expressing support for affirmative action were Tom Ridge of Pennsylvania and George Pataki of New York. Meanwhile, Christine Todd Whitman of New Jersey and Tommy Thompson of Wisconsin warned the party against strong opposition.

19. Lemann, *The Big Test,* 309–30.

20. R. Michael Alvarez and Tara L. Butterfield, "The Revolution Against Affirmative Action in California: Politics, Economics, and Proposition 209" (working paper) Pasadena: California Institute of Technology, 1999.

21. The question of whether to advocate the use of race-neutral alternatives to affirmative action preferences also was the subject of debate within the Bush administration. Brian Jones, the Education Department's general counsel, dismissed worries that colleges could be sued for discrimination for preferences based on class ranking or family income, but Gerald Reynolds, the department's assistant secretary for civil rights, said his department and the courts might look askance at any approach that clearly used some close proxy for race "to make an end run around" antidiscrimination laws.

22. Bush's approach to the cases so angered some conservatives that, three years later, they opposed the idea of seeing Gonzales or longtime Bush aide Harriet Miers named to the Supreme Court, partly out of suspicion that the two played a role in talking Bush into taking his split-the-baby position.

23. The University of Michigan asserted that its minority enrollments fluctuated too much for a quota to be at work, but the Bush administration's brief said such fluctuations simply reflected Michigan's inability to precisely predict acceptance rates.

Chapter 12

1. Among the few precedents was, notably, the *Bakke* case.

2. Unless otherwise noted, the quotes from sources and summaries of briefs contained in this chapter are based on my reporting for *The Chronicle of Higher Education,* and, in some cases, are taken verbatim from my *Chronicle* coverage of the *Grutter* and *Gratz* cases. In some cases, full texts of the brief were downloaded from the web site of the *Chronicle* (http://chronicle.com), where they have been made available to subscribers.

3. Tony Mauro, "Stevens Offers an Inside Look," *Legal Times,* Oct. 6, 2003.

4. Three years later, the Pentagon and many of the top law schools that had rallied behind the University of Michigan would end up on opposite sides of another legal battle that had made it before the Supreme Court. At issue was the law schools' refusal to allow military recruiters on campus to protest the Pentagon's prohibition against openly gay people serving in the military ranks.

5. Will Potter, "Many Hispanic Students Live in States That Already Ban Affirmative Action," *The Chronicle,* June 6, 2003.

6. Will Potter, "American Indians Seek a Voice in Affirmative-Action Debate," *The Chronicle of Higher Education,* June 6, 2003.

7. Nicholas Lemann, *The Big Test: The Secret History of the American Meritocracy* (New York: Farrar, Straus & Giroux, 1999), 203.
8. Alexander W. Astin and Leticia Osequera, "The Declining 'Equity' of American Higher Education," *Review of Higher Education* (East Lansing, MI: Association for the Study of Higher Education), 336.

Chapter 13

1. Unless otherwise indicated, this chapter is based on my reporting for *The Chronicle of Higher Education* and in some places liberally borrows from *Chronicle* stories containing my analyses of the Supreme Court's rulings in *Grutter v. Bollinger* and *Gratz v. Bollinger.*
2. Daniel Golden, "For Supreme Court, Affirmative Action Isn't Just Academic," *Wall Street Journal,* May 14, 2003; James M. O'Neill, "Justices' Pasts Factor into College Debate," *The Philadelphia Inquirer,* June 16, 2003; Daniel Golden, *The Price of Admission: How America's Ruling Class Buys Its Way into Elite Colleges, and Who Gets Left Outside the Gates* (New York: Crown Publishers, 2006), 251–54.
3. Golden, *The Price of Admission,* 253–54.
4. U.S. Supreme Court, *Gratz v. Bollinger,* 539 U.S. 244 (2003).

Chapter 14

1. Unless otherwise noted, this chapter is based on my reporting for *The Chronicle of Higher Education* and borrows from articles printed there.
2. U.S. Representative Steve King, an Iowa Republican, briefly revived the legacy debate in early 2006, when he offered an amendment to the Higher Education Act requiring colleges to report data showing how much preference they were giving applicants based on legacy status, ethnicity, or race. His proposal was opposed by higher education groups and overwhelmingly rejected by House members in no hurry to stir up what the Supreme Court had seemed to settle.
3. Transcript from, "Equity and Excellence in American Higher Education" forum, April 29, 2005 (Washington, D.C.: Brookings Institution).
4. Christopher Avery, Caroline Hoxby, Clement Jackson, Kaitlin Burek, Glenn Poppe, Mridula Raman, "Cost Should Be No Barrier: An Analysis of the First Year of Harvard's Financial Aid Initiative" (NBER Working Paper 12029, National Bureau of Economic Research, Cambridge, MA, 2006).
5. Karin Fischer, "What Works Best to Expand Disadvantaged Students' Access to College? Aid Officials Share Ideas," *The Chronicle of Higher Education,* Sept. 14, 2006.
6. "Equity and Excellence" forum, April 29, 2005, Brookings Institution transcript.
7. Ben Gose, "Questions Loom for Applicants and Colleges," *The Chronicle of Higher Education,* Feb. 25, 2005.
8. In an interview for this book, Richard Sander, the economist and law professor at the University of California at Los Angeles, said he has found the casual use of "race norming" in his analyses of admissions practices at law schools. Colleges' pursuit of racial and ethnic proportionality in selecting classes from their qualified applicant pools is discussed by Jennifer L. Knight and Michelle R. Hebl in "Affirmative Reaction: The Influence of Type of Justification on Nonbeneficiary Attitudes toward Af-

firmative Action Plans in Higher Education," *Journal of Social Issues* 61, no. 3 (Sept. 22, 2005), 547.

Epilogue

1. John C. Jeffries Jr., *Justice Lewis F. Powell Jr.* (New York: Charles Scribner's Sons, 1994), 487.
2. Alan Krueger, Jesse Rothstein, and Sarah Turner, "Race, Income and College in 25 Years: The Continuing Legacy of Segregation and Discrimination" (NBER Working Paper 11445, National Bureau of Economic Research, Cambridge, MA, 2005). A separate study by a University of Chicago economist has projected that, absent major changes in public policy or in the economy, the earliest the black-white skills gap will close is 2050, and it is equally likely the gap will remain significant for the rest of the twenty-first century; see Derek Neal, "Why Has the Black-White Skill Convergence Stopped?" (NBER Working Paper 11090, National Bureau of Economic Research, Cambridge, MA, 2005).
3. Alexis de Tocqueville, *Democracy in America* (New York: Library of America, 2004).

Index